Sow the Wind

by

Peggy Larken

Published by WRITERSWORLD

ISBN 1-904181-25-2

WRITERSWORLD
47 Churchill Road,
Chipping Norton,
Oxfordshire,
OX7 5HR,
England

www.writersworld.tv

Synopsis

This memoir spans the first seventy years of a long life. In this vivid account Peggy Larken describes her childhood as a doctor's daughter in Bushey, Herts before the First World War, growing up in wartime, her first job in London and an exciting period in Jamaica in the 1920s. Her marriage to Tom, an officer in the Royal Navy, provides the thread that links many adventures and experiences in this country and overseas. For almost 20 years their home was the Five Sisters, a Thames barge in which they sailed as far as Paris and Holland before finally anchoring in Yarmouth, Isle of Wight. Through all her experiences, some tragic and many entertaining, Peggy's unique combination of courage, determination, unfailing humour and humanity shines through.

Peggy Larken wrote an enthralling account of her experiences in the Thames barge Five Sisters. This was published in 1970 by Robert Hale & Co as 'Five Sisters'. It is out of print in 2004.

About the Author

PHOTO BY PHYLLIDA ACWORTH

Peggy Larken was born in Bushey, Hertfordshire, early in the last century when fields and lanes surrounded the villages that have now been submerged under the spread of London. Her father was a doctor of an Irish family of Quakers, the Shackletons. When just grown up she went to Jamaica, where her maternal grandparents' family had been planters since the last century and she stayed on her grand-uncle's plantation.

She returned to England and became secretary to an architect in London and in 1936 married a young Naval Officer, Tom Larken. They spent their honeymoon in Germany, walking in the Black Forest and as a result, when her husband was at sea, she returned to stay with a Wurttemberg family and to argue with the Nazis under the mistaken idea that if only ordinary people got together the war could be prevented. When the war did finally break out she had given up this apparently abortive idea and was living in .Plymouth with her husband and nine-months-old son. After the war Tom Larken returned from the Far Fast where he had ended up in 1946. Faced with further separation they bought and converted a Thames Sailing Barge and made it their home for eighteen happy years.

Peggy's first book (which went into two editions), records hers and Tom's life on board the barge Five Sisters, and the many cruises and adventures they enjoyed in the fifties. When they finally came ashore, they bought a gasworks on the Isle of Wight, and converted it into a boatyard, which brought new challenges into their lives.

These memoirs take Peg almost up to the present day. Sadly, Tom died in the mid sixties, but her life has been full, and she has provided a pivotal centre of support for her large family and many friends. In 2004 she is in her ninety seventh year, and has recently been busy adding newly remembered stories and photographs to the memoirs, on her computer.

Sow the wind and you reap the whirlwind.

To Jeremy, who shared the whirlwind with fortitude and humour.

Acknowledgements

This book has taken a long time to write but here it is. I appreciated enormously the efforts of many people in getting my book to publication. I would like to express my particular gratitude to Tim Parkinson whose enthusiasm, technical knowledge and encouragement have brought it to light. My goddaughter Annabel Grey not only retyped the text, but also rescued a third of it following a digital disaster. Anthea Larken proof read meticulously, helping get the structure organised from an early stage. Lisa Parkinson, with her linguistic talent, restored grammar to my errant German and French, languages in which I have for years been inclined to chatter in an undisciplined way. Lisa, Annabel, Anthea and my niece Muff all devoted much time to the final text. I am delighted with the cover design by Wendy Larken, who understood exactly what was required. I thank everyone who reads my 'track' down the last ninety years or so, years during which such tremendous changes came over our world. I hope it will give something of the pleasure it has given me in the writing.

Table of Contents

Part I Between two Edwards

The Beginning

It being the month of May, the huge old wisteria which embraced the house in its strong branches would have forced its new young tentacles into the upper windows and thus would have shed some of its powerfully evocative scent around the bed on which the baby was being born. This must have been the beginning, because all my life whenever possible I have planted wisteria to climb over the many houses in which I have lived.

The real beginning, where my memory is secure, is being a little girl of say three years old, pushing a doll's pram up and down on a narrow strip of grass that ran along a sumptuous garden border beside an old apple orchard. The pram would either be filled with teddy bears and dolls or with kittens forced into doll's clothes, who at any moment would make their escape into the undergrowth regardless of the encumbrance of the clothing.

My companion in whose care I spent many happy hours of childhood was Albert, our gardener. Albert, a young man not yet twenty from Oxfordshire, came to my father as a groom-gardener. It was the month before my father married my mother, a girl of just eighteen. The year was 1897.

My mother's family had been in disarray. My grandfather, a doctor, had been seriously ill during which time his practice had suffered and drifted away. In those days there was no provision for such circumstances – one made the best arrangements possible – and so my father came as a locum to assist my grandfather to restore his practice and gather his patients together again. My grandfather had been a colourful figure, enjoying life and much popularity but also enjoying good living in a style he could not really afford. Thus my grandmother had needed all her wits, and in a quiet way she had many, to make ends meet with a sick husband to nurse, and a large rambling house to manage on a diminishing income. To help financially, she took in foreign girls who came to learn English. My grandparents had two daughters: one serious and academic, who became a beloved aunt, and my mother who was an attractive, mercurial impish child of only fifteen when my father arrived. Bea, her sister, was two years older. They were educated at home by a German governess.

The two sisters were intrigued to find the new doctor's top hat on the table in the hall. "Well," said my aunt, "at any rate he has bought himself a new hat." My mother put it on – it came down to her nose. At that moment the two doctors emerged from the study and everyone laughed, my grandfather feigning disciplinary disapproval. My mother took the hat off. My father fell in love with her.

My father was twelve years older than my mother, who was almost a child-bride, he having waited for her to grow up from the schoolroom where he found her. Her father remained a semi-invalid: he had in fact ruined his good health due to a terrible mistake when he administered himself in error a dose of strychnine instead of a tonic. His life was saved by his friends, doctors from nearby practices who pulled him through the gruelling crisis that ensued. And so it was that on marriage my father and mother took over the old house while my grandparents moved to a smaller one in the village.

My father had not originally intended to stay. When offered a partnership he had refused it. He had a great love of the sea and had signed on as ship's doctor on a ship bound for Australia. He wanted to see the world. However, having bid the family farewell, he changed his mind in the train to London and returned next day having cancelled his commitment with the shipping line. He was delighted to find that the offer still held and was content to bide his time. When my mother was seventeen he proposed to her and on the 2nd June 1897 they were married.

The old house that the young people moved into would have been sparsely furnished. My father had a struggle to build up the practice. My grandfather died soon after the marriage, leaving large debts which were paid by his business friends, to my father's great relief. It was perhaps fortunate that they were not immediately blessed with the children for whom my father, from a large happy Irish family, yearned.

I imagine that his pretty young wife may not have shared this enthusiasm at that time and would have been disinclined to give up her new found freedom, the glory of being grown-up, married to a good looking young husband. The marriage met with full approval in the village, as did the young doctor. My mother told me that in those days, when a young bride was invited out to dinner, she wore her wedding dress and was taken in to dinner by her host, often, in my mother's case, a contemporary of her father's. My mother also told me that a chaperone had to be a married woman so that my young mother-to-be of only eighteen, and the young doctor, were in great demand to fill this position, being sought after by other young girls who were not married, some probably older and wiser than my mother. It was clearly considered a basis for an enjoyable evening out.

The village was Bushey in Hertfordshire, then still enjoying rural life with farming the chief occupation. There were country houses and estates in the surrounding countryside still in the ownership of old families who had lived there for generations. The countryside was particularly beautiful. Change however was on its way. The building of the railway, the London and North Western, had made the country very accessible from London, particularly for businessmen from the City who built large houses where they established their ever-growing large families. These houses had large sumptuous gardens, scrupulously planned. Some owners dabbled in farming, some hunted with the Old Berkeley. They sent their sons to nearby Harrow or other public schools and for girls there were governesses. They made an entirely new population who laid the foundations for the later suburbia.

In addition, there was another set of people for whom the district made an ideal setting, a group whom my mother found interesting and amusing – artists studying painting at the school founded by a young German painter, Hubert von Herkomer, later to be known as the Professor. The Professor was an enterprising man and his school prospered. He was the son of a German craftsman who recognised his son's potential and sent him to art school at an early age. By the time he came to settle in England, he had already made a name for himself. Having designed and built the school, he housed his students around the village: shopkeepers and cottagers were glad to take lodgers. He then set about building himself a rather dreary house modelled on a Bavarian castle, the stones used being dug from the bed of the Rhine. For many months the village watched the sturdiest carthorses available haul the stone laden drays up two steep hills from the station. He named the house Lululund after his wife Lulu. It stood incongruously amid meadows until the Second World War when all but the gatehouse was pulled down.

The school attracted students from all over England, the Continent and America. A couple from the United States, James and Nell Montgomery-Flagg became life long friends of my parents, although Nell, my godmother, sadly died when still comparatively young. James became a famous illustrator in America. The four of them spent holidays together, one in Paris and one in Holland which I remember being talked about. I found letters to and from Nell in the 1890s and later from James until his death during the second war.

The railway made it possible for yet another group of people to take up residence – actors found the midnight train from Euston enabled them to snatch a quiet night in the country after the fall of the last curtain. All this company greatly amused my mother, but the social life that it entailed put something of a strain on my hard-working father. Nevertheless, his practice began to prosper. My mother was young and frivolous but she also had another side: she played the piano happily – until her father's illness she had been going to study music in Dresden. Theosophy interested her and she studied French. Then she was passionately behind the suffragette movement, though not actively marching or chaining herself to railings. Both parents were supporters. Since she was young and outspoken, I imagine that some older people at those dinner parties may have looked askance at the young bride's boldness which they may have taken for impertinence.

Another interest that the Professor brought to an astonished village was the cinema. He was fascinated, experimented and wrote his own plays for his students to act in – jumpy erratic melodramas. He constructed his own cinema for showing the films and once even Ellen Terry and Henry Irvine were guests.

In June 1904 my brother Pat was born.

Pat and Peg

My brother's entry into this world in June 1904 gave the greatest possible joy and delight to both his parents. There had been several disappointments on the way – in fact there might have been many more of us, which would have pleased me, who always wanted a big family, but my mother had been unlucky. Perhaps, however, the delay was an advantage in one way, as by the time the nursery was set up my father had triumphed and his practice was well established. The house was well cared for by Big May and Little May, the latter was Albert's daughter. Albert himself had a garden boy to help, who in those golden days cleaned the knives and the shoes while he whistled the current music-hall songs. All boys whistled in those days, particularly the butcher boys as they delivered the meat. Anyway, contentment reigned and the household was carried forward on a wave of fragrant happiness.

And fragrance was what I most remember about the home into which I arrived four years later. Our house always smelled right at all seasons – the garden came inside. The wisteria, which embraced it, suffused it throughout with an unforgettable scent in spring. Lilac, wallflowers and roses followed and the flowers of the moment were ever with us. There was a certain lyricism about my mother, who had inherited a love of the soil from her own mother, our grandmother. She loved nothing more than to let the soil run through the fingers of her beautiful hands, hands that also had that instinctive aptness of knowing how the flowers wanted to look in the house.

A short distance from the house was a bank on which three old chestnut trees grew. They hung over the bank creating a cathedral-like space beneath, gloriously shady in hot weather and giving two effective harvests – white candles in spring, conkers in autumn.

The top part of the garden nestled round the house. There were various outhouses, a stable with two loose boxes, a harness room which always smelt damp and mildewy and was dark and cold, a coach house where my father's dog-cart was kept, later to contain the de Dion Bouton in 1912. After the coach house the garden narrowed and continued down a considerable hill to the bottom of the valley where there was a stream in a little wood which was not ours but where we nevertheless played. And to the right and west of the garden lay an enormous meadow, which my father rented from the Manor opposite, owned by an army officer serving in India. In the meadow Nobby the horse grazed, when not in the stable or out with my father on his rounds. Jane, the donkey, kept him company. These were our means of transport: the dogcart and Nobby for my father, Jane and the trap for the family.

Jane, like all donkeys, was no fool and had a will of her own. One day we were out with our Aunt Beresford in the trap with Jane. Auntie very kindly got out to walk up a hill to ease the donkey's load. At the top of the hill she placed her hand on the door of the trap but Jane, sensing that the easy time was over, dashed away and did not stop until we reached home. My brother and I, quite unable to control her, were shaken like peas in a saucepan. Our aunt had an anxious and ignominious walk back.

The field was a big one and had a pond in the middle. It had a barn and a pigsty – we kept pigs and piglets. Albert, the son of a country cottager, knew the true value of pig keeping. Most cottagers in those days kept a pig, valued with pride and affection until the sad day came when it was killed, providing the family with meat, bacon and lard for months to come. "Well, pigs is pigs." was one of Albert's favourite sayings to my father, if he suspected him to be wavering over the next litter. We also kept chickens, which wandered in and out of the barn. Today this might seem an enormous property yet it was what was necessary for anyone who was obliged to keep a horse or even horses to carry on with their livelihood, as my father had to do. The field provided hay for Nobby and Jane : this was stored in the loft above the stable. It also provided enormous fun at the hay harvest for us and Albert's sons.

Into this gentle pattern my early life fitted. Then, when I was four, change came. Nobby fell in the pond and the pond was deep. Albert was alerted to the accident by the faithful Jane, who cantered wildly round the field eeoring at the top of her lungs until help came. Alas despite Jane's effort and all Albert's loving care, Nobby developed pneumonia and died, mourned by us all.

Then came the de Dion Bouton. My father was beginning to lose his objection to motorcars. Gone were the days when he had driven his dog-cart in a cork screw winding motion up Watford High Street in front of a car in order to register his dislike of the invention. So he became converted or succumbed to a de Dion. It was the last model to be produced with only one cylinder and this had an unfortunate result for my father. He found that he could be heard all over the countryside as he puffed along and was therefore continually stopped on his way by anxious mothers who had not sent for him – "Just in case, Doctor.", they would plead. The de Dion was the outcome of Nobby's tragedy which, although we did not know it at the time, presaged the end of the style of life which I have just described.

My recollection of those first few years of my life is of the garden and of course of Albert. 1911 was one of those exceptionally long hot summers. I remember hanging about the coach house while Albert put the finishing touches to the dogcart and harness for Nobby – both were turned out with pride by Albert each day and were ready waiting for my father to come out from his morning surgery. One day Harry the garden-boy teased me by putting me into my pram which he was cleaning. The pram was lined with American Cloth, a forerunner of plastic, and it was burning hot to touch. I screamed not so much with pain but more with frustration. "You didn't ought to have done that, 'Arry," said Albert, "look you've put her in a rage." No doubt I was often in a rage. At my christening the verger is reputed to have said to my aunt "Don't she 'owl?"

I think I was difficult. There was a nanny whom I did not love and she did not love me. I remember being pushed out in the pram in the afternoons, a practice greatly encouraged for all nannies to get them out and the child to sleep. Nanny was often accompanied by a tall young soldier resplendent in a scarlet coat. This made it difficult for me to drop off to sleep as required. Nanny would lean over the pram and administer a sharp slap to the covering with the exasperated cry of "Go to sleep." The practice was quite unnecessary as, if she feared I might give away her secret, I was quite incapable of doing so at that age. On the other hand, I assumed this to be normal treatment until one day I was pushing my doll's pram in the garden and lent over smacking the occupant, a doll not a kitten, saying "Go to sleep". An elderly cousin remarked: "What a cruel mother – your baby will never go to sleep if you slap her like that."

I don't know if my parents found out and disapproved of Nanny but she disappeared. Little May left, I think to be married, Albert's children all married young and happily, and Emily came as a nurse-housemaid. All these distinctions among servants were carefully drawn up by agencies that supplied them. Everyone knew their place – agencies, employers and maids. It had simplicity. Now it is considered that the contracts for employment were very one-sided in favour of the employers, but the maids had board and lodgings which people tend to forget and their work clothes, uniforms, and often a happy household to live in. Although I agree that wages were ridiculously low, the house reverberated with life, it was full of people – the kitchen was a place of friendship for children, with fun as well rough discipline as meted out in the cottages from which the maids had come and where life was hard. This taught us a lot too.

It was a great treat when the maids asked if they might take me home and I saw the other world: life in cramped conditions in a small cottage with many children of all ages sitting round the table eating wonderful stodgy suet puddings soaked in gravy and vegetable – lots of turnips. Afterwards we would go for walks along the lanes and in the woods and gather flowers, and then after a hot cup of tea it was time to go home. I was shy but I learnt a lot.

Then, when I was four, I went to school where Pat was already among the bigger children. I joined the kindergarten. My first day, I well remember because I was given a bundle of little coloured sticks which I was told were units. Now our grocer was called Mr. Unit and of course I lost myself in my own game. I saw his white apron, his neatly trimmed beard in my imagination and made him a white stick while I arranged his brothers, sisters, aunts and uncles in groups from the other colours.... My first lesson in mathematics thus utterly failed as I did in that subject from that day on.

When a little older I was a fairy in A Midsummer Night's Dream. A boy called Peter Murray Hill was an elf, one of Puck's followers. We both wanted to relieve ourselves while waiting off stage in the garden and we did so behind a large peony. What we did not realise was that although we were sheltered from the view of those off-stage grown-ups who were busy dressing us we were in full view of the audience. This mishap landed us in dire trouble after the event.

I wonder if it was the school's fault or mine, but it was at this school, nice as it was, that I began to experience a lack of confidence – I was short of what was expected in those days of "Character". "Character" always had a capital C to Victorians, and had to be encouraged into us. True, we were now in the reign of Edward VII, but the grown-ups in our lives had been reared by Victorians. When asked if I had been in the raspberry bed I lied, but my stained pink lips betrayed me – it was very grave: I hated batter pudding and laughed at lavatory jokes, whereas in later life smutty jokes have always alarmed me in case I miss the point. I made friends with a girl whose parents were in India and who was the ward of the headmistress – together we wasted our time playing pranks I think, and were probably a damned nuisance. My mother was a friend of the headmistress and it was agreed amicably that if we were separated we might learn something and so I was the obvious one to go. In after school-life it served me well as I boasted that I had been expelled from my first school which gave a spurious cachet to my standing which I freely indulged as well as the fact that I had two webbed toes on each foot.

My mother on the other hand had to find an alternative education and I joined a family of four children who had a governess – Miss Cowderoy from whom I learnt to write but not to read. Their parents were very intelligent, their father an editor of the Manchester Guardian. The children were young and spirited; we played most imaginative games with dolls for whom we cooked and dyed clothes, making our own dyes from flowers. After a little time they went to the local grammar school and another family was found.

This was during the Great War and the children of our neighbours, the Wheelwrights had lost their mother, a very talented artist. Their father was at the front. However he had married again, a most interesting outstanding woman who gallantly decided to teach her stepchildren and enlisted others to join. I was very happy there in this small school and the family became life-long friends of my brother and myself: the family of Wheelwright; there were four of them – Dorothy, Tiggy, Betty and Jack; after the war there were two more – Joan and Tony. This was the time I learnt to read, among many other things.

It is impossible not to include Miss Dack in the story of our growing up into adulthood. Miss Dack – "Miss E.C. Dack", as her bill heads announced. Miss Dack was the daughter of the church verger who died before we children knew her. She kept a little shop in one of the cottages opposite the church. She sold all sorts of things from reels of cotton, handkerchiefs, pens and pencils, writing paper, books and ran a circulating library costing two-pence a book, sentimental stories or poetry which she loved. After her father died and before the shop was established she often came to our house to look after my brother when he was a little boy. Pat led her a fair dance, I think, but she was always game. Once when my mother met Pat coming in alone from the garden she asked "What have you done with Miss Dack?" "Oh" was the reply – "she's up a tree being Pallas Athene but can't get down".

For me, she was a great friend and ally – I would escape to her shop when Mademoiselle arrived to try and teach me French. Also when Miss Dack wanted to shop in the village she would ask me to keep shop – a hugely enjoyed treat. She was very small and her clothes were always too big so, as she "ran up the village" the clothes jumped up and down on her. When we grew older it became a custom to visit her on Sunday evenings. She was the bane of my father's existence – she adored him and when she heard our front door shut as he walked out she would run out to catch him for a chat. Much later in life my mother-in-law lived in the cottage next door. Early in the second war a bomb fell on the village destroying the church's lych-gate, the memorial for the first war and also killing a soldier billeted in our house. My mother-in-law rushed out to see if Miss Dack was all right, but the blast blew her back into her own house, breaking both her wrists. Miss Dack got up and swept up the glass and went back to bed. When I visited her in my middle age she asked me how old I thought she was. I turned this over in my mind – well, when I was little you must have been at least seventy so now you are well over a hundred. Fortunately I did not reveal this assumption – she proudly said she was eighty. Then, one day near the end of the war, we buried her in a quiet corner of the churchyard. The coffin looked so tiny.

I return to a cryptic date in my childhood – 1914. But before this came 1913 which brought into my life a great-uncle from Jamaica. My parents had gone on a walking tour in Switzerland. My brother was at a boarding school in Seaford and I was sent to stay with my grandmother, who lived with our aunt in a little house in Bushey. For some days the small household was excitedly preparing for a visit from a beloved brother after years of separation. I unfortunately went down with some childish complaint and was confined to bed when the great day arrived, which of course may have been a benefit for my grandmother. She brought him up to see me and a small, slightly built, charming man peered down at me with twinkling eyes like my Granny's. Together they joined in and played some game I had invented to pass the time.

I did not know it then, but this visit was of great moment. My grandmother had been brought up with her brother and sister on a plantation in Jamaica. There had been a terrible drama when she had run away to marry my grandfather, an Irish doctor, causing her father to disinherit her, his favourite daughter. Now her father had died and this visit was a re-establishment of the family connection and bridged years of lost affection between brother and sister. It was also to have a bearing on my own life in the long distant future.

The Great War I

"Vive L'Angleterre!" came across the water to our retreating ship. From every window along the street that borders the harbour in Dieppe and from the intensely crowded breakwaters that enclosed it like two encircling lobster's claws, the French waved and cheered until we could hear them no more. And we in our turn put up in unison from the overcrowded ship a cry – "Vive La France!" This overwhelming fraternity was only about four hours old. Up to that point we had been distinctly unpopular – the villains – perfidious Albion in fact. It was 4th of August 1914.

My mother was a Francophile and wished her children to be so too. She determined to take us for a holiday in France and Pourville, a little seaside town a few miles from Dieppe, was selected as suitable. My father booked rooms in a small pension – "Aux Deux Routes" – for the family and my Aunt Beresford. Some friends of my parents and their son had also come with us. My father was to join us later. My poor brother at school in Seaford had chickenpox and was not able to join us as we crossed from Newhaven. He was, however, to travel later with my father.

There exists a post card – Carte Postale – written to my father in my mother's handwriting post-marked 27 July 1914. It reads "Please try and come on Saturday – there is a war scare on here – today the Banks will not take B's gold. Do please come!". There was, as we now know, more than a war scare in the Chancelleries of Europe. That postmark is very significant: it was only a day or two before Lord Grey's famous statement "The lights are going out all over Europe." The Germans were already packing their trains with troops bound for the Belgian frontier, while the great powers ganged up for or against each other in a tangled web of hostilities that followed the murder of the Austrian Archduke in Serbia at Sarajevo. The general public had very little idea of what was happening and this included my mother.

While we children played on the beach, swam and ate the enormous meals provided by Madame at the pension, the grown-ups either sat rather decorously in groups in deck chairs on the beach or went for walks. They had endless "boring" discussions. There was a German waiter whom everyone liked at the pension, 'Fritz', of course, and every time the guests assembled for meals they would light-heartedly ask him if he had his orders yet. This was not a serious inquiry but served as a means of practising their foreign language ability. The orders meant that he must make for the frontier of Germany at once or run the risk of being interned in France in the case of war. This and the Bank's refusing to exchange gold to francs made anxious conversation for the guests. Then, one day, to everyone's dismay, Fritz replied to my mother "Mais oui Madame, il faut que je parte de bonne heure demain matin."

By five o'clock next morning Fritz had gone. But he came back: the waiters from the Grand Hotel with whom he was to travel had not waited for him and had already gone. Madame, with tears of grief, was however the proud owner of an automobile and she put it at his disposal: she bid him another tearful farewell, promising to keep his trunk safe until after the war. It was Saturday, and that afternoon my father arrived. It was 2nd August.

That evening I walked hand in hand with him down to the sea front. As we wandered along notices were being pasted up on all walls, trees or in conspicuous places. "Mobilisation Générale". People crowded round to read them and all the men, young and middle-aged, were scrambling to be off to their units by any means available. My father remarked "I am afraid there is going to be a war," to which it is alleged that I replied "If I had known there was going to be a battle I would never have come."

Somehow next day, 3rd August, we got to Dieppe. Madame regretted that she could not help but a farmer with a trap was willing to take us. Once in Dieppe we met the full force of our national unpopularity. "C'est la guerre". Where was perfidious Albion? Steamers had been cancelled. Passengers for England who were arriving by every train slept that night on the hard benches in the Customs House. "Surely," pleaded my mother, "you can let us have some milk for the child (me)?" She then ingeniously found a bed for me and slept herself on the floor.

Next day we wandered disconsolately about the town. We found a hotel, which grudgingly gave us coffee. It was beside a huge square – La Grande Place – where the military were examining horses which the farmers had brought in for possible war service. I jumped in and out of a low window and ate lumps of sugar wrapped in paper. My mother irrelevantly complained that the white frills on my drawers were getting black.

We huddled on the beach throwing stones at a cairn my father had constructed. Then suddenly, in mid-afternoon, we saw to our relief a ship high in the water, because of a lack of her usual ballast. She was empty of passengers but turned out to be the packet from Newhaven sent to pick up the stranded tourists. We gathered our things and made for the harbour and watched the ship berth. As she did so, sailors on board threw great bundles of English newspapers on to the quay. Everyone scrambled to get one and there in enormous letters was the headline announcement that England had dispatched her Ultimatum to the German Embassy in London, to the effect that if Germany did not withdraw her troops from Belgium by 11 p.m. that night England would declare war on Germany. In seconds our status changed, arms stretched out to embrace us, restaurants opened their doors to us, milk for the child as well as that of human kindness flowed. By about 8 p.m. we were ready to sail and the ship pulled away from the quay amidst the cries of farewell to comrades in arms. Eventually we could no longer hear "Vive l'Angleterre!" and our throats no doubt were dry.

By the time we approached Newhaven the Ultimatum had run its course, it being by then midnight. A bossy little tug came out to meet us and through a megaphone her captain informed ours that England was at war with Germany. Had we any Germans on board? This put people into a flurry of confusion. The last thing I remember is putting my feet to fit a pattern on a carpet in a hotel in Newhaven at 3am on 5th August 1914, while my parents finished a late supper.

The Great War II

During the remainder of those summer holidays, which were fine and hot, soldiers continually marched through the village of Bushey en route for camp in Watford. They came from London and were Territorials or Reserves. As our house was set back from the road, they generally broke off at that point and sat down, those who could leaning against the house. We kept a barrow of apples always ready and out my brother would wheel it, to distribute among the relaxing men. They asked our names and made much of us, thinking perhaps of the children they may have left behind. We also offered cigarettes – "Three Castles". Then at command they would drag themselves to their feet to fall in and off they would march. After a few paces they always swung into song. They always sang as they marched. I remember on one day when they did not fall out but marched on, a cottager from across the road ran out with a jug of water which they passed along the lines as they marched, and I thought what a clever thing to think of. Some weeks later they would return on their way to London to entrain for France. I think they were known as "The First Hundred Thousand" or perhaps that was the name of a book I read by Ian Hay which filled me with tears because so many, nearly all, were killed.

Since those days and quite recently when watching a TV programme describing the outbreak of the Great War, I discovered that, what I always thought of as my mother's rather foolish foible in her unpreparedness for war, was universal – no one had any idea of what was going on, least of all in the capitals of Europe. The great empires were deciding what to do next in the most haphazard sabre-rattling way. The Kaiser up to 2nd August was hesitant and did not really want a war. Russia, still smarting under its defeat by Japan, was eager to prove a good ally to Serbia. France wanted to protect her own land once more from assault by Germany. Britain did not decide to declare war until 4th August. Perhaps it was really the legacy from Bismarck which finally won the day, so that all Europe went to war.

The years that followed were punctuated by my mother's dramatic announcements chiefly of the terrible disasters that befell and overtook the Allies. There were the everlasting casualty lists which devastated the village, as sons and husbands were killed. Also among the wounded and killed were some of our own relations and friends from further afield. But despite these tragedies, our house was a happy place, bustling with life.

One of the greatest treats was the usually unexpected arrival of people on leave from the Front in France. Two Irish-Canadian officers made their headquarters and temporary home with us. A young man who had spent his school holidays in our house because his father was a colonial governor somewhere, also came to us for leave: Archie, at school at Fettes in Scotland, had been too old to notice me or I him, except occasionally when I was allowed to see his model train set up in the attic. When war came he resolutely remained in the ranks and wore a very scratchy uniform. His brother Edward, a regular soldier, was taken prisoner and spent a bitter war in a prison camp in Germany. A luxury hotel, Bushey Hall, became the training school for recruits for the Brigade of Guards, and I remember a very lonely young man, a Welsh poet, took refuge within our house whenever possible. Among my mother's letters are some to him at the Front. I do not know if he survived.

Meanwhile, my mother worked in Watford, making bandages and she became head of the Red Cross Depot's Bandage Room. Albert left for the Front in a labour battalion and used to write postcards to us. Forever after he regaled us with stories of France, to our delight as they were made up of army gossip in the ranks. This left us with the garden and my mother in her element as she loved gardening and sometimes she and Albert had not seen eye to eye. She sent him parcels of food to complicated addresses in France. In fact, I think that she, like many people in wartime, thoroughly enjoyed her full life. I have found countless letters to men at the Front and then sadder ones from their relations edged with black – life and death were closely intertwined at that time. With all this intensity a lighter side to life emerged, captured with such words as flappers, knitting, (children knitted khaki scarves with irregular curvy sides as the stitches varied in number – some got dropped) the foxtrot which was to give birth to the Dancing Years, rationing and baked beans, Harry Lauder, Chou Chin Chow, I think, and George Robey whom my mother adored.

My own life proceeded in a fairly even way. At home with my mother so often out at the Depot, the maids were my playmates or I visited my grandmother where Aunt B would teach me how to write in Braille for the blinded soldiers. This was fun and absorbing. I remember I was digging a grave for a dead bird when my mother announced in a voice that was like one of Jove's thunderbolts, that Kitchener had been drowned. Later my father's friend in the Ministry of Information told him that a telegram had been intercepted which ran "Shall Herbert enter the London Academy next December" making the word "Shetland", close to where Kitchener's ship had been torpedoed. This was a subject to be discussed over Sunday lunch with much intensity.

Sunday lunch, I regret to say, for us was a feast. The butcher made it quite plain that "we cannot let the doctor starve" and accordingly sent a sirloin of beef when possible. To mitigate this luxury it was generally shared among many guests, including soldiers.

There was a big wedding at The Manor House when the youngest daughter, Nora Gabain, was married. The Manor House grounds were opposite our house. Two of my school friends and I were bridesmaids. My chief memory is that the Bishop of London who officiated and later kissed the bridesmaids had not shaved very well – he was prickly. A cloud hung over the proceedings as the only son of the house was missing in France during the enemy's last "big push" as it was called, before the Allies managed to turn the tide of war – this was August 1918. He was never found.

But the tide did turn and November arrived. At the eleventh hour of the eleventh day of the eleventh month, after four years of continuous activity, those monstrous guns across the water fell silent and peace broke out. On 11th November 1918 the armistice was signed.

At school our friend and teacher, my friends' stepmother, waved a cup of cocoa and sent us home, hooters from the laundry blared out and the church bells began to peel as I bicycled home. My brother and I hung out our flags – the Union Jack, The Irish Harp on Green with its Union Jack in the corner, and a Red Ensign, emblems of patriotism of the sort that everyone possessed. Influenza had begun to sweep through the world and my father was rushed off his feet. At the same time my brother's school had closed and he was home so that he, my mother and one of the Canadians back on leave and I set off for London where we found the town madly and chaotically "en fête."

I saw the end of both wars in London, but this was a celebration to end all celebrations, as well as an end to all wars. The next one was more sober-minded – we had seen it all before. In 1918 we got into Trafalgar Square Tube station before the celebration resembled a riot. Children including myself were lifted and passed over the heads of the crowds trying to get in to the Tube station. My mother feared that she would never see me again but she did. As we trudged up the hill from Bushey Station the church bells were still peeling at 10 o'clock and my father was putting the car away after his long day. And this was only the beginning of the 'flu epidemic. We felt very happy, but of course very humbled, as we sat down to drink hot cocoa.

School

In January 1919 my friends, the Wheelwrights, and I all went to a school in Watford. The big double-decker buses that ran from Edgware to Watford had been taken to France to be used in speeding our soldiers in the great advance, chasing the Germans back across their frontier. As a result lorries did service for the absent buses – it was a cold winter and one was wrapped up in huge scarves, I remember, pinned behind one's back. Once at Watford Junction we had a half-hour walk and then the reverse journey at 4 pm. Once home, there was homework to be done. After a year or so of this our parents decided to send us as boarders.

In some ways I enjoyed this school chiefly because I found I was able to be naughty. At first I was horribly homesick as a boarder and found a little-frequented lavatory at the top of the house in which to cry. One of my friends, who had come from the same homely school in Bushey and I, got us into the most ridiculous trouble in our first term. The dormitory was divided into four with long curtains for privacy like those drawn round beds in hospitals. The grown-up world was still imbued with Victorian ideas of decorum – even children must never see each other's naked bodies.

There was a good custom at the school that after games in the afternoon everyone had a "sponge bath", so that under every bed was a small papier-mâché bath, a little like a modern washing-up bowl, which we filled and splashed about in the water before dressing in our tidy frocks for evening. On this particular afternoon we were playing about with water as children do and my friend was peeping into my cubicle, displaying her tiny bottom to Matron who at that moment came in to see what the noisy laughter was about. I was making a waterfall in some ingenious way but the trouble was our nakedness. We were taken when dressed to the headmistress who said, "No nice children would do such a thing." and we were allowed no jam on our bread for a week. Freud's ideas had not yet penetrated English girls' boarding schools but to our credit this did not affect our lives in adulthood as the old rogue might have expected.

There was another friend in our village with whom I had played ever since I was seven. Her father had been killed in the war and her mother, much reduced in circumstances, managed gallantly to bring up on a pittance two boys and a girl, who was my friend and two years older than I was.

Babs joined us as a boarder at the school in Watford and she and I came home every Sunday after Church and returned in the De Dion in the evening. At least we were not in the De Dion but outside it. There was a special arrangement for passengers: a back seat was lifted on to the car's stern by Albert and my father and screwed down on a flat area behind the hood. Whoever sat here was high up – one could catch bits off trees as one drove under them. It made a strange profile – the bonnet with its magnificent brass lamps beside it, then my father and mother, (my mother in summer wearing a veil against the dust) then the hood folded back, then us on the back seat. My brother and I had many journeys on the back seat.

One happy memory of my friend was on an island we pretended we owned in the middle of a pond in the Manor House garden where we were allowed to play. It was small but a delight. We sowed seeds of flowers and mustard and cress and spent hours there. One day I managed to fall in when crossing on a branch of a tree, our only access. The wartime addiction to knitting was still a rage and our two mothers had knitted us dresses. As I walked home from this ducking my dress stretched to the ground. I felt grown up. Although my mother re-knitted my dress, this initiated a great game of dressing up in our parents' clothes, borrowed unbeknown of course by them. We then tottered out into the village street on unwieldy high heels and with rouged cheeks and lipstick, to various houses where we paid an afternoon visit – such things still existed. Sometimes a bewildered butler would inform us that Madam or even on one case Her Ladyship was out – we chose big houses and giggled our way up or down their drives. We never managed to get past the servant at the door. I remember Her Ladyship was wife of a recently made peer and new landowner. I take it that it is his grandson about whom I sometimes read and who is now deeply involved in the politics of Europe.

After a year or so at school in Watford we all, except Babs, left for other schools. There were defects, which our parents did not care for and they sought for alternatives. Mine was Sherborne, but looking back I missed the fun of the Watford School. My final departure turned into a riot. My dormitory had planned a midnight feast which entailed getting day girls to buy food which we stored in the chimney. Then one day we found that the chest-of-drawers that hid our hidey-hole was pulled out and our stock removed. All hell broke out, complicated by my mother arriving in the hall one evening bringing a special assortment of cakes for an allowed farewell party. The evening was Maundy Thursday and her visit coincided with that of the priest who had come to hear confessions – (the school was ultra High Church which my parents thought excessive). My mother was unknowing of the midnight lark but she was overcome by the odour of sanctity and dumped the cakes in the hall and rushed off. "Can you imagine the deceit of it," said the headmistress, over the telephone next day "she hid the food in the chimney." To which my mother wisely replied in her slow engaging way "I don't suppose she had anywhere else to put it, had she?". I was proud of my mother, but she did not encourage me to feel in the right. All very girlish fun, encouraged by such writers as Angela Brazil whose books were favourite Christmas presents – "The Madcap of the School" I seem to remember.

I also remember one occasion when one of my exploits paid a very happy dividend in my favour. I can't remember why I was in disgrace but I was not allowed to go to the firework display at the boys' school which was exactly opposite our school. I was to go to bed instead. Well, what the authorities forgot was that my dormitory overlooked the boys' school and from my window I had a wonderful view. At the same time, the maids who were the only other occupants of the house took it into their heads to bring me up a special supper and to join in the firework watching. Maids were splendid in their tolerance of children and nearly always took their part if they felt a child was ill-used by their standards. On the other hand they had a robustness which was very straightforward.

Sherborne was a very different kettle of fish. It was at the other end of the spectrum as regards religion – it was a last stronghold of Protestant England. It had a dear old head mistress, Miss Mulliner, who had been schooled in the teaching world by those truly admirable women, Miss Beale and Miss Buss of Cheltenham Ladies College fame. "Miss Buss and Miss Beale, Cupid's darts do not feel – how different from us, Miss Beale and Miss Buss" is now famous but their spirit dominated our upbringing at that delicate stage. Their mission was to establish the right for girls to have the same advantages in education as boys had. English, mathematics, history, geography, a little science and languages etc, filled our days, which began and terminated in prayers, good wholesome prayers I must add – petitions to make us better people. We played games, engaged in matches, and were taught sportsmanship and to be self reliant – like our brothers, we were told. But here was where a discrepancy crept in – contact with our brothers or with other people's brothers was not encouraged, the boys' school was out of bounds. Parents with boys at the boys' school were asked not to take their girls there for fear of infection, which must have been very irksome for the parents. Letters even to uncles were regarded with suspicion.

Sunday was a day encased in the Bible. It began with prayers before breakfast, after which we wrote our letters to our parents. That over, we set out in crocodile formation for the Abbey. Here there was apt to be a two-hour service, fortunately in beautiful surroundings. During the long sermons one could read the Ten Commandments which were written in stone each side of the main aisle – just as Moses wanted them to be – on tablets of stone. The services were of what was called a "low church" variety of simplicity, which was rather charming, if dull.

We returned ravenous to our houses for a very good traditional Sunday lunch. After that we had two whole hours of scripture homework – one hour for the Old Testament and one for the New. Following that, we could go for a walk in crocodile formation or in summer, if hot, we were allowed to stroll about the school grounds. These we never left except to go to the Abbey on Sundays and with our parents when they were able to visit us.

In those days epidemics were very prevalent and a nightmare to schools, especially after Christmas. Nevertheless this theory of "infection" from other schools played an out-of-proportion part about which we had our suspicions. It was rumoured at one time that our headmistress had written to the boys' headmaster requesting that, if the boys, while out on a run, should find themselves passing a crocodile of girls, would they please not turn to look at them. The result was that when such a thing did happen, the boy in charge issued an order "Eyes left!" and to the girls' disappointment they all turned their heads away. I think things are very different today.

In fact the system had started to creak. Just before I left there was a sudden inexplicable happening – the big outside world made its first step in encroachment. The fifth and sixth forms were invited, and the invitation was accepted, to attend a performance of Julius Caesar at the boys' school. The preparations for this undertaking were prodigious: our house matron gave us minute directions for our dress. We were to wear our confirmation dresses – white, of course, and to take our shawls. We would wear our overcoats and tam o'shanters and snowboots (these were worn when going over to the schoolhouse for lessons) but these three things were to be left in the hall. All girls must wear their thick green games tights as a precaution against the cold, our matron rather curiously added. The evening was a great success as far as the girls were concerned – we all fell in love with Cassius.

Oddly enough the story does not end there. In late life, sixty years later, I went to a naval dinner party. The great man of the occasion revealed that he had been at school at Sherborne and of course I said that I had too. I then told him the story I have just written and we both laughed. "But", I added, "we all fell in love with Cassius." to which he replied "I was Cassius." Astonished, I looked, and there I could see in this good-looking man the once gangly youth, who had captivated us sixty years before.

After three years at Sherborne, I was moderately well educated for a non-academic child. I managed to come away with my School Certificate with five credits but these were in “soft” subjects, as my young son told me in after years.

In this innocent atmosphere, combined with our own natural innocence, I was wholly unprepared for adult life, was horribly shy and quite out of place in the home to which I returned, which had become full of my brother's young friends from Cambridge.

The Nineteen Twenties

In 1925 I left school. At the same time my brother in his third year at Cambridge fell in love and became engaged to a most beautiful girl, Eileen Crofts. She had connections with Bushey having been to school at St. Margarets but she hailed from Westmoreland in the Lake District I was seventeen and my brother's friends were all about twenty-one and more. I was desperately shy amongst these seemingly alarming people with all the savoir faire which I entirely lacked. I had stepped into a world where the rules for living instilled into us by all those dear teachers, those innocent women who had gone straight from school to be sheltered at university and then returned to school again to teach, did not apply. Our teachers, whether they wanted it or not, were for the most part condemned to spinsterhood, the men they might have married had been killed in the war. Our scholarly and deeply religious headmistress hoped that her girls would become missionaries in darkest Africa or failing that "There is," as she said in her pep talk to leaving girls, "the profession of teaching; nursing is a noble calling or nowadays one can even become a doctor." At this point she paused, sighed and looked out of the window. "Then there are others," she went on, "and you need not despair. For you, there is the home." Beyond that there were no more categories. A very pretty Welsh girl, more knowledgeable than most of us, added as we broke up "What about the street?" I got the impression that our revered headmistress had no idea as to how her pupils had arrived in this world.

So there was little guidance in all this for life as I found it in the 1920s. Nor were the books that everyone seemed to be reading to be found in the school library – books by such people as Michael Arlen and Aldous Huxley. In my bewilderment I used to go for long walks with my dog and return in a filthy old mack which I did not take off as I sat in the drawing room amongst those Adonises and pretty young women and was offered drinks like gin and orange, a new "in" drink, (I can't believe my father approved), of which in shyness I drank too much.

My mother, who had greatly looked forward to my return and who unrealistically did not appreciate my ineptitude but wanted me to play a part as daughter of the house, struggled gallantly to cope with my uncouthness and inelegance. She set off with me to a London dressmaker but here we met more trouble – I was the wrong shape. It was the day for flat chests when women battened down anything they had in that line with the same vigour as the previous generation had gone in for tight-lacing their waists in corsets. Waists now were round the thighs: the result was a profile resembling a pencil – the so-called "boyish figure". With pins in their mouths the dressmakers tut-tutted as they draped pieces of material round me and I stood mesmerised with dismay by my bulging reflection in the mirror – a plump seventeen-year-old with bosoms the size of small melons – no wonder I thought I was deformed. This brings me to the strange fashion in language for this part of the female anatomy. We had busts to be flattened, the Victorians found friendly bosoms to be cried on by friends in trouble, later breasts became fashionable, particularly with someone called Sabrina (by which time ironically I could not fill the bras on offer in shops) and now the word is boobs which can be accepted with ease or not, according to the attitude of the developing adolescent.

On another front (my head) a kindly hairdresser shingled my locks and chatted as if to a normal being. My head in the mirror looked quite a promising shape when he had done. My father expressed sorrow when I returned without plaits, or perhaps it was some years earlier that I became bobbed.

I remember that my lovely sister-in-law-to-be sympathetically took my hand and steered me from the harrowing dressmaker experience to the hairdresser. Nevertheless, despite her kindness I could not disguise from myself at that moment that it was also her perfect lines that induced my fear of my own deformity.

The next effort of my mother's who had always had big ideas, fulfilled a long cherished wish of hers – she took a party up to Cambridge for May Week. My brother found rooms for my mother, his girl and myself and he included an undergraduate friend to make up our party. The friend was also very attracted by his beautiful young woman which made it interesting – I managed as best I could to feel at ease. I might have succeeded better if I had not met my first horsefly during a picnic.

We had set out in punts on the River Granta passing a party which consisted of Jack Hulbert, Cicely Courtledge and Leslie Henson, then at the height of their fame in the musical comedy world, exciting to all of us. I enjoyed paddling a canoe. We had lunch in a field. It must have been here that I was stung. The evening of the next day was the Pembroke Ball, the highlight of the whole enterprise, my leg started to swell as we returned from the picnic and by next morning was the size of an elephant's. Treatment of my leg became the central preoccupation of our whole party. Nothing seemed of any avail until my brother got hold of a bucket into which he placed my leg and then he filled the bucket with nearly boiling water from a kettle straight from the hob. I might not have danced very well, but I did go to the Ball, carrying this diminishing bolster leg through the evening.

The next day we went home and I found happiness traipsing across the fields with my dog once more.

These were the dancing years. Everyone danced. It was the day of Thé Dansant. You could go to a restaurant in almost any town and there would be a small band, hopefully with a saxophonist, a piano and any other musician that could be engaged. Tea, bread and butter, hot buttered toast, sandwiches, even watercress and elaborate cakes would be ordered, and between mouthfuls, people would jump up and take a turn or two with their partner around the prepared space. If women had no men at the table they would dance together, men of course were always in short supply. At night the big towns blazed with dance halls, Palais-de-Danse; partners could be hired and the competition between bands was a great factor. In London there was Ambrose, the Savoy Orphians and several others. In private houses or studios a record could be put on the gramophone and people would start to dance until the record suddenly groaned itself to a dying halt. The needle then had to be changed and the record replayed. All sorts of needles were invented but the principle always remained the same until the stylus came and we called the instrument a record player.

At this point it is time to mention Aunt Elsa. Aunt Elsa was not a real aunt but she had joined my mother and aunt for lessons with their German governess in their childhood. She was the same age. I have already mentioned Professor Herkomer who ran the famous Art School in Bushey. The Professor married three times and by his second wife he had a son, Siegfried, and a daughter, Elsa. After this wife, Lulu, died, he married again, causing something of a scandal because the third wife was the sister of Lulu, an alliance forbidden by the church. Aunt Elsa always maintained that their stepmother neglected them, putting all her energy into the students and the school. In fact, she claimed they would have fared very badly indeed if my grandmother had not taken pity on them, fed them odd meals and suggested that they share her children's governess. It was because of this that Aunt Elsa considered my mother was the nearest she ever had to a sister – my own Aunt Beresford and Elsa were less allied.

And so it was that throughout my childhood Egyptian cotton arrived to be made into dresses for me and every summer Aunt Elsa and her husband, Uncle Charles, came to spend some of their leave from Egypt staying with us. This was not always pure pleasure for my mother. Aunt Elsa, like her father, the Professor, was eccentric. We had other eccentric aunts, real ones, from Ireland, but Aunt Elsa's eccentricity was very noticeable, in fact embarrassing. She always held strong views and voiced them wherever she was. The most tiresome quirk in these visits was Aunt Elsa taking over the kitchen, which she did on arrival. Owing to the climate of Egypt and the difference between Egyptian and English stomachs, she brought back a rule that all vegetables must be washed in permanganate of potash before being cooked. She forgot, as she took control, that Albert's vegetables were beyond reproach, grown in good honest London clay and that none of us suffered from the home cooking. You can imagine the nightmare this became to my mother as she explained the complications to Ellen, our cook, who became grumpy and offended and apt to give notice.

And so it was a terrible shock on the day I walked into the house, having left school for good, to hear (almost amidst my mother's greeting) that Aunt Elsa had invited me to spend a few days with her in London. Uncle Charles would be away visiting his relations. To my consternation my mother had agreed that I should accept.

I was stunned with alarm. The reason for my mother's decision was twofold: one very deep and real reason was sympathy: poor Aunt Elsa and Uncle Charles had lost a very sweet little daughter a year before, which devastated us all. Another reason, I suspected, was my mother's desperation at the chaos in the house. So it was that I found myself for several terrifying days, the first of the summer holidays, staying at a very grand hotel, the Mostyn, somewhere near the back of Selfridges in London.

It was indeed a grand hotel: I was a very young and inexperienced seventeen: the decorum of the dining room was awe inspiring: the hushed voices of the diners (other than my aunt's imperial tones), the immaculate starched table cloths sculptured to the sizeable tables with napkins made to look like waterlilies and the supercilious head waiter in his white tie and tails, a true monarch of his realm, bending over Aunt Elsa while he and she studied the menu. At the very first meal my worst apprehension was fulfilled – Aunt Elsa took the head waiter under her wing, explaining just how she wanted her meal cooked, almost threatening to show the chef in his own kitchen her methods. At this point I felt the apparent silent ears of the other diners had somehow become focussed on our table.

To me Aunt Elsa was kindness itself – everything was arranged for my entertainment. At the same time she could not resist giving me some tuition in how to get my own way in public and my first lesson was at Selfridges. We were in a department that dealt with tropical kit – Empire days. We very soon had the staff of the whole floor in attendance while Aunt E explained how she wanted a parasol lined in green against the glare of the desert sun. Suddenly she demanded a chair. Now Selfridges had just gone over to the

American idea and had done away with those nice chairs against the counter once found in English shops when you could do your choosing blissfully sitting down. So persuasive was Aunt Elsa that eventually a huge wooden office armchair was brought down from Gordon Selfridges's own office upon which she sat like King Canute regarding the rising tide of amused shoppers, who now gathered round us. It was impossible for me to try and pretend I was one of them as Aunt Elsa called to me to open a parasol and walk round with it so that she could judge its suitability.

We went to two theatres, which was fun, and to the nearby Wallace Collection. There was one difficulty when out and about, which seemed to me to be very tedious. Aunt E did not trust the hygiene of any public convenience – loos now – and so we had to take a taxi back to the hotel when we wanted to relieve ourselves.

In the evenings after dinner, we went out dancing – "Whom shall we dance with?" I asked, fearing that we would have to dance with each other. "No worry on that score." said Aunt E with a mischievous look and when we arrived at the Mayfair Hotel Ballroom, I think it was, a beautifully dressed young man, in white tie and tails like the head waiter, greeted us. "Good evening, Madam." and Aunt Elsa introduced me to Marcus, our hired partner, a gigolo.

It was lovely to dance with Marcus, but difficult to talk to him. He always began the evening with "How's your auntie tonight?" after which conversation languished, as I was too intent following his steps. Aunt E insisted that I danced first, then I would sit out at our table and watch as she whirled energetically around the ballroom taking Marcus with her. She wore a wig – very unusual in those days, but as she said, it saved many tedious hours at the hairdresser – and the wig used to become a little tippety before she sank exhausted down as the band stopped. I would try surreptitiously to straighten it for her.

Looking back, I think I was too inhibited to enjoy the extraordinary experience and in my ridiculous adolescent way I was thankful that there was no one from my school there to witness me dancing with a gigolo who was really very nice and earning an honest living giving fun to two odd lonely women.

Aunt Elsa came into my life again in the far distant future.

Further Education

During the next autumn of 1926 my Mother wisely sent me to learn housecraft at the National School of Cookery in Buckingham Palace Road. I was boarded out rather oddly in a home for fallen women in Streatham. The reason for this was not a reflection on my morals nor a terrible warning should one stray from the straight and narrow. I was to stay in the house of the Warden, a clergyman with a large family of six children and his very nice wife. They were friends of friends of ours in Bushey. The wife was a sister of Ben Travers, a playwright of farces then in vogue – "The Cuckoo in the Nest", "Rookerynook" etc, with Tom Walls, Ralph Lynn and Mary Brough. This family was anything but dull. They ranged from ten to twenty-one and were very lively. The three months passed happily enough.

I became vaguely proficient in laundry and basic cooking of the suet-pudding variety but the best skill I brought away which paid dividends later in life was making loose covers for chairs and sofas. There was however one conspicuous failure due to the fact that I found I could get a seat at the Old Vic for 8 pence (8d about 10p today) so missed afternoon lectures. As a result I was never able to change a washer on a tap. But I saw Frank Vosper as Anthony which was a very fair exchange. I paid considerably more to plumbers down the ages than the price of my seat at the Old Vic.

After Christmas it was suggested that I should join two of my Irish cousins in Switzerland. Geoffrey Toone, at school in England, was feared to be suffering from lung trouble and in those days a spell in the Alps was the recognised treatment. He was at a school in Chateau d'Oex and his sister Cicely and I were to stay with an English woman, a Mrs Bull, recently widowed, and her friend Madame la Comtesse de Messey, from whom we were to learn French. The latter was an extremely fierce lady and rather masculine, tweeds, collar and tie, who became violently hostile to the suitors who surrounded her friend Mrs Bull, a lady of good looks and charm.

We were an odd party. The nicest thing that happened in Chateau d'Oex was an outing on toboggans towed behind a sleigh drawn by horses with tinkling bells on their harness. We stopped to drink delicious hot chocolate in a village before returning in the gloaming through woods of pine trees.

After a few weeks, it was decided to travel to Italy and this we did, stopping at Milan and Florence. I think it was a great burden for our hostesses to find accommodation that suited our parents' purses, so we stayed in some very grotty boarding houses. In Florence we seemed to be kept securely in our bedroom a great deal of the time but we got friendly with some sellers of ice cream and used to let down a basket on a string, with much fun displayed at each end of the string.

Of course we paid visits to museums but I was a complete philistine and became appalled at the fates of the poor martyrs depicted bathed in blood against imperial purple. So for me a great opportunity was lost. I think our hostesses did their best but were inexperienced themselves both in art and in interesting or inspiring the philistine young.

My mind however ran on other things. It was in Florence I thought romance had passed me by for all time. Geoffrey's housemaster from England came out to Florence with two other boys from Charterhouse and we all met. One of his friends invited me to join him on Sunday to visit the Uffizzi Museum. I got over my aversion to museums in a trice and was very excited at what I felt was my first invitation from a young man. Then, to my dismay, Mrs Bull decided that Cicely must accompany me. That might have passed well enough, had not Cicely been so well briefed in chaperonage that she took my arm in hers at the beginning of the outing and we glided like Siamese twins throughout the whole expedition. Finally we returned. The young man I remember stood up in the fiacre in which he had driven us home with an amused expression on his face and took off his porkpie felt hat first to one and then to the other of us. In my frustration I could not speak civilly to my cousin for some days – my life would never recover.

However it did and I quite forgot the young man's name. Then a short time ago I was recounting this ridiculous episode to Geoffrey himself, now in retirement after a long career as an actor. He gave me his friend's name. It was Hervey Benham. I had read his book "Down Tops'l" and had even met him in the fifties. He owned, as we did, a Thames Sailing Barge, with which he actually traded. He was a splendid man of the sea with whom my husband had much in common, so once more I was out-manoeuvred but did not happen to mind.

On my return home, my parents were rather appalled at my lack of progress in French, after quite a lot of expense. I am no linguist and later regretted the opportunities I had missed. My mother even signed me on once a week at the French Institute in London, where I managed to learn a delightful and famous poem by Ronsard about an old lady sitting sewing of an evening by the fire in her old age, who is not to forget "que Ronsard me célébrait du temps que j'étais belle". How charming I found this.

My Home and Albert

By the end of the summer of 1927 I felt something must happen, other than a round of tennis parties and the chickens. My father had set up chickens in a small way: a friend had built a magnificent hen house, all to give me occupation at home. I loved my home but I was stifled. My happiest times were spent helping Albert in the garden. There was no garden boy now, Albert was getting older, the field and Nobby had long since gone but the pigs remained.

The pigs were always a prime consideration with Albert Andrews. From time to time he and I would set off, I had learnt to drive, to call on various farms to arrange a marriage for Betsy, our sow. Albert wearing a collar and his jacket sat upright as suited a Lord Chamberlain scouring the courts for a suitable consort for a royal princess, and Betsy was royal. He turned down many possible husbands as unsuitable. Getting into the car after one visit he remarked "Well, Green's 'OG is like Green – lazy and don't know 'ow to take 'is pleasures. Drive on, Peg, to Turpins." So we drove on until an eligible mate had been found. A day or so later Betsy was got into the cart and amidst squeals of protest was driven off to her nuptials. Then a few more weeks passed before the little piglets arrived and happiness reigned in the garden.

Albert loved talking and reminiscing about the past. My life was enriched by his conversation as we worked. He told me how, as a boy of nine, he had taken the family cow out in Oxfordshire to feed along the verges by the roadside, thus providing milk for the large family of his brothers and sisters. The roads were very adequate for this, there was little traffic, the railways having taken it from the roads, and incidentally also from the canals. When he first had a job it was with his father's employer, Lord Jersey, for whom his father was forester. Albert looked after the youngest daughter of the family who was a cripple for whom her father had bought a special little chaise. Albert had care of it and the pony who pulled it and the young lady as she drove out.

Albert's father had taught his son to fell trees with the utmost precision. Albert having gauged the height of the tree would bend down until his head touched the ground and from this position he would note the tiptop of the tree and would put a stake in the ground where his head had been. Later after some hours of sawing and adjusting ropes etc the tree would fall, the tip would lie on the exact spot that had been staked.

When the field was sold, my father let a metal merchant take away some iron railings. This remained a source of deep sorrow to Albert. "You don't remember them there iron railings." he would say as we set out on some job, and I could see how handy they would have been. But there was an implement which seemed to cover all emergencies – it was Iron Bar and it belonged to Sexton in the churchyard, Our garden ran down the hill parallel with the church yard and one day I was sent off to get Iron Bar but I returned with the message that Sexton said "No". Albert's head went characteristically to one side as he said, "Mm, I'll go." Off he went and returned with Iron Bar. I never knew what had taken place from his comment – "Funny chap, Sexton."

He would tell me stories about the war and "what we did in France", but they were only everyday things. "Be first at the tap mornings but fourth with the stew." "Let the fat go to the other fellows." and so on. "Lousy as a 'edge'og." is another useful phrase when describing someone unpleasant.

In civilian life he was a fireman and when the whistle blew off he would run to the fire station in two minutes and we would not see him again for some time. His wife was a pretty woman, daughter of the shoemaker. She was a small, vivacious and proud person who brought up her family of two sons and four daughters with care and good sense on the sparse wages it was customary to pay. They did have lots of good vegetables, however. Looking back they were very happy and in comparison we were spoilt.

The meadow lay adjacent to our garden and although no longer ours it played a rather irksome part in our lives. The owner, the absent Lord of the Manor, offered it to my father for £20. It was a big field – say seventy acres or more. It was about 1913 and my father considered the offer; Nobby had died and the Dion Bouton had been bought. The hay harvest was a great labour and expense to my father, so the offer was turned down. The butcher, whose son was known as Greasy Harry because of the oil that plastered down his hair, bought the field. We had two butchers in the village but this one was one of my father's pet aversions – he had a few enemies, carefully selected whom he considered to be corrupt in some way or other.

Unforeseen in 1913 was the huge development that would take place between the wars when the railway was electrified and suburbia spread over England's green and pleasant land. So Grease's father was on to something good: he became very rich as he filled the field in the 1920s with many houses. This wealth however was not the bone of contention to my unacquisitive father. It was the hoarding – an enormous hoarding at least twenty feet high, which was erected along the High Road displaying garish advertisements. My father rightly objected: they were destroying the environment. During the Second War these horrors happily disappeared from the countryside lest they proved guides to an invading army or to the Luftwaffe.

"Hoist on his own petard" is a wonderful expression. My father had made his views against advertising so clear to everyone that when in the 1920s the London Midland and Scottish Railway offered to put some discreet advertisements, beautifully designed by Paul Nash, on our barn, which also faced the High Road, he felt bound to refuse.

My mother had been delighted at the idea – the rent would, she said, have paid for our summer holiday. My father was adamant and remained unmoved by her arguments. The crisis became very stormy one day at lunch. Finally my mother, realising that she had lost, rose majestically from the table and as she swept from the room remarked "Well, to the pure, all things are rotten."

My parents had a great many friends – our house was an open house at teatime when people from many sides of life came to see them. Our round table was spread with scones, sandwiches and cakes, my mother sitting beside the teapot. It was a satisfactory way to entertain as people sat down. This was much more conducive to conversation than stand-up drinking is today. There seemed to be a great deal to talk about. As well as the painters and writers who still lingered in Bushey and sometimes dropped in, many people came back on leave from abroad – district commissioners and their wives with tales to tell of lonely places in Africa or India. Real people, very different from the supercilious officials displayed on the television representing Empire Days – they were local people who had gone into the Colonial Service, probably marrying local girls.

One who was always very welcome was Oriana Wilson, the widow of Edward Wilson, who had been with Scott on the tragic expedition in which they both died. We had other connections with Antarctica, as Ernest Shackleton was a cousin. He returned in 1916 after his ship, the Endurance, was crushed in the ice and broke up. The most dramatic and historical journey by his crew, crossing the Weddell Sea in a small boat, the James Caird, and the final rescue was all hot national news. We were very proud of his achievement. His brother, Frank, we also knew but that was another story.

Our uncles and aunts from Ireland visiting England stopped off with us. It was possible to have breakfast in Dublin and tea on the same day in Bushey. For some reason the Irish Mail for Euston stopped at Watford.

But despite all this life at home, it was not mine and I yearned for mine to begin. The question was where and how. I was able to travel to London easily and signed myself on with some parish centre in the East End of London at Old Street. A friend of mine from school recommended it as a job. There was no pay: it was a time when people went as volunteers to try to help in the slums – a forerunner of today's Social Services – it was amateurish and very difficult to make any headway. Conditions were appalling – bugs where the paper had come away from the wall, I remember, and so much distress among the women I spoke to, trying to encourage them to keep up their children's hospital treatment and so on. I had to report my efforts to the committee made up of health workers and clergymen. Impossible to forget the plight of people living under such conditions. Later in life I spent some time in a very different East End of London where happiness reigned – Cable Street, not far from Old Street.

Then one day I took myself to an agency – Universal Aunts – and at once landed a paid job. Miserably, I gave up the voluntary work but I needed to earn. A kindly fat lady offered me work at £1 a week as an office girl. "The hours are 10 to 5 – tell your parents." she added to reassure them. This made me cross, as at seventeen I must have looked as gormless as I felt.

The following Monday – a glorious crisp October morning – I walked on air to the station. I was going to find my own adventure and to see the world.

Albert must have added care of the chickens to that of the pigs, but he didn't complain.

Office 10 to 5

My job was the office girl – the dogsbody – in a very scruffy office on the top floor of a building in Lower Regent Street. The business was run by an ex-army officer and comprised an insurance agency for brother officers and others. He was a rather ramshackle man, it seemed to me, and terribly old, but in reality in his fifties, I should think.

He shared the office with a retired Naval Commander who worked an engineering business and who was to the staff rather a shady figure: I was learning about what today would be called 'sleaze'. Both were kindly employers. My job was to stamp the letters, post them, file the papers in rather tatty envelope files of the Major's making and put them in alphabetical order on a very dusty shelf – in old offices there was always thick dust. I made tea and answered the telephone and did other things but I forget what. I learnt to type. There was a very nice girl secretary, Hilda, who took letters down in shorthand and typed them in the small outer office where we worked. We had one excitement that came up from time to time and that was going to dog shows.

This we did, whenever there was one in London. The Major bred Bedlington Terriers and they were a passionate interest to him. Sometimes I went with him – we took it in turns: Crufts, The Ladies Kennel Club and others in Olympia and the Crystal Palace I remember. On one occasion our stand was beside one displaying toothpaste and a girl stood at it saying "Can I interest you in Kolinos toothpaste?" "Can I interest you in Dog Insurance?" was my cry. We held out our respective brochures hoping to attract passers-by to our stands. Then on the second afternoon we relieved the monotony and she said "Do you insure your teeth?" and I said "Do you clean your dog's teeth with Kolinos?" The Major was not amused when he happened to return, but he forgave me. It was a very feeble joke.

I rather enjoyed myself towards the end of the shows when I would nervously go up to the winning dogs' owners and try and get them to insure their valuable dogs – a new idea in those days. There were many Americans and we tried to persuade them to insure their dogs for the sea passage to the USA. It was fun to chat them up with, I suspect, the annoying arrogance of youth. Having nothing to lose after an arduous day's work, one lost all shyness.

I spent about a year and a half at this office, enjoying myself up to a point. The friends I had stayed with at the home for fallen women came into my life again, as one of the boys took up with Hilda's successor in the office.

I spent my summer holiday with the family in Dorset. The Reverend met me at Axminster, I remember, in one of the original Henry Fords, a real Tin Lizzy. A hazardous journey – to brake you put your foot down fully on the accelerator whereas to go forward you put it only half-way down. In any case, the Reverend was an erratic driver. The holiday was fun.

It was not really a healthy life, going up and down on the train to London with lunch in very cheap places – strict rules of hygiene had not become obligatory in any restaurant. After working for nearly two years, I developed a form of typhoid during the second summer and was quite ill at home. The best thing about this illness was that it took me far into the summer and during convalescence I lay in a hammock in our orchard reading lots of books and gazing up at the blue sky through branches of the apple trees. In September our Great Uncle and Great Aunt from Jamaica paid us a visit.

I must recall that when a child this same Uncle Townshend who it was had come to visit my grandmother, a visit that had healed an old wound – my grandmother's marriage had distanced her from her parents who had cruelly disinherited her. Since that original visit we had established further bonds with our Great Uncle Townshend and Great Aunt Sara after my grandmother had died in 1917. This was their second visit to England since 1914. My brother however had visited them in Jamaica the year before: thus was the restoration of happy relations further established.

In 1927 Pat had suffered what was a severe blow to a young man. While at Cambridge he had played soccer for the University, but sadly, just before the great match with Oxford with a Blue dangling before him, he was in hospital where his knee was operated on for the removal of a cartilage. My brother was devastated, the more so because at the same time his engagement to his lovely girl fell apart and she left England for Chile, where she joined a brother who ran a boys' prep. school in Valparaiso.

Our Uncle had no children and as well as healing the family wounds he wanted the younger generation's co-operation, possibly as inheritors of his plantation. Anyway he invited Pat to go and convalesce in Jamaica and my brother accepted with alacrity. I think possibly that at the back of my Pat's mind was the notion that Jamaica was a little nearer to Valparaiso.

As events worked out my brother became well again and managed to enjoy himself enormously in Jamaica. He had a great ability always to make friends. There was a very beautiful dusky girl by name Carmen Pringle. Once, when wandering along a beach after a picnic she asked him if gentlemen really preferred blondes – Anita Loos's book of that title had just come out – to which Pat replied "I do not know, but if so I am no gentleman", or so later I was told. He left a reputation for gallantry and charm.

Well, when he went down to Kingston to take his passage home he found the ship alongside his was billed to be going to Valparaiso that night. This was too much for my brother: he took his luggage and got on board somehow squaring his ticket. The effect on my parents was devastating but after much adventure he returned to England. Having got across the Andes, he signed himself on to a cargo boat as ship's doctor. Our parents forgave him and I remember that the night of his return the fatted calf was served for dinner with all the trimmings. I found to my dismay that the Bible story of the prodigal's brother was true. I was as jealous as hell, having spent weeks cheering up my parents during his escapade. He then concentrated on becoming a real doctor. In the course of time he married his dream girl, Eileen, when she returned from Chile.

Now back to my own experience. The same invitation was issued to me that my uncle and aunt would take me back with them. I had saved a little of my earnings, which had been minutely increased, and my father gave me money he had not used for my education. So in October (the season known to be less invaded by hurricanes) we embarked at Avonmouth on the good ship Patuca for Kingston, Jamaica where a real adventure might begin.

Stones Hope, Jamaica

It was a very bleak moment: the sky was grey, heavy with rain to fall, inside the ship seemed a strange place with its maze of white steel corridors, now to be called companion ways, filled with people and luggage, people all talking in raised voices, commanding voices, that made what they wanted clearly understood. They wanted everyone to realise that this was the case; they had done it all before. The answer was to go up on deck, but here the scene was depressing in the extreme – miles and miles of colourless water stretched between mile after mile of grey mud flats. The ship chugged steadfastly on, over that flat, flat water until land on either side slipped quietly out of sight into the distance. The ship began to roll, then the sound of the engines suddenly changed into power as we lolloped into the swell of the Atlantic Ocean. From then on the ship would pound, day after day, her relentless way westward. I was terribly sick.

After several miserable days lying in my bunk, the top one, luckily, in a cabin I was sharing with a sad widow returning to the place of her honeymoon, rather unwisely I thought in my youthful arrogance. She had a very large cabin trunk, a speciality of those days of shipboard travel that made a small wardrobe of itself when stood upright. It took up a great deal of room in our small cabin for two. The poor woman used to unload some of her nostalgia and grief as I lay feeling horribly ill in the top bunk.

After a few days the steward suggested that I try some food and to my horror brought me some rare steak and an orange. Amazingly I swallowed both and felt suddenly better, got up and dressed and went on deck. All this time my uncle and aunt had visited me with kindness and encouragement, telling me that my seasickness would eventually pass – and all would be well again and at last I discovered that they were right.

On deck warm sunshine greeted me and the islands of the Azores, really the tops of sunken mountains, rose abruptly beside us out of a benign blue sea. Flying fish streaked out of the water, flashing their blue sides before plunging in again. From that moment on I took to life on board, played deck games, swam in a tiny pool rigged out of tarpaulin and ate a great deal too much. The good ship SS Patuca was a banana boat which carried sixty passengers.

The passengers were a mixed collection of people and colours: planters and business people returning to Jamaica after a holiday in England. It was the proud boast of those known as the plantocracy that there was no colour question in Jamaica. This meant that those with a splash of colour or even those with quite deep dark skins, testimony to the old slave days, and who had been successful in commerce, farming or business, were accepted by whites as equals. My uncle had many friends and business acquaintances of all shades, many of whom would drop in to see him and take breakfast with us when we reached Stones Hope. A Planter's breakfast was a great occasion. There were many Portuguese who traded in Kingston and ran the local newspaper, the Gleaner. I made friends with one such family on board, the De Costas.

Despite this seeming open-mindedness, I fell foul of my uncle when the ship dropped anchor to deliver supplies to the minute Turks Island, a cable and wireless station just outside the West Indies. I was in a crowd waiting to climb down into a tender to go ashore, when my uncle over-heard people using my Christian name. "I forbid you to go ashore with these people," he said. My uncle and aunt still referred to each other as Mr. and Mrs. Ronaldson. Now this was the first sight of land for thirteen days and the first tropical island I had ever seen. It was totally flat and lay in a turquoise sea of unimaginable blue. My deeply felt mortification was luckily short-lived. Aunt Sara arrived, a tiny woman of eighty, took my hand and led me to the embarkation spot. "I told Townshend he was ridiculous – this is not the last century, it is 1929. Of course you must go with the young people."

During the night of the fourteenth day out, as I lay in my bunk I watched through the porthole the dawn break to the south east of us, the horizon became a blazing streak of red, greens and purple. I was excited. Then suddenly the ship's engines stopped, cables rattled out through what I later learnt to call fairleads and the ship's anchors fell with an almighty plop into the sea near the Pallisadoes in Kingston Harbour. As soon as I could I clambered on deck, but to my great disappointment the Island was shrouded in the thickest heavy mist. A dog barked on the nearby shore, I remember, and I turned in dismay to my uncle who had joined me. "Oh dear," I cried in my anguish "you told me this would be the most beautiful view on earth and now I shan't see it." "Don't worry," he replied, "the sun which will soon be up will disperse this mist and you will see the Blue Mountains in all their glory." He was right. The engines started again and we edged our way into Kingston Harbour. Then the mists rolled back and there beyond the green misty plain of Liganee towered the Blue Mountains. They lay like the richest blue velvet piled up on a draper's counter, a few skeins of mist clinging to some of their folds, a sight of the utmost breathtaking beauty.

Little black boys dived for pennies thrown down by the waiting passengers – aboard and on shore chaos appeared to reign. After noisy hours of landing things bought in England for the plantation, clearing customs and other business, we left for the long drive up to the mountains of Manchester (a very dull name for my first experience of the tropics) to my uncle's retirement home, Stones Hope, in the hills near Mandeville far above the old sugar plantation where he had battled for his living from boyhood.

Stones Hope lay in the hills that rose above the plains of Vere, with its great sugar plantations. The property was planted with pimento, a crop rich in oil from the leaves of trees that looked like olive trees. One could see the house from what was the top gate; the road wound its way down for about two miles. At the bottom the land levelled out into a large saucer before descending further down the mountain and here, beyond a huge clump of bamboos, stood the plantation's buildings: barbecues for drying coffee and a small factory which extracted the oil from the pimento leaves, then general sheds. In the centre of the saucer on a little tuft of high ground stood the house. A little fence surrounded it, with some steps leading from its entrance to a small gate. The house was one storey surrounded with verandas dripping with orchids. Behind the house, still on the high ground, were the kitchen and servants' premises. It was very neat and well cared for by the black servants who came out to greet us. The greeting was enthusiastic – myself considered to "favour Marsa Pat," but the joy of the returning Marsa and his Missus was the greatest joy.

Next day I had my first tour of the plantation with my uncle. Behind the domestic buildings was a plantation of banana trees, beneath which grew coffee enjoying the shade given by their large leaves. Under these, pigs rootled. This was my first lesson on plantation economy. Besides the chief pimento oil crop, all kinds of other things were grown on a small scale. My uncle had had a serious struggle growing sugar when a young man after the emancipation but now, in his retirement in the hills, he loved to experiment with fruits and vegetables for the table which was a very good table indeed.

His ancestry went back some way in Jamaica on his mother's side. On his father's side, some land had been bought by his paternal great-grandfather, a merchant sea captain. In 1840 his grandfather, a wine merchant in London, sent out his eldest son, Uncle Townshend's father, as a young man of twenty to manage the estate. This was a difficult time in Jamaica after the emancipation of the slaves, when the original big sugar landowners sold up and left. Our great grandfather managed successfully until trouble came from his brothers in London. They were a family of twelve children, two of whom became known as the 'wicked uncles' to later generations. They managed temporarily to ruin the Jamaican estates. However, Uncle Townshend's expertise and extremely hard work saved the day, he recovered and became a planter of distinction. But I have put all that, together with my grandmother's runaway marriage, into a novel, whose foundation must have seeped into my subconscious mind at that time.

I was now twenty-one and eager to absorb all I could while living in a household which contained four people in their late seventies and eighties, and two in their forties, the Busha and his sister, whose mother of eighty had joined them, making the average age in the house seventy, including me, aged 21. Busha was the title given to the second in command on a plantation: a very important man, second only to the Marsa, in this case my great uncle.

I was lucky, in that my room looked out on to a perfect tropical view. There was a break in the lip of the saucer which cradled the house and buildings, through which one looked down to the shimmering lowlands below, where the sugar plantations lay and to Carlisle Bay, the old sugar and slave harbour. The blue, blue sea was edged with yellow sand, a perfect bay, many miles below. One of my aunts told me that if Carlysle Bay ever looked as if it was in the garden there would be a hurricane. On my last visit to Jamaica years later, on the very day of my departure that was just what I saw and it was true.

I slept in a four-poster bed. The furniture throughout was mostly of mahogany as was the house itself, which made it very dark. In contrast, the verandas decked with flowers were a riot of colour. The dark house was a relief from the strong sunshine outside. As well as the sunshine, around the house one seemed to be bathed in the laughter that seems to be built into black people with the sun.

The pattern of life flowed very evenly. The day began at about 5 am when a wonderful freshly picked orange arrived with the most delicious coffee presented with gales of laughter by the maids May or

Maud. At this hour, my uncle and Busha were out in the plantation before it was too hot. Below my room was my Uncle's office to which black people would come to consult him in a steady stream. They brought all their problems to him – asking for a loan to buy land for themselves, which he encouraged, whether to marry, how to discipline their sons. One marriage floundered: the lady had a wooden leg so my uncle's bad advice came back on him: "at least she won't run away," he had commented. However in the event, when they got into bed, she took the leg off and beat her husband with it.

The nicest story of all is about a much revered headman called Wood for some reason always referred to as Old Wood, though like all black people he looked young. He asked for leave to go and bury his grandmother. This took him a long distance over the mountains, but to Uncle Townshend's surprise he returned much sooner than expected. As in Ireland a wake was of great importance. "Old Wood – how come you back so soon?" asked my uncle, to which Old Wood replied; "Oh Sah – I get there, but old lady not dead so I buck up with a disappoint". This phrase I find covers so many situations in life, as have many of the Jamaican sayings that I learnt.

The three elderly ladies, Aunts Sara and Gertrude and Busha's mother, Mrs. Thursfield, all had specific work to do, each managing a department of the house, garden and poultry yard. They did this before the planter's breakfast. They also made cakes for the huge influx of visitors that arrived nearly always for afternoon tea. The buggies and cars could be seen weaving their way down from the top gate. As well as local people, since it was considered to be a show property, many people arrived with introductions from England. Aunt Sara, strict teetotaller, used nevertheless to brew a very strong pimento dram which, being made of home-grown pimento, she considered to be unintoxicating, despite the fact that it was laced with rum. Some of the visitors whose ship had called into Kingston and who had been persuaded to take the long drive to see the plantation, would gladly accept the dram, but were driven practically unconscious back to their ship – possibly carried on board.

For me, while all the morning activity was going on I would find the horse, Dobbin, saddled by Michael, the dear roadman tethered beneath my window for me to ride, which I did, travelling some miles accompanied by Uncle Townshend's dog, Speckles, a Great Dane. I was perfectly safe among the friendly population, who called out 'howdies' to me as I passed. Once, Speckles was lazy and returned without me. Michael ran for about five miles lest Dobbin and I had come to grief, which was not so.

I have left out the most important moment of the day, the planter's breakfast. This took place at about 10 o'clock, after much had been accomplished in the cool early hours of the day. It consisted of porridge, followed by such things as 'accis' and salt fish, pancakes with sardines, snapper fish, bacon and eggs and masses of fruit, mangoes, pawpaws, pineapple and strawberries. And, of course, the most delicious coffee.

Replete from this wonderful meal, the next big event of the day came – family prayers. The family sat with their backs to the windows, the servants opposite against the dark mahogany wall. The effect of this was that, as they were black, one could see only the whites of their eyes. The prayers were simple and occasionally amusing. When I was invited to Kingston to a great ball and complained about my wardrobe (skirts having gone from short to long since I left England) Uncle Townsend happily read from the gospel, "Behold the lilies of the field, they toil not neither do they spin, yet even Solomon in all his glory was not arrayed as one of these." After prayers were over he went to his office and emerged with a cheque for £10 for me, which was a huge sum in those days.

At times it seemed to me that I was living in unreality, that I had lost contact with modern life. But in reality I travelled over a tremendous span of time: the stories of the old people covered life from the mid-nineteenth century to my own life of the twentieth century and even further back to the eighteenth, if their own recollections from their parents' memories are taken into account. I learnt a great deal about old Jamaica, sitting in the House of Assembly in Spanish Town where my great-grandfather had sat, saw where my grandmother had danced in the old King House in the golden days of splendour and when she had watched the Southern Cross rise over the Rodney Memorial when the ball was over. They took me to visit many very ancient properties with such happy names as Money Musk, Rippling Banks, Amity Hall and my family's own Hals Hall and Springfield. In the cool of the evening my uncle liked to walk up to the top gate and I used to be invited to join him when he would talk about the past. How much I now regret the things I did not ask him, particularly why Admiral Rodney presented a beautiful silver cup, known as a Rodney Cup, to a sea-faring forebear. It is rumoured that, commanding his armed merchantman, he was drawn into the Battle of the Saints. Owing to my negligence or scattiness, I forgot to write it down so that it is lost in the mists of time, yet the Rodney Cup remains.

Despite all the wonder and novelty, I thirsted for some company of my own age. When I was invited by people I had met on the ship to stay in Kingston (despite their having called me by my first name) I was delighted. I was driven off by Clarence, the chauffeur, to Williamstown to catch a train. The roads were ramshackle and full of dangerous turns as they descended clinging to the mountains, a precipice on one side. Once in the train in the early morning I remember that I saw the sun rise three times in different valleys on the same day, as we descended to the lowlands. I also remember that at Maypen, girls came along the platform, carrying trays on their heads with the most delicious cashew nuts.

One lovely old property I stayed in was also with friends from the boat. We played tennis and swam. All plantations had water tanks to provide water for cattle and these made delightful swimming pools. On another property lived a young girl, Agnes Crumewing, who oddly enough had been to my school in Watford, and, with her brother, we rode early each day around Rose Hall in the lowlands.

Towards the end of my visit, after Christmas, she and I were invited to King's House in Kingston. This was the most extraordinary and alarming experience. The Governor's wife was a most charming person called Lady Stubbs and she used to invite young girls to stay whenever the American or Royal Navy ships were paying a visit to the Island. It was this invitation that gave rise to my initial anxiety as to what to wear and to Uncle Townshend's prayer, "Behold the lilies of the field etc."

At the first evening's dinner I was placed next to a Field Marshal, Lord Methuen, who passed the time demonstrating with cutlery how the British Square had fought prior to the Boer War. He was kind and obviously wanted to help me. It wasn't all like this: the young had plenty of fun, swimming and dancing. Once we were mounted on mules and taken up the Blue Mountains to Newcastle, myself fitted out with riding breeches from a Colonel. There were two American girls and a young English naval officer, Nigel Nugent. The girls asked me if I knew anyone in America. I did – Jean Crawford, her grandparents lived in Bushey. Well, hard to believe, but astonishingly, that particular Jean Crawford lived in their street "back home". As a result, I have been a bore all my life. If anyone is from Australia or South America, I ask if they know a friend of mine out there.

On the whole, all these experiences went to my head and I gloried in the luxury of the high society, once I had got over my first shock. It was during one of these visits that a most unfortunate mishap took place, which certainly took the wind out of my sails. It was a night when Lady Stubbs was too exhausted to accompany her husband to a ship's party. My friend Agnes was not there. When the time came to get into the car, I sat next to the Governor in the back – the ADC in front. The car drove into the dock-yard and alongside the ship, HMS Durban, I think. I followed the Governor up the gang-plank, the ADC behind me. When the band struck up God Save the King (Governors represented the King), the Governor was on deck and the ADC and I were still at the top of the gangway. At that moment the trade wind struck, as it was apt to do at that hour, and my dress, bought with Uncle Townshend's £10, shot up over my head so that I stood motionless with my white dress like a tulip floating above my head. My only comfort was that I was wearing some particularly attractive knickers that my mother had given me – they were pale green, suitable for this flower motif. The Governor, sensing that something unusual was going on turned round, but by that time the anthem was finished and I recaptured my dress. He was a nice man of few words, with, luckily, a gutsy sense of humour.

When I returned to Stones Hope in the hills, any illusions of grandeur I had collected were soon squashed. My relatives greatly distrusted the authorities from England. Ever since the abolition of slavery in 1833, the Colonial Office in London had treated the West Indies most shabbily and this neglect benefited the United Fruit Company of America who in 1930 were buying up old properties that slid into debt.

Up in the hills there was quite another side to colonial life: a gentle paternity reigned where servants and their masters affectionately teased each other. One could come into the dining room and find the maids hiding under the table. We played the same game and sat down and waited, wondering where they were until they burst out laughing. They were very caring and loyal – when Busha returned from the war Michael, the road mender, was overcome with affection.

As I have said, there was a healthy independence of officialdom. Uncle Townshend, when he was a member of the Legislative Assembly, crossed swords with one of the Governors, but he managed to remain a friend. There was simplicity in his dealings in business and with his employees. Mandeville was the nearest town to Stones Hope and because of its pleasant climate it had attracted many retired expatriates often from India to settle there. It became a Little England with a club, library and English Church. My uncle did not go to their church but instead supported one called Snowdon on top of a steep hill whose incumbent was black. Services were very long, very well attended and the congregation very enthusiastic, singing with full heart and lungs. I cannot leave without telling one of the nicest stories from Jamaica that I know.

It was Whitsun and Mr Swaby, the Vicar, had a brilliant idea. He would let a dove loose from the trap door in the attic of the church during the final hymn – "Come Holy Ghost, our hearts inspire . ." It was not a very well kept secret because as the hymn began, accompanied on the harmonium, all eyes turned to the roof as Joseph, the verger, climbed the ladder to the trap door. For some time nothing happened, the hymn was replayed twice, and then again. At last Joseph appeared and descended the ladder, stumped across to the Vicar and in a hoarse whisper that echoed around the church, his hand to the Vicar's ear, announced "Oh Sah, the puss hab niambed (gobbled) the Holy Ghust".

So I saw the British Empire in its gentle evening of decline or perhaps more accurately of reconciliation. In Kingston, as far as I could judge, there was equal concern for the welfare of the colony – for hospitals, education and, of course, trade. The Governor and his wife were the most dedicated people it has been my good fortune ever to have met.

In May 1930 I sailed home with my Great Aunt Gertrude and Busha, both wanting a holiday in England. This time the whole voyage was delightful as Agnes, my King's House friend, was on board too. I remember that I had a flirtation with the third officer who was a nice young man. I was still a confused late developer.

Toulon

In early spring of 1931 my brother married his beautiful girl, Eileen who had come back from Chile. This was rather well timed in fact, as while he had been a medical student at St. George's he had had a happy flirtation with my school friend and friend for life, Eileen Harley (later Freeman) – I had two such friends. She, however, wisely considered that the dream girl was the one for him and withdrew. She proved to be right and both she and he found their ideal partners.

Although I still felt I had not resolved my life, it did not stand still. I came back from Jamaica and signed on for a secretarial course at the school of Miss Cassandra's in London – in Piccadilly. Before I actually started there, an invitation had come through Aunt Elsa to visit a family in France. They lived in Toulon. Madame Dormoy was a recently widowed lady whose husband had worked in a French firm in Egypt. The Dormoy family had lived next door to Aunt Elsa and Uncle Charles in Egypt and became good friends. Two of their three daughters had already paid us a visit in Bushey. The elder of the two, whom I had liked very much, had become engaged to a young Englishman, George Morris. I found myself invited to be a bridesmaid at the wedding.

This was another awe-inspiring challenge and to Toulon I felt I had to go and did so with much panic. As always, it seemed for some reason that it would be foolish to reject the chance. I postponed my attendance at the secretarial school for a month and set off once more by train across Europe.

There was also a very nice eldest sister who had two small boys. She was separated from her husband and had returned home. At that time the sorrow of the disastrous marriage hung over the household and was constantly referred to in lowered voices. Later she married again with the rather depressing surname Le Mort, but this time it was a happy marriage. She had great charm combined with chic. Then came Susanne, my friend, the bride, and her younger sister, who was extremely spoilt, attractive and dominating. Roger, the youngest was an adolescent who was in revolt against the establishment – represented by none other than his poor bereft mother. On the whole they were a tempestuous lot with charm. There was too a married son who came with his wife and small boys for the wedding. As always in France, the household possessed a " femme à tout faire", whom everyone bullied.

When I arrived, the marriage arrangements were causing considerable dismay. The bridegroom was Protestant, which was the cause of the trouble. This fact prevented the couple from enjoying certain joyous practices for weddings in the Catholic Church. For instance, there were to be no flowers and the ceremony could not take place in front of the High Altar, music was out and there were various other disadvantages. In fact it sounded pretty bleak. This was in the early 1930s. Distressed as Madame Dormoy, a faithful Catholic was, the girls did not seem to be such ardent followers, perhaps having mixed in Egypt with non-Catholics. Then the whole situation changed when they discovered that there was an English church in Hyères, only a few miles away. With an English bridegroom, what could be better? They became reconciled and abandoned Catholicism with simple alacrity.

I soon discovered that this created a curious dilemma for myself. The bridegroom was due to arrive on the eve of the wedding and until then I was the only Protestant. Thus I became the authority on the English marriage service on whom everyone now depended. Having thrown away their own service, they became very open-minded about ours. I was hazy myself and had no prayer book to consult. Luckily, when George arrived it had all been settled, for he knew even less than I did.

Discussions had gone on far into the nights. There was a huge stove in the salon which,before we went to bed, constantly consumed papers with all the arrangements that had been agreed that evening. So we always started again the next morning. The Grand Cortège was a very thorny subject for dispute.

The girls, including myself, were busy with dressmakers' fittings and hair appointments. We had rather pretty dresses in blue chiffon with hats – but I forget what they were. We were each to be escorted by a young man as a "garçon d'honneur". These were all friends, young lieutenants in the French Navy. Mine was very handsome and called Charles La Fargue.

The great day dawned and we drove to Hyères and assembled in the English Church. To my dismay, I found that I was still the authority on procedure, both with the French congregation and with the very English verger who did not know what to make of "this lot". The service got off to a good start, however, and seemed to roll along nicely. Then the moment came when the bridesmaids, led by their Garçons d'Honneur, received donations – "Bread for the Poor" (Madame's choice). We each carried a little basket decorated with flowers. Then suddenly came the crunch – I was faced with an insoluble problem as we stood in an indecisive group holding our baskets. "Where," asked the French "is the Sainte Vierge?" "What," asked the verger, "do you want to do with these baskets?" I was aghast – the Reformation of course. Impossible in those few seconds to give a brief course on our English history, the disappearance of the Blessed Virgin Mary and Henry VIII's quarrel with the Pope. The verger pointed out a harmonium in a corner – I wished I had thought of the font but perhaps that would not have been suitable, being too suggestive and far away, so "faute de mieux" I succumbed regretfully to the indecorous harmonium. We returned into the church to find a cousin singing a solo.

The final exit from the church with the Grand Cortège went off very well – it had been the subject of such bitter dispute. Madame was escorted by the General, a much-discussed friend, resplendent in uniform. We tripped along with our Garçons d'Honneur behind the bride and groom, as in any English wedding.

I stayed on in Toulon for another week dominated by the second daughter, who spent much time in a little gazebo above the street playing a ukulele. This brought many young men into the garden creating a very jocular atmosphere. Then there was a ball at the naval base to entertain an English Royal Navy ship, HMS Queen Elizabeth. I was completely deserted by Solange, who was supposed to be my escort, but fortunately I was invited to dance by some French officers which restored my confidence. Also, I found among the English Naval contingent a friend from Jamaica and this saved my evening.

Kind Madame Dormoy wanted me to go on to Paris, but my time was up: my mother urgently wanted me home and I was due to start at the typing school.

London

I arrived home on a Friday and it was springtime. My mother explained that there was a local wedding next day to which I had been invited. I was hesitant to go, not knowing the people concerned very well. The reception was to take place in a big house of friends of the bride's family, where I had often played tennis. In the end I decided to go and dressed myself up with particular care in as much of a French style as I could, as often happens after a visit to France. The occasion had all the trappings of a popular social wedding. There was to be a dance that evening in the house, to which all the young people were generously invited by the very elderly owners.

When I was at school at Sherborne, my parents paid extra for me to have dancing lessons. My mother had become very disturbed when she found that modern ballroom dancing had not been included. The foxtrot was definitely forbidden by our dear old puritanical headmistress. We floated about doing Greek scarf dances or bumped around in English country dancing. Nevertheless, we had a spirited dance mistress who dared to teach us the Black Bottom. It was a well-guarded secret. This whole attitude was incomprehensible to my mother, both she and her mother had adored ballroom dancing which she considered absolutely necessary equipment for entry into modern social society. Fortunately there was a young woman living in the village who taught ballroom dancing and my mother arranged lessons for me in the holidays. I went twice a week to the studio of Florry Laurie.

Then one day at the close of the lesson, Florry said "I have got a partner for you next time. It's no good if you can only dance with me." So when I turned up for the next session there was the partner, a very tall boy, terribly gawky with enormous hands and the cuffs to his sleeves well up his forearms – he must be growing too fast I thought. Without a word we began with a waltz – one, two, three, turn – and "now reverse" – one, two, three and so on. After a short time she said that she would ask the artist from the studio downstairs to come up and see what a good dancing couple we made – this of course to encourage us – one two three turn etc. After this we then set to on the dreaded foxtrot.

When it was time to go, she asked if we could come the following Tuesday but the gawky boy explained that he had to go back to Dartmouth that day. I felt relieved – we had not exchanged a word and I did not think we ever would. We were both about fifteen years old then.

You can imagine my amazement when an extremely good-looking young man in exquisite white tie and tails invited me to dance with him that evening of the wedding. Beneath this finery I recognised the gawky boy of some five or six years ago. He had indeed grown very tall – well over six foot.

"Do you remember the studio with Florry Laurie?" we both began, then stopped and laughed. Conversation did follow but not with any great ease, at any rate not on my side. He had been away in the Mediterranean for two years, serving as a midshipman and then a sub-lieutenant in the Navy. Instinctively I thought: "You are far too good looking – everyone will be after you". He was enjoying himself enormously as brother of the bride -cocky no doubt, I decided.

I went ahead with my secretarial training but was terribly bad at shorthand. However, when I finished the course with lamentably low shorthand speed a request came in for the sort of job I wanted – secretary to an architect. His office was across Piccadilly in Vigo Street. I went for an interview and to my surprise and pleasure was accepted. For the next three years I worked there endured, I have always thought, by my boss.

My boss was Brian O'Rorke. His was becoming a famous name – a young up-and-coming architect. Before I left the office he had won the competition for the National Theatre but it was sadly never built. With the Second War the whole project was dropped.

It was a job that was particularly suited to me because there was very little shorthand. I used to write the letters for my boss, once he had told me what he wanted to say. This made me feel very important despite my lowly position behind the typewriter. My worst and detested work was typing the architect's instructions to the builders – specifications – these were all in special formulae and transferring them to my typewriter was my worst headache. It kept me sometimes long into the evening before I could deliver a satisfactory copy. I had learnt to type quite fast but it was just before touch-typing had become the custom. Touch-typing meant that you did not look at the keys but at the text and so got along much quicker and more accurately. My specifications had to be carefully doctored with clever India rubbers.

The Office was on the sixth floor of a building in Vigo Street. There were three apprentice architects. They worked at drawing boards in front of three large windows looking down Sackville Street. Another draughtsman, a particularly nice New Zealander, Paul Pascoe, sat on the further side of the room where my desk was also. I faced the door and could rise to receive visitors and clients. We had a scruffy cloakroom next door – adequate but not up to today's standards.

As well as letter writing, I had also to deal with the telephone as diplomatically as I could – the boss did not like to be disturbed. But best of all I was sometimes sent out searching for fabric patterns from various designers and warehouses. O'Rorke had the contract for fitting out the interior of the Orient Line's new prestigious modern liner, SS Orion, then under construction in the shipbuilding yard. This was of tremendous interest to us all and was most exciting. The interior decoration was to be in an entirely modern style employing new materials and techniques – far removed from the Victorian or Edwardian styles of liners up to the present. The old style would be of vintage value now and by today no doubt would be preferred.

By far my most agreeable and restful job was colouring plans for the clients reminiscent of the gentle pleasure enjoyed in childhood of colouring on a wet afternoon. This came my way in the office from time to time.

After a few weeks I found a room in London in what was then Oxford Terrace. Oxford Terrace faced Cambridge Terrace and ran from Edgware Road up to a rather grander district called Sussex Gardens and now the whole place has changed to that name.

The two terraces faced each other across an elegant wide street: a line of shrubs ran down each side giving to each a private inner road to their front doors (neighbours could not spy across on each other's carriages). It was a pretty oasis that one turned into from the colourful vulgarity of the Edgware Road, but it had become shabby and had lost its innocence. The elegant eighteenth-century residences had turned into boarding houses bordering on the red light area around Paddington Station. Once, when my mother was staying with me, she and I were walking back from Paddington Station along Spring Street. Two girls stood talking together as we passed. Said one: "Seen Rene lately?" "No," said the other, "where does she walk now?" My mother's expressive eyebrows went up: "Where have you brought me to stay?". A Victorian childhood made no fool of my mother – her sense of humour absorbed the situation.

My lodging was a true find: it came from a suggestion made by a very old friend – the mother of the children with whom I had shared Miss Cowderoy, the governess, when very young. Her name was Mrs Saxon Mills. Her sister-in-law, Mrs Haslam Mills, had been recently widowed and had bought a house which she filled with lodgers in order to help pay for her children's education. I had the tiniest possible room with a gas ring upon which I could boil a kettle. Breakfast was brought to our rooms, which was wonderful because our redoubtable hostess was North Country and generous, so breakfast was a lavish start to the day.

North Countryness broke through in many ways It was a lively household. Mrs Haslam's husband, like her sister-in-law's had been a sub-editor of the Manchester Guardian and the eldest son was a successful playwright. I hoped to conceal my ignorance (squareness today) in such intelligent society, but it was essentially a warm-hearted household. There was always an undercurrent of drama running from day to day. Our hostess, as a first time house-owner, coped with the slings and arrows of outrageous fortune that spilled over the house: boilers blew up and roofs leaked etc. We were offered dinner round a family table for half a crown if we wanted it, when all the day's gossip and mishaps were revealed, There was a cook, Mary, who ruled below stairs: a cockney with a strong contralto voice who entertained at the Christmas party singing "Poor old Jo". The only day when there was no dinner was Derby Day, when she took a taxi of friends to Epsom.

The nice thing was that on fine days I could walk across the parks to get to work. Once or twice during a hot summer, when Brian was away, the whole office took a bus to Kensington to the new Lido in Hyde Park. George Lansbury, a socialist MP had established a Lido for the people with facilities for swimming, picnicking and boating. He was a very public spirited man. We were all very left-wing. Everything conspired to make us so: wages were only just adequate for a very simple life – lunch cost me sevenpence and dinner half a crown at Oxford Terrace or at Lyons Corner House or the ABC, this last very down market. I welcomed invitations to dinner but had to absent myself from time to time from Oxford Terrace, lest it be thought I was too clinging or lacked friends. But half a crown went a long way. It could buy you a seat at the theatre in the Pit for which you queued.

The office life was on the whole fun. The young apprentices chatted away while working which made a congenial atmosphere. During the afternoons when things often slowed down the great preoccupation for those at the windows looking down Sackville Street was watching the clientele coming and going to and from the famous tailors' houses. These were generally young men able to afford this luxury, which those in our office could not. They were therefore derisively described as Lancers or Hussars, with some exaggeration put into the expression.

But the most interesting point about the whole entertainment was reporting on the tarts who emerged just in time to forestall these "blades" as they might be called, as they left their tailor.

"I say – just look at Nelly's new fox fur." would be a sudden cry or "Ruby looks a bit down in the dumps today – that fellow yesterday must have been a dead loss."

The architectural journals of the day fostered left wing views. There were the Dolfus Flats in Vienna for workers; Russian and Continental design was away ahead of what we were doing. We were spreading suburbia in a most unimaginative way over our beautiful countryside. We had not yet stopped cutting down all the trees to lay out small plots – ten houses to the acre for instance in poor Bushey, Hertfordshire and Metro-land snaked out into the country with its electric trains. It was however a world of conflicting but exciting theories and new beliefs: on the one hand you had the Bolsheviks in Russia, on the other there was the rising tide in Italy and Germany of Fascism; in England Sir Oswald Mosley had minimal success. The Spanish Civil War split the two opinions down the middle and men went out to fight on either side. Russia swept up some of the intelligentsia:, Bernard Shaw and the Sidney Webbs visited the Soviet Union, returning in a state of euphoria. Then concurrently in England there was a tremendous phase of disarmament of the fighting services for which we later paid dearly.

During my time in the office, Germany's return as a political power became evident. On the top floor of 66 Oxford Terrace lived a German girl, Lilli, who was secretary to the German Naval Attaché. She was very friendly and proud to proclaim her country's new flowering. Whenever there was a bank holiday one young man in the office dropped a bulging rucksack, with huge boots attached, for us to fall over in the cloakroom. He used to go hiking in Germany and came back with tales of the welcome of the youth hostels where he had stayed and of the wonderful pattern of life for the young.

At weekends I went home to Bushey and drank in country air. I always found notes for me inviting me to play tennis at various houses – it was the most frequent form of entertainment. Nowadays people have swimming pools rather than tennis courts. One recurring invitation to play tennis was from the once gawky young man. Then these were still the dancing years and there were many places to dance on Saturday evenings and people to take one. My brother had joined my father in his practice and he and Eileen lived nearby with their baby daughter, Desna ("Muff"), which made it very congenial. My parents enjoyed their first grandchild.

For me it was a time of arrival I suppose. I had been a late developer. Now I think I felt in tune. I could enjoy myself for enjoyment's sake – I find that Diaghilev once said, "It takes a long time to become young." which I find very true, but I found life desperately interesting too. There were people and there were ideas. Nevertheless, at the back of life was a perpetual problem which I hoped one day would be solved.

There lived at No 66 Oxford Terrace a very gentle old lady who had a psychic sister. She told my fortune one evening, A fortnight later I found she had come to dinner.

"How is my fortune tonight?" I asked her – all young people fall for this, I think.

"Well, it has changed," was her reply.

I pressed her after this but she looked unhappy. She said perhaps she was wrong but that my life would change after the coming weekend. This was disconcerting, as I was going to spend it with my brother and sister-in-law in Cumberland, where Eileen came from. I hoped nothing would go wrong.

We had a long drive to get up North in one day and started very early, stopping for breakfast at Grantham. Here in the hotel was a polished table at the entrance and on the table a bowl of freshly gathered buttercups from which one petal had fallen and was lying cup-like and reflected in the table's shining surface. What a good omen for summer.

During that drive two things occurred which stuck in my memory. The first was that we read in the daily papers that a new stage star had been born the night before, taking London by storm – she was Vivien Leigh – I forget in what play. Then, during the afternoon, there was a tremendous drop in the temperature as the weather became horrible and it snowed hard.

Next day, coming down from a long walk over the fells in very cold wet weather which, despite all, we enjoyed, I told them of the fortune-teller's prediction and we laughed. Nothing untoward had occurred.

Pat put me on the midnight train for London at Carlisle and I slept all the way to London. I got to the office on time. Then a call came for me from my mother. She told me that my father had had a stroke on the Saturday – he had been caught in that sudden change of temperature without his overcoat and now was very ill. I was summoned home. He never recovered and died two weeks later. So the fortune-teller was right and my life did change after that weekend.

The blow was of course tremendous. My father's death was a shock and a grief, not only to his family but to everyone who knew him: "Bushey loses a beloved doctor." said our local Watford press. He was a beloved doctor – not a spare seat in the church at his funeral service. Consultants came down from London.

He died when the Great Depression was at its worst. One of the early economies was for people not to pay their doctors. Our father had educated us very well but he was denied the chance to make up this expense. My poor mother found to her dismay that she was almost penniless. Owing to the odd arrangements for doctors, who charged their richer patients but not their poor ones, my mother constantly met people who, to cheer her up, said: "What a wonderful man your husband was – he never charged us a penny". My practical mother became a little disillusioned at this. Times have now changed in every way. My life had also changed as the sooth-saying lady had predicted. The whole era of growing up had ended and I had lost my very loveable father.

Goodbye London

That summer I stayed for a time with our favourite aunt Beresford in Highgate. It was good to be alone with her and we both worked. Then I returned to Oxford Terrace where life there and at the Office went on as before, with one exception. The erstwhile gawky youth, now a man and a splendid one, took to coming up to London from Portsmouth for an evening out. These evenings, spent of necessity on a shoestring, were fun. Half a crown went a long way; a seat at the theatre in the pit, some way to a bottle of wine, a plate of Bisque d'homard (lobster) soup at the Hungarian Restaurant in Lower Regent Street, followed by an omelette (five shillings, that was two half crowns) and half a crown took a taxi home. Evening dress for the Hungaria of course, but girls could make their own fairly cheaply.

There was a special occasion in the Office when I asked for a Saturday off to go to Torquay. "Why Torquay?" asked the architects. On Monday when I returned, stuck above my desk was a front-page view from the Times – this was a feature in those days and it took up half the page. "The Fleet at Torbay" was the subject on that particular Monday.

Then Tom came up to London on leave and joined the architects and me on one of our escapades in the lunch hour to Lansbury's Lido in Hyde Park. Fearful lest he would not be accepted, coming from the Services (echoes of Hussars and Lancers, but the Navy was different) all went well. I need not have worried. Tom came through with glowing colours. We all swam and ate pork pies, and then we climbed onto the top of a bus to get us back in time.

There was a pub opposite to the Office which had bay windows. In the bay on the top floor was a table; we could look down on to it from Brian O'Rorke's window. Tom had a delightful habit of buying a nosegay from the flower-sellers in Piccadilly Circus. He would then settle himself, his hat hiding the nosegay in the middle of the table. My watchful eye would look down and know when he had arrived.

One Friday evening Brian was giving me much to do. "Tonight?" I asked aghast at the prospect – it was quite late. Brian leaned over and looked into the pub. "Oh I see. No, tomorrow will do." So my secret was out all round and the architects office were all to come to the wedding.

As I have said when my father died in June of 1935 England was enduring the terrible depression known as "The Slump". Although the Practice now had four partners there was no money to support my mother: fees due did not materialise for the firm. Curiously we could not pay for our shopping in the Village immediately after his death because of probate requirements.

However, fortunately that winter my mother was given a trip to visit her Uncle Townshend in Jamaica. She returned in March of 1936 to sell our house which had been occupied by Albert and his family meanwhile. My mother's situation was now complicated by Tom and myself wanting to get married. Both our mothers were recently widowed but despite the shortage of funds both set their hearts on a slap-up wedding. With no house it was impossible to be married in Bushey but the Navy came to the rescue. Tom was doing a course at the Royal Naval College at Greenwich and had left a suitcase at 2 Lamb Lane to meet the requirements for residence in the parish. Thus it was that we found our way to the King Charles Steps on the River Thames as man and wife in May of 1936.

Part II To Stop a War

Der Schwarzwald

"If I'd 'uv known what nature of a job it was" said the boatman, "I'd 'uv brought a better boat – red plush seats and all, a real smart little job it 'uv been".

But no. The boat was perfect: small, a trifle shabby but a hard working clinker-built dinghy with an outboard engine.

The gap was growing ever wider as he spoke between the waving people ashore and us as we swept away in the swirling ebb tide of the Thames at Greenwich.

A perfect getaway for a sailor after his wedding, one might think, from King Charles steps at the Palace of Greenwich, the Royal Naval College. It had however a spurious panache.

Downstream we turned the bend of the river into the next reach, once out of sight we drew alongside some steps and jumped ashore: we were instantly arrested. We looked round in dismay – Daisy was nowhere to be seen. The police who surrounded us were adamant – no one had been that way – they would not have been allowed to anyway; this was Woolwich Arsenal – quite the wrong place. I was escorted to the Guardroom while Tom set off between two policemen in another direction.

In the Guardroom several policemen sat drinking tea from large thick mugs. The tops of their uniforms were undone and they looked at ease. They took no notice of me and went on reading their newspapers.

After some time one of them offered me a mug of tea, which I gratefully accepted not having managed to drink one at the wedding. After this another, older than the rest, addressed me without looking up.

"Have you recently been married?"

"Yes," I answered eagerly , "This afternoon in fact"

I fingered the rose in my buttonhole and glowed in my new clothes for the occasion and felt hopeful.

"More's the pity," came the disconcerting reply, "It only brings trouble".

However another one gave me a tip for the Derby, Felstead, and to my everlasting regret I forgot to back it and it won.

After what seemed an interminable time my beautiful brand new husband returned, having established his credentials satisfactorily, and what was better still, with Daisy.

Daisy was our Morris Cowley car, twelve years old and bought off a scrap dump for £10. Her predecessor, the Yellow Peril, had been older, snub nosed, so that to us Daisy was modern. She was a two-seater with a dickey at the back, which held our luggage and had a folding seat for passengers. She had side screens to keep out the rain and of course a hood, which went up or down according to the weather. She was endearing and adequate; she carried us far for several years to come.

The evening light was slipping away so that it was dark by the time we reached Dover. Among my souvenirs I have a label – "Lord Warden Hotel" on the back of which is scribbled "One bottle Champagne left in room No 27 – Gertie."

I hope we were able to recompense Gertie adequately for her abstinence as it was presented to us on our return to pick up a suitcase two weeks later. We certainly had little money left after our honeymoon in the Black Forest in Germany.

Next day Daisy was slung up high over our heads in a net and lowered into the hold of the channel packet and crossed with us to Calais. From then on we rattled our way over the uneven and never ending cobble stones – old French pavés – to Brussels. Daisy had long ago lost pride in her shock absorbers. The experience was shattering.

In Brussels we lingered for a couple of days to recover from the shock of the pavés, also from the shock of the step we had taken. We managed to see at least one museum and to eat some wonderful dinners. When we had recovered our equilibrium, we set out for our main objective – the Black Forest, where we had planned to walk.

Daisy excited incredulous interest as we chugged along the Rhine from Cologne to Heidelberg, Freiburg and on at 30 miles an hour. There were few cars and anyway nothing like an old Morris Cowley had ever been seen: The Peoples' car was just emerging – I think too the Opel was being made.

By the roadside, children held out bunches of flowers hoping we would buy them : they were lilies-of-the valley, 'Maiglöckchen' (May bells), which we were delighted to have and their scent filled our various rooms each night.

It was terribly exciting to see the German landscape, little towns and pretty villages. A Hohenzollern Schloss, high up a mountain, dominating the skyline and overshadowing a vast valley, was awe-inspiring and conjured up old fears. And so our days rolled by. In the Black Forest area we gave lifts: people undismayed climbed into our tiny dickey. I remember one old woman with a goose she was taking to market was great fun. Then there were three young ex-army men who somehow squeezed in and became extremely friendly. They were wandering about the country in search of work which, we learnt, was a general pattern after the first war. We parted in extremely happy accord, swearing that from now on there must be no more wars: politicians made these, we agreed, not ordinary people. We took their photographs with our Brownie Cameras, promising to send them copies to some odd address, which in fact we faithfully did.

Eventually, we reached the Feldberg where we left Daisy, comfortably covered up against any bad weather and set off on foot, after a night's rest, to explore. My German adventure had begun in the office days. The young apprentice who took his holidays hiking with the 'Strength through Joy' – the Hitler Jugend (Young People's Movement), came back with food for thought, backed up by my friend Lilli, secretary to the German Naval Attaché. The world was facing two opposing cultures – Communism from Russia and Fascism from Italy and Germany, so we were very eager to meet one of them first hand. This we were able to do more easily on foot.

Next day between St Blasien and Waldshutam-Rhein the spring weather left us and was not to return during our visit. Never in living memory had weather in June been so bad. I have since learnt that England is not the only place to have a rebellious climate.

Waldshut was a picturesque little town, medieval in architecture. A gatehouse enclosed the main street at each end. In the centre on one side was an imposing Rathaus or town hall from which hung a gigantic Nazi swastika flag. Smaller flags hung from nearly all other buildings – the town in fact was 'en fête', in honour of the showing of the film of the latest Nazi Rally in Nuremburg. We decided after dinner that night to go and see it.

The effect, particularly on me, was traumatic. Tom, being a member of the fighting services, was already aware of the ugly shape that the world was taking. He was less surprised.

Since those days, we have become more accustomed to great rallies showing military strength, tanks bristling with guns, lethal weapons of terrifying power, moving in mass formation which the Russians also indulged in. In those days, England was accustomed to more docile processions from the Empire, including lovable elephants to celebrate their monarch's jubilees etc. Hitler's rasping voice and the adoring cheering crowds finished the illusion. I thought of the 'entente cordiale' we had had with our three young soldiers from the First World War, only a day or so before.

The rain poured down. I plodded along paths between dripping pine trees, which were enveloped in a dark vapour, which, incidentally, gives the name to the Black Forest. In front of me, an enormous figure – six feet four in height – was a yard or two ahead and above me, the rucksack hiding his head from view. This headless giant strode steadily on and might, I feared, disappear into the mountain mists and be lost forever. "That is Mein Mann", I promised myself, as I struggled on, wondering whatever I was doing. Rain trickled down my neck.

I must admit that I had harboured an idea, despite his very many qualities, that in some respects my education had been better, possibly broader than Tom's. That a Dartmouth education was a technical seafaring affair and not at all intellectual. How wrong I was. His English master was Neville Coghill, an excellent Chaucer scholar who produced the play of the Canterbury Tales in the theatre in London a year or two later. Tom spoke very good French, taught him by Père Vert (Mr. Green) and knew exactly how to make arrangements for whatever we did in Brussels. In English he also had an endearing habit of producing the 'mot juste' throughout his life, which was very entertaining. He read books of great weight, both in content and size, as I found to my concern as time went by. As he fell asleep, a huge tome would often fall on my head. All this was to follow later, suffice it to say that I soon discovered that le petit déjeuner was ordered with complete savoir-faire on the hotel telephone. So here I was, wet and bemused.

However, I was to discover that he was not speaking real German, merely making himself understood amid gales of German laughter. So, as we left Basle by train, we got into an express instead of a local train. The result was that we started to climb the Blauenspitz on our way back to the Feldberg, later in the day than intended. The rain poured down.

As night began to fall and no habitation, as described in the guidebook, appeared my confidence in Meinem Mann began to wane. I shouted some despairing acid remarks into the wind, as fear of nightfall began to build up – we had already passed a place where some people had recently perished from exposure. At last we came to an open space with bushes for shelter. We found a seat and could read a notice on it – "Schöne Aussicht" (beautiful view) – and pondered if anyone ever saw it. It did, however, indicate the summit. Then suddenly, over a crag, we spied a light some feet below. Clambering down we literally fell into a Gasthaus and into the arms of three very pretty girls, fair-haired deutsche Mädchen. They tore our wet clothes off and threw them into a tiled oven to dry. We put on pyjamas and were served a delicious dinner by candlelight. The girls plied us with red wine, which we all shared. They made everything a great joke and were, I think, delighted to have custom in such shocking weather. At last we fell into bed – without the girls – and between lovely linen sheets slept like logs.

On our way home, we made a social call on a Professor and his Frau living further down a valley at a place called Maxime. He ran an establishment that coached young Englishmen in foreign languages. His comfortable, middle-aged and sharply intelligent wife helped. The weather had begun to soften and the fragrance of hay and early summer filled their house, which stood in a green garden beside a waterfall. There was a delicious tea with a great variety of cakes and newly made strawberry jam.

A recent student had been Terence Rattigan, the playwright, and from his sojourn with the Professor had stemmed the play then running in London "French Without Tears". This intrigued and pleased them both very much. As in the play, the daughter of the house had married a naval commander. It was to a friend known as Shorty Carlill in real life and his wife, Helga, that we owed our present invitation. We left this delightful and highly civilised oasis in our honeymoon with reluctance, for the long haul through the industrialised areas of the disputed Rhineland and home.

Wayside to Newcastle

Wayside Cottage was an idyllic cottage in perfect surroundings. "You'll never better this", said a friend, experienced in moving house. Another friend had filled the deep windowsills with foxgloves from the woods, so we were enchanted as we stepped over the threshold.

The cottage belonged to a Mrs. Pettifer who was going to visit her daughter in America. Mr Pettifer was boarded out – "Not fit" said his spouse, "to look after himself – can't even boil an egg." But he could grow vegetables in the tiny garden from which we profited, being allowed to help ourselves.

The cottage was part of an estate and we had a superb view beyond our own boundary over the garden with ornamental trees. The Major who owned it was kind and not obtrusive. On the other side was a field from which larks rose and sang from morning to night.

We arrived with our belongings on Sunday night. At 7 a.m. next day Tom left for work at Whale Island, the Gunnery School in Portsmouth. I spent the day unpacking our wedding presents and placing them around. I began to cook dinner from a book called "Dinners for Beginners" but it was for very elaborate eaters, demanding many courses, so all pots were boiling but nothing was ready when Tom returned. It didn't matter because his first words were "We've got to move and almost immediately, I'm afraid."

I looked round in incredulity at the home I had tried to make all that day.

"Where to, for heaven's sake?"

"Newcastle-on-Tyne."

We had about six weeks in this Elysian paradise during which time I learnt about a few of my husband's foibles which were both infuriating and endearing. The first concerned our bed. Tom had an impractical idea that our bed would always move with us, like Queen Victoria's. It had proved difficult to get it upstairs in Wayside Cottage.

It was a splendid bed which my mother had given us from her spare room. It had a very good large box spring. Unfortunately for succeeding generations, in the 1930s brass bedsteads were out and we discarded what today would have been a very collectable item. Instead, Albert had a friend who would make us a portable frame in wood. His name was "Young 'Oare" – he was about sixty. Albert proudly showed me the finished job and very courteously but with avuncular roguishness he wished me much happiness and many children to be born in that bed.

Despite Young Oare's work, it was the box spring that proved the difficulty – it could only just be wheedled into our bedroom at Wayside Cottage, which was lucky. Tom decided that to meet future needs he would have to cut the box spring in half – rather drastic, I felt, to cut the marriage bed in half after only three weeks, but I agreed.

The operation began after supper one night, at about 9 o'clock. The whole thing would be completed by midnight and we would be comfortably tucked up soon afterwards. I was to learn that my husband was a very bad estimator of time. He had brought back with him a roll of canvas from a sail-maker, a bunch of rings for threading rope through on sails, a punch and die, together with a mallet borrowed from the sail-maker. He also had a palm, needle and thread so that I could stitch away making flaps for the two raw ends of the box spring once it was cut in half. It was ingenious.

At three in the morning I was holding the punch and die in position, while Tom very deliberately struck it with the leather mallet to place the rings. At last we were ready to thread the rope through to draw the two halves together. At about 5.am we fell into bed and lay on the finished article. At 6.30 the alarm went and I also learnt that sailors can miss a night's sleep without turning a hair. They can also, I found later, spend all day without a meal and then eat an enormous amount at one sitting and before sleep.

A second foible grew out of necessity. In those days the Admiralty cherished an idea that the state of matrimony was not for junior officers – for Commanders, yes, but below that rank you rubbed along as best you could. In any case the Navy did not pay like the other two services until after the war: there was no marriage allowance, nor help in moving house. Nor any houses either – you found your own if you followed your husband. The wife generally found it, as she usually got there before the ship.

It was a good idea, therefore, to have a trailer for our possessions to fix behind Daisy for her to pull. Tom found a coach-builder who would make one for us. The trouble turned out to be that he was accustomed to providing for a lighter load, such as one calf or a pig, whereas we had so much, including the famous bed.

The day came when we set off and stopped for the night in Bushey, after which we wound our way on to the Great North Road en route for Newcastle, which we hoped to reach that evening.

It was, I remember, an uncomfortable journey. For one thing we were nostalgic for our first home and I was apprehensive about our next one in the North, quite wrongly as it turned out. I had also fallen victim to a most disagreeable attack of boils and had one arriving on my back. My dog, Jock, a dear, clumsy, large Airedale, sat on my lap. Outside, a dreary drizzle turned to heavy rain. Windscreen wipers had not reached Daisy – one had to open one half of the windscreen.

Then, crossing Yorkshire in the late afternoon, there was a nasty crump noise from the rear: the trailer and Daisy had parted company. The trailer had sunk down on its haunches, refusing to go any further. There was no sign of life in that bleak countryside on a wet Sunday evening.

"All we need", said my redoubtable husband, "is an acetylene welder." and he set off in Daisy to find one.

Jock and I huddled beside the trailer drawn to the side of the road and I wallowed in woe. I had to keep things from running into the trailer in the bad visibility. Beside us, not far away, I could see slag heaps and huge kiln-like funnels outlined in the murk. Their size made me feel even more lonely, deserted and depressed. In my uncertainty as to what might happen next, I began to wonder disloyally whatever had induced me to marry "Mein Mann".

Then suddenly the miracle happened: Daisy returned. Inside were Tom and an acetylene welder carrying his apparatus for acetylene welding. I could not believe it. He had been drinking in a nearby pub, The Fox at Brotherton, the most obvious place for Tom to look for help – a pint had settled everything. Within half an hour Daisy was once more swinging along the Great North Road, with the trailer in happy pursuit. Some people do have luck, I thought. To my great pleasure, a little time ago, I was travelling along the new motorway when I suddenly saw standing high up above the down lane, by itself but reverently preserved, the Brotherton Fox. I wondered if a very old acetylene welder still drank there. A short way away I also spied two kiln-like funnels still there to remind me of the despair of long ago.

Late that night, long after expected, we slipped into Newcastle and found our way to 61 Kenilworth Road, off the Scotswood Road. Most of the surroundings have been swept away but I believe this road still remains. Despite the late hour, we were very cordially received by our landlady, a gentle, quiet, middle-aged woman, whose husband and two sons were out-of-work shipwrights. She served us a very welcome supper of bacon and eggs in the front room which was to be our sitting room.

Next morning Tom left for the Vickers shipyard where HMS Newcastle was being built. I was left to take stock of my situation.

My sense of humour was miles away as I sat and contemplated our sitting room. Thirty years earlier it might have been a bride's dream of elegance. There were dark green velvet drapes everywhere with tassels and bobbles and a tremendously cumbersome over-mantel with shelves holding paired vases. All could be collector's pieces now, as fashion has swung back, but to me, in 1936, from a generation who had thrown away Victorian tastes, fresh from an architect's office where horizontal lines, wrought iron and glass tables and even white carpets were fashionable, we seemed to be living in a dark green cavern. Nottingham lace curtains at the windows kept the daylight away.

Upstairs we had a back bedroom. One could just get round the four foot double bed by going sideways to get to the dressing table.

Next day Jock and I set out to explore the streets outside. Kenilworth Road was one of many that rose up the side of the steep gorge of the River Tyne from Scotswood Road which ran along beside the river. These side-roads resembled giant staircases, each house a step towards the skyline. The houses were heavily Victorian, each the width of one room and a passage. Front rooms were uniformly all draped in Nottingham lace curtains.

Further afield, there were acres and acres of streets all exactly alike. They were entirely deserted by women – no one was shopping but at all street corners stood groups of men, shabbily dressed in dark suits and wearing cloth caps, their hands deep in their pockets. Resentment seemed to be expressed in every line of their bodies as they engaged in desultory conversation. This was indeed the Slump. We came, with relief, to a small public garden. Asphalt paths ran around it with several long seats in strategic places before a little lawn with beds of begonias. The seats were crowded with men. They fell silent as I passed and I felt suddenly garish in my gingham frock of blue and white check. "What do you feed that dog on?" one of them called after me and I felt ashamed of Jock's well-fed comely form. There was nowhere to go where I could hide my prosperity and softness from the South, in comparison with the utter degradation and despair in the shipbuilding world of the North. Of course I knew about the unemployment, but I had never imagined scenes like this. We retraced our steps back to the green cave and I began to knit Tom a pullover against the day when the good ship Newcastle would go to sea. Meanwhile Daisy was our salvation, carrying us at weekends to Hadrian's Wall or to explore the town and country of Durham or castles on the Border. We bathed at Blyth where coal seams crumbled on to the beach to be gathered into sacks at the foot of the cliffs. The tides rolled them into balls.

Rightly or wrongly, we thought that our presence in the house in Kenilworth Road made a change for the better for the family there: we paid five pounds a week for board and lodging. The trouble was that I had nothing to do all day, except take Jock for a walk or sit and knit or read in the little green front room. It was not possible to get a job as young wives might try to do today – it was hard enough for the locals. I missed my architects and life in the office. Jock missed the country, which oddly enough led to our release.

One morning, our landlady dashed upstairs to tell me that Jock was eating the leg of the table in the front room. I leapt downstairs and found the place in disarray and Jock's expression conveyed – "Come on, I've had enough". I took him out and tied him to the front railing while I went to examine the damage. I offered to go and get a joiner to put it right. Then I discovered that Jock had begun on the front door as well. We set off as fast as we could and miraculously found a joiner who came at once to repair the damage. The whole episode was taken with admirable fortitude by our landlady, but the next day she had something important to say to me, hoping I would not be offended. Their daughter had had a baby and was coming to her parents from hospital. Would it be possible for us to find somewhere else to live? They were fearful of having such a dangerous animal in the house with the new baby. Jock never did such a thing again, the vet I took him to see only laughed and said he was constipated and needed exercise. He was a crafty dog.

For us it was happy news, as we were longing to find somewhere nearer the country. By this time, with the Government's change of policy and the Admiralty's new contracts, the shipyards were crying out for shipwrights – full employment had suddenly returned – the Slump, in fact, was ended while England prepared for war. The men of our house went back to work.

We took up residence in the salubrious suburb of Jesmond, a stone's throw from the spacious Town Moor where Jock could exercise several times a day.

There were great advantages in our new home; we were able to have some of our things in a light and airy room. There was a pastry cook where they baked in the shop and where Tom was able to buy his favourite éclairs on his way home. We ate them in front of our cosy fire, watching the crimson December sunsets through large windows without Nottingham lace.

There must have been especially fine sunsets in Northumberland because I remember so many, particularly when we visited a shipyard down on the Tyne. Alongside the destroyer we were seeing was another skeleton ship on the next slipway, her beautiful frames outlined against the setting sun. Riveters throwing red-hot rivets to each other were working overtime: the tide had definitely turned and you could smell prosperity returning to the town. Paradoxically, the joy was not to be everyone's. We made many friends in the North but mostly, of course, with other officers who came with their wives while other ships were built. Tragically, of those couples – our first married friends – only widows survived when the war was over. There was one exception and he had mislaid his wife.

We used to play golf on the Town Moor for free, until we gave up in despair: Tom had a drive long and straight down the fairway until it suddenly turned at right angles and continued just as far into some undergrowth or woodland. We tore ourselves to pieces looking for lost balls and quarrelling. There was a repertory theatre with a flourishing company which nurtured many well-known actors. Edward VIII's abdication took place in December of that year and I heard George V1 proclaimed from the steps of the Guildhall in Newcastle.

At the time of the abdication Tom was testing the telephone communication system on board HMS Newcastle. He plugged in to speak to a gun turret. In answer to his question "Who is speaking?", the inevitable reply was "Mrs Simpson, Sir".

In our lodgings I was listening on the Radio to a mid-morning programme. Claude Dampier was a comedian whose stock-in-trade was an imaginary character called Mrs Gibson. That morning he unfortunately sang "She has sex-appeal – Mrs Simpson"....The BBC faded out into silence. Soon the announcer's voice came through to the effect that the BBC apologised for the bad lapse in taste due to the strain of the news announced that day.

In the spring, I think in March, the good ship HMS Newcastle was complete. As she steamed down the Tyne on her first journey to the sea, the shipyard workers, who were now working flat out, stopped work to cheer her on her way – she was the first naval ship to be built on the Tyne for ten years.

Leaves

Leaves, or furloughs as the railway tickets called them, came and went, but their arrival was as welcome as the leaves on the hedgerows in spring.

The Home Fleet spent three months at sea, followed by one in port. The time in port was divided up, one half of the ship's company going on leave and then changing over for the other half to have theirs. I have explained the "days-on" routine when at Holland Farm, which had to be borne, but our leave period belonged entirely to us. At this stage without a family, we made the most of our time.

There was a wonderful bonus for the English: travel abroad on the Continent was so much in our favour. Germany had a system of issuing special Deutschmark for foreigners visiting the country. In France the exchange was greatly to our advantage. This served us well: it was cheaper to go abroad than to stay in England for the two weeks at our disposal. Naval pay, before the war and until 1947 or so, dated from the days when younger sons with a family behind them went either into the Church or the Navy, subsidised from home. The popularity of a Naval career suited the Admiralty, so the system remained unchanged until after the War when they were forced to make Naval pay commensurate with that of the other two services. Anyway, the glorious thing was that we had this wonderful opportunity. As the black clouds gathered over Europe, we determined to see what we could of the world across the Channel.

We did not travel in luxury but became adept at night travel on hard third class wooden seats. An aircushion under the hip, a pillow hired from a trolley on the platform for the head, and a bottle of red wine for the tummy, induced a reasonable night's sleep.

The first summer, however, we had no need of trains – we borrowed a boat, on terms, from some friends and sailed over to France. We bobbed in and out of harbours around the Baie de la Seine. The boat was a Bermuda rigged cutter of four tons called Fidget. She belonged to a syndicate of Tom's friends but later became owned solely by Colin and Maurice McMullen.

Tom and I had sailed with friends in idyllic weather off the East Coast some years before. Now there were only the two of us and I was inexperienced. All cruises in small boats produce a saga and the mystery is why people ever go more than once to endure the discomfort of being cold, wet, hungry and perhaps frightened. This suffering is entirely offset by the joys of arrival in port, the drying out, eating and, of course, the recounting of the saga.

Our trip in 1937 contained a normal mixed bag of adventures – getting becalmed, going through a tidal race, getting stuck on the mud (my fault) and shopping happily in French markets. Three events stand out vividly in my memory. The first was a wonderful uplifting sensation to the spirit. We had been becalmed in a fog for what seemed like twenty-four hours. White walls of fog surrounded us as we lay heaved to, waiting for the fog to rise. Ghastly chuggings of ship's engines came near to us. We feared we were in the shipping lane and beat on a bucket with a hammer to warn of our existence. However, the ghost ships slipped by. I was sitting at the helm in the early morning, feeling very disconsolate when suddenly there was a whirl of wings on all sides and thousands of gulls, who must have been floating on the water all around us, rose as one. Within minutes the fog rose too. A feeling of elation came over me, possibly this was how Noah felt when the dove returned with the leaf in its beak.

There was the never-to-be-forgotten fat lady having lunch. We had arrived at Barfleur at 2 p.m., hungry but late for a mid-day meal. There was an inviting little restaurant beside the harbour. It had a striped sunblind, green plants and two tables outside each side of the door. We sat down at the one empty one and with great affability were served a four-course meal for the equivalent of two shillings each. At the other table was a party of about six people who were finishing their meal amidst gales of laughter produced by a large fat lady recounting some long story. We could not understand but nevertheless fell under the spell of her infectious laugh as she included us by gestures in a most courteous way. Finally she rose from the table and, turning towards the inner restaurant, still helpless with laughter, she bent towards our table and as she passed remarked, "Madame, j'ai le corset qui monte" (I have a corset that rises) and disappeared. Presently she returned, presumably having re-arranged her corset but began immediately a further story so that the garment must again have been in jeopardy. We took to her.

We had a somewhat hazardous return. A situation prevailed which I subsequently learnt always to expect when returning from France. With leave coming to an end and it being essential to return on time or be in trouble, the weather turns foul. French fishermen watched without encouragement as we beat out of Fécamp harbour, rising and falling over the incoming swell.

That night, the sea calmed down a little and Tom entrusted me with the middle watch while he snatched some sleep. I sat fairly contentedly watching the night sky with the wind sharp upon my cheek. I felt happy but sleepy. Then suddenly with a jolt I looked up – the stars were all in the wrong places – I must have dropped off – we were sailing back to France. Stealthily I crept about trying to retrieve the situation undetected, but the flapping of the sails as I put the ship about brought a voice from below – sailors only cat-nap – "Darling, you're wonderful.", came up to my guilty ears, followed by "My God, you're not.", as Tom's head emerged.

The next day, in poor visibility and driving rain and wind rising to force 6, Tom was up forward taking a reef in the jib, I was at the helm holding our course with all my might and main – in fact my whole life depended on it, as I did not want to lose my perfectly good husband by some stupid error. Then suddenly the Nab lighthouse, which we had not been able to locate, flashed past only a few yards from us and we were able to make Portsmouth Harbour.

My husband's derogatory statements always managed to cheer me up. For example, "Darling, you are plain". You might think it could break a marriage but it entirely restored my 'amour propre' – I knew I was a winner.

In January of 1936 Tom took me to ski in Austria. We had spent our second night on a train; the first had been from Newcastle to London. From Victoria we set out for a small village, Hochsölden. Despite the comfort of aircushions etc we were tired, bedraggled and tatty by the time we reached a little village at the foot of our mountains. Our clothes were rather unconventional to meet a European winter. Tom wore a remarkable carriage coat, Victorian and called 'Uncle Frank' after a distant forebear who had owned it. It made him look like Sherlock Holmes. I wore an old fur coat which my mother had relegated to feeding chickens in. The train from Victoria was full of people bound for winter sports and included a large party of very smart girls, sixteen of them with four accompanying young men. At every change in our journey they were always there until at a small station they seemed to have disappeared – Bludenz I think – where there was an empty bus waiting to take us on the final stage of our journey. We got in and settled down to wait and to read our books in peace. The driver arrived and got in, at which point a door of a café opened and out poured the same party who, we were hoping, had been carried on in the train. They were in better shape from second class travel than we were, spruced up and revived with coffee. Immaculate in their rather twee skiing outfits they clambered all over us with shrieks of merriment and sat down, ignoring me but eyeing Tom with possessive charm, "Oh dear, how unfair on our first holiday." were my thoughts. But 'Mein Mann' managed to continue to read some extraordinary tome that weighed our luggage down. Then he turned, looked at me and out came this remark, which warmed my heart – "Darling, you are plain." I didn't have to worry. In the end, of course, they became tolerable, staying in a different hotel. They were in fact the second tour made by Ingham who accompanied the party and laid the foundation of the now popular agency.

Skiing was a problem to me. Tom held to a fallacy on the subject. This was that if you ever got on to the nursery slopes you would never get off them. Instead, he took me on tours which I always spent on my bottom. In later years at Gargellen I rebelled and took myself off to join a lowly class and made progress. Tom would go off on his own and would later appear at the top of the slope. "Achtung!" would cry the mothers to their children, "Herr Thomas kommt!", and Tom would come straight down and over a small bridge to the steps of the Heimspitz where we stayed with the family Thony. I was then able gently to join him on very happy expeditions.

Devonport

At 7 a.m. on a grey morning in March I stepped out of the night train on to the platform at Devonport in a state of extreme desolation. On the train from Newcastle to London Jock had become extremely ill and in London a vet had diagnosed galloping consumption. It appeared that there was no alternative but to put him to sleep and, rightly or wrongly, I agreed. The antibiotic M & B had been discovered but was not available for use by vets. Jock had been mine for some years and had come as my dowry and was beloved.

I took a bus around Devonport to fill in the time before the busy world woke up. I looked with unhappy hostility at the grey, squat little town. Later I became fond of it and mourned as it fell to ruins under the enemy bombardment. The bus passed the dockyard gates and I wondered what was happening within. The ship, I knew, would have arrived. I found some breakfast and set out to look for house agents. I cannot remember if there was any choice but I settled for No 4, Hilary Terrace in Stoke, a small town midway between and linking Devonport and Plymouth.

It was a first floor flat owned by Miss Collins who lived on the ground floor. She agreed to let us have the flat for 30/- a week instead of 35/-, on condition that we watered her aspidistras, one of which stood in a life-sized china swan. We watered her aspidistras daily, as well as her hats.

In the bathroom there was an extraordinary contraption of a type I was to meet years later in Malta. A large copper pot like a harvest-home tea-urn stood over a gas ring. The tap which filled it ran so slowly that one was bound to go away and start cooking bacon and eggs in the kitchen. A scream from Miss Collins below would precipitate a rush to the bathroom to turn off the tap, followed by my apologies and a mopping up process began. Miss Collins kept her hats on top of her wardrobe immediately under the bathroom. I suggested that she moved them.

In addition to this almost daily douche of water, the flat was extremely damp, like many west country houses. Our house was Jerry-built and had many depressing shortcomings, linoleum that never quite fitted and was apt to turn up at the corners. The first night that Tom was home, he came into the kitchen and flung open the window. The window and the whole frame fell into the garden below, shattering glass over the cabbages and winter greens. Despite the flat's and our shortcomings, Miss Collins remained on friendly terms, which speaks volumes for her generous and stalwart character.

Time passed not unpleasantly and Tom had leave during this stay. He found a small sailing dinghy which he hired from a fisherman in the Barbican and we sailed for a week of his leave, exploring the creeks around Plymouth Sound. Each night we left the boat pulled up in some quiet place, often made fast to a tree, and returned home by train. This was a freedom you could not risk today. Each morning we would return and find all in order and would set out again to continue our exploring.

For some reason we made no arrangement as to what I would do when the ship left for its summer cruise. I did not want to think about it, nor did I want to stay alone in the flat in Stoke. From Plymouth Hoe I watched the ship steam out to join the Home Fleet. A newly commissioned cruiser of a new class, she had all the trappings that the occasion demanded: the decks lined by sailors, the Royal Marine Band playing and her newly painted sides glittering in the April sunshine. There is something terribly emotive about the stately progress of a warship leaving or entering harbour, either carrying away or bringing back husbands, fathers or sweethearts. Few cynics would, I think, be able to remain unmoved.

Dolefully, I returned to the flat to pack up. I noticed with dismay that the aspidistra in the swan had turned a nasty yellow. Tom had insisted on pouring dregs from beer mugs as well as my tea-leaves. I hoped that Miss Collins would still remain friendly, which luckily she did. She was a gallant woman.

Very late in the afternoon I set off in Daisy. She and the trailer had come round in one of the Newcastle's empty hangars, as the ship's planes had not yet arrived. We left the trailer in a lock-up garage packed with our unwanted possessions. Ill-luck befell it.

I don't know how I discovered Holland Farm near Plympton in the gloaming. I turned down a deep lane to Sparkwell. I found a deeper lane with a farm gate left invitingly open and turned in. The banks were covered with primroses picked out for me in Daisy's head-lights. At the bottom of a slope was a rather stark stone farmhouse. Finding my way through a mucky farmyard I came to a low wall where upturned buckets and milk churns stood in neat rows. I opened a gate and then knocked apprehensively on a very heavy looking door. The door was opened by a smallish woman who invited me into a flagged kitchen. Around a long wooden table opposite an old fashioned range, the Perraton family sat eating after a hard day's work. On the range stood open shallow pans of clotted cream in the making. Despite the hour of my intrusion and the general shyness on both sides, it was agreed then and there that I would be welcome to stay.

Holland Farm: this began a happy association and gave us another of our many homes. We spent nearly all the leaves there, when the Home Fleet was in harbour over the next two years. All that is, bar one, which is a tale in itself. Every three months the Home Fleet returned to base and half of the ship's company had two weeks' leave, turn and turn about. During the time on duty, watches went in rotation and it worked out as one night on board in three – more, if one was unlucky. The company at the farm reduced the loneliness of the days "on", which worked out as two days and a night. I discovered bird watching.

The many advantages outweighed the disadvantages at the farm. Among the latter was the cold in winter. The sun never actually penetrated into the rooms, which had tiny square windows in walls three feet thick. Against this, the pleasure of sinking into a feather bed on a winter's night was hard to beat, taking no account of the courage required next morning to get out of it. I remember one Christmas of intense cold when even the lamp which we carried up to bed to augment the candle-light was bliss to the hands held near to it. This was how the English had always lived until the Americans came over in the war and left their mark with central heating and beef burgers, food far removed from the delicious fried egg and potato of Mrs. Perraton's breakfasts, the farm steak and kidney pies, the home-cured ham and creamy butter.

I can smell and feel the farm now. Outside, geese hissed, turkeys gobbled and hens cackled through most of the daylight hours. Before daylight actually broke, the hobnailed boots of young George, the son of the house, could be heard on the kitchen flagstones and soon the traction engine in the yard would spring into noisy action. He would drive out to farms requiring power for threshing etc. at 5 a.m. and would roar along the lanes without meeting traffic. We could hear him for miles.

Gentler memories are of the beautiful white hands of Mrs. Perraton and her daughters, softened by milking and making butter, which they did by hand. I can smell the wood fires and hear the welcome crackle of green sticks as the sitting room fire "took" (afternoons and evenings only). We learnt to mull beer by putting a hot poker in a nearly full tankard.

The seasons came and went and during the harvest I was allowed to lead the heavy mare, as she pulled the float on which the stooks were being loaded. I was mocked for my difficulty in getting her moving. "Go on – you've got to swear at her." Her name was Violet and I swore at her. This I did as loudly as I could, which was unfortunate as my mother-in-law's name was Violet too and she was staying with us at the time.

My mother-in-law was a charming, innocent character guided by a determined will. Her visit to us was in the spring and on her first evening we took her for a walk. It was Market Day and as we climbed the deep lane to the gate Mr. Perraton hove into view. Now Tom's father had been a pillar of the Conservative Party and after his death his wife loyally gave her services to the local branch of the party.

Mr. Perraton swayed noticeably on his stick as he plunged down the lane for home. It had been market day and his rather blood-shot eye roved over us and an introduction was unavoidable. It was part and parcel of my mother-in-law's determination that she never missed an opportunity and here an excellent one presented itself. "Now," she said, "Mr. Perraton, you can tell me what farmers think of the Milk Marketing Board." Mr. P. swayed on his stick and there was a moment of consternation on our part. His blood-shot eye roamed round the lane then it came to rest and lit up. "Do yew really want to know", he began, "what I think of the Milk Marketing Board?" Then came the blast – "They boogers up in London......" followed by a richly obscene condemnation from which we gathered that Devon farmers had no love at all for the Milk Marketing Board.

Finally, Tom managed to say "Come, Mother, it's time we got on with our walk and let Mr. Perraton get home." His mother's comment as we walked on: "Do you know, I didn't understand a word Mr Perraton said. What a difficult dialect it is." The next day she was a little disappointed that he passed her without recognising her. "How odd, he was so pleasant and talkative last night." This closed the matter and no doubt the Conservative Ladies back home were none the wiser.

Mrs Perraton gave me a story I could vividly imagine. As Mr. P. was tying his black tie while dressing to attend his father's funeral, a fox streaked across his land, followed by the whole pack of the Modbury Harriers in full cry. This had never occurred on his land before. In any other circumstances he would have been with them. Despite the smallness of the window to his bedroom and the excitement outside, the richness of his language was distinctly heard above the commotion of the hunt.

There is only one further story to tell because it relates to an old tale. Mice sat on a beam behind the mantelpiece over the fire. There was a gap in the old building and the mice hung their tails down through it. I regret to say that Mrs. P was annoyed by this and took the scissors or carving knife to cut off the tails of the poor mice. I have always wondered how the farmer's wife was supposed to have managed this and now I know.

It was from the farm that I set out in the autumn of 1937 to fulfil my plan to complete my agreement with the three young Germans whom we met on our honeymoon. The time was now ripe: Tom was going to sea for the autumn cruise.

Deutschland Über Alles, Part I

On winter evenings in Newcastle and again at the farm, we pored over Hugo's Self-Taught Course in German, quarrelling over my pronunciation. Nevertheless I persevered, so that in the autumn of 1937 it was time to put my idea into effect and to return to Germany. My idea was that if only ordinary people of the two countries got together, political differences would fade away.

The Frau Professor at Maxime, our friend's mother, found a family who would engage me as an "au pair" girl. On the Hoe in Plymouth I watched the good ship Newcastle leave for her autumn cruise and then I left for London. Here my mother was in St. George's Hospital following an operation. I felt extremely uneasy and guilty, but all I can say is that I felt compelled to pursue my course and to Germany I went.

At 6 a.m. on a beautiful September morning I stepped out of the little mountain train on to the station platform at Herrenalp, a pretty little village in the Black Forest. The aches of a night's journey on wooden seats began to fall away.

In the middle of the long platform stood a very spruce middle-aged couple, Hugo and Irene Böppel. (I spell Irene as in English but it was pronounced Irena) They looked remarkably spry and elegant with the sun glinting on Irene's fair hair. Both were good looking and well dressed in the style of the Forest: well tailored grey-green suits and rather ridiculous Tyrolean hats on the side of their heads.

The village lay in an oasis of the Forest along a small river that wound its way between the little fields and wooden Alpen houses. The Försthaus was above the village, tucked in beneath the Forest. It was a pretty, colourful house with its windows wide open to the valley and sunshine. Inside it was very snug – gemütlich, as I learnt to describe it. I fell asleep in a room at the top of the house, to the sound of waterfalls from all around. I also fell asleep in love with my first impression of Herrenalp.

Hugo was a solidly built man, already showing signs of middle-aged tubbiness. His position as Förstmeister made him a man of consequence in the whole area. He was good-natured and strong-willed. On his expansive chest he proudly wore the Iron Cross, Germany's highest award for valour on the battlefield. His face also bore scars from sabre cuts won in duels at university and these were equally proudly borne. In 1923 he had been with Hitler in the Biergarten Putsch which had failed in its objective. Hitler had served a prison sentence, but Hugo had escaped. His loyalty to Hitler was devotedly steadfast.

Irene was a tall attractive blonde and was very vivacious. She, too, was a devoted follower of the Führer and upheld the régime with energy. Trotting behind her when out shopping round the village, I used to try and gauge the true response to her unfailing greeting – "Heil Hitler" – as she entered a shop, her voice high and clear. The replies were often mumbled and were usually followed by "Grüss Gott", the old country greeting.

My duties seemed shamefully light, or else I was very negligent, but I found myself treated by my charming bosses as one of the family, or even as an honoured guest. I did some light housework, which salved my conscience, prepared vegetables and cooked a few English dishes that I knew – my repertoire was slender – and I learnt more from theirs. I began to find that I was a valued curiosity from England on whom the ideas of the new German Reich could be tried out.

"What do you think of the new Germany today?" was the first question I was asked by every new person I met. The Böppels took me with them whenever they went to visit friends in other villages beyond Herrenalp. Between the houses in the village itself was a constant flow of people. Sometimes in the evenings we would congregate at the Hotel Post, an inn with a beautiful wrought iron sign, a short distance from the Försthaus. Discussions were never far from the subject of politics, at home or abroad. For the first three weeks I was very impressed by the freshness and order of everything and the enthusiasm expressed.

There were some great friends who lived in Stuttgart, the curator of the War Museum there and his talented wife. Both spoke perfect English and the curator had an Oxford degree in Anglo-Saxon. Despite their obvious intelligence, the conversation followed the same lines as at Herrenalp: the unfairness of the Treaty of Versailles, the loss of their colonies, the devastation in the aftermath of war with the wandering population without work (like the men we had met on our honeymoon) and the resultant fear of Bolshevism. Out of this chaos, I realised, had come the rising Adolph Hitler to bring order and dignity back to the country. One and all expressed their amazement at England's attitude, her short-sightedness, the stupidity of people like Winston Churchill and Vansittart, two people I had not thought much about but apparently regarded here as enemies of the Reich.

There was one heinous crime and it was this: "In England gibt es viele Lords, die Juden sind."(in England there are many Lords who are Jews). There was no denying this, but what did it matter? Despite this criticism of my country, the last glass of Glühwein was raised to the toast: "Germany on the land and England on the sea and the whole world is ours". Expressing my horrified doubts, I would spend a night after such discussions tossing and sleepless. Any love affair I may have entertained for the new style Germany and its influence on the progress of the world, faded. Stopping a war was to prove no easy matter.

One day I was taken to a gathering in the village that was the equivalent of the Women's Institute in England – the Frauenschaft. Here I listened to all the same arguments, this time read out from an edict from Hitler himself. A huge map was unrolled to show the iniquity of the English possessions overseas, the Imperial pink on the map which was accurate at that time. But then came a gross inaccuracy: they pointed out the route in the Mediterranean along which the British Navy had transported Russian Communists to fight in the civil war raging then in Spain. It was useless for me to protest that it was not so – "Das ist nicht wahr". They knew better. However, they politely and jokingly asked me to tell King George on my return about the colonies they wanted back.

I used to take myself for walks in the forest. I had dabbled in ornithology at the farm in Devon and here in the forest I found many species less seen in England: redstarts, for instance, were plentiful. There was one very pleasant pastime and that was climbing with Hugo up into the Hochsitz, a tree platform high among the trees to watch for deer coming down to drink below. They had to be culled so it was a necessity for Hugo, as well as a sport. Luckily we were unlucky on that score when I was there: I am hopelessly on the side of the hunted. Once, when I was beagling in the school holidays, a hare ran along a bank immediately above me. When the huntsman asked if I had seen the hare I sent him off in the other direction. The terrified animal had, I thought, looked me in the eye. What was wonderful in the Hochsitz was the fact that one could observe the birds in their natural habitat in the top of the trees, where they did not expect us to be.

One day I came in from a walk to find that a rather surprising arrangement had been made for me. A couple who lived not far away were great friends of the Böppels and we had all made an expedition to Münich in weather conditions that must have equalled those that produce the Fall in America. The part of the Forest we crossed was ablaze with the autumn and I learnt all sorts of descriptive superlatives as we motored along. It had been a long day with too much to see and so it was now suggested that Hans, the husband, and I should spend a weekend there while his wife was in Berlin on some business, perhaps political. We would stay the night and Hans would show me München in detail. I was assured that this was his Frau's special wish and with her blessing we set out. Hans was an amusing young man whom I rather liked, flirtatious too which made it fun. I enjoyed his company as he showed me around the complete Nazification of the city. There were two museums which faced each other, one for what I think was called 'The People's Art', which was extremely boring. It was full of pictures of peasants working in happiness upon the land, or young people performing other laudable things like helping the sick and the poor – good, clean occupations. The other Museum was advertised as showing 'Debased Art', some of which was pornographic, but amongst its paintings were several of the French Impressionists. I remember Van Gogh among other famous names. 'Le Déjeuner sur l'Herbe' would certainly have been there, if they had been lucky enough to have it.

It was nevertheless fun. We lunched on German sausage and dined on schnitzel and goulash, drank more wine than was good for us, but not too much for me to make sure that the communicating door between our two rooms was securely locked that night.

When we got back to Herrenalp I found that yet another plan had been hatched by my kind friends and by Han's wife in Berlin. It would be possible for me to go as an 'au pair' to the house of a general – Field-Marshal Von Blomberg, the head of the German Army in Berlin at that moment. I began to think the term 'au pair' was becoming slightly ridiculous. Field-Marshals did not exactly fit into my idea of ordinary people getting together, but the overriding reason why I turned down this offer was that time was running out and Tom's ship would be returning to Devonport. Nothing would prevent me from going home for his leave.

It was borne in upon me that argument was quite useless. My friends found it hard to understand, things seemed to jangle which was frustrating. "But you will meet the Führer himself in the Field-Marshal's house", said Irene. This did not appeal to me at all. I had come to regard all the photographs of him as ridiculous. One day, Irene sat at the table gazing with affection at a photograph of the Führer, "So ernst." (earnest) she exclaimed. I thought he looked a silly little man. Looking back on it, this consignment to the Field-Marshal's might have been very dangerous or disagreeable, had I accepted. I set about making arrangements for my journey home.

Before I left, I enquired of Irene about a battalion of young men who marched past our house every day. They wore drab uniforms and forage caps and carried spades over their shoulders in military fashion. They sang as they marched, but they did not seem to be a very spirited lot of young men. They were, she explained to me, on Arbeitdienst – young men on National Service and they were engaged in building new roads – Autobahn in fact – down which later the army was to drive its massive equipment for invasion. The odd thing about the singing was that they always changed the song at exactly the same place each day. Irene's explanation was also odd, "Well, it is always good to sing – bad people do not sing". What bad people I wondered? I noticed that these young people were never to be seen off duty in the village. What sort of camp did they inhabit?

In spite of their incredulity about the chance I had thrown away in Berlin, I was befriended by my friends and bosses. The day finally arrived for my departure. Hugo and Irene saw me off, as they had met me, on the platform of the little country station. They had been wonderfully kind to me. I was sad to leave them. They repeated their plea to the end, despite my dismissive arguments, "Don't forget – Germany on the land and England on the sea and the whole world is ours." I laughed and waved as the little train rounded a corner and began to descend to Karlsruhe and the Rhine, leaving the Schwarzwald and all its beauty behind, as I thought, for the time being.

During my journey home, the sinister side of Nazism raised its ugly head. For the first few stops, I was alone in the carriage and I had time to think. As the train descended the carriage began to fill up – everyone began talking and, of course, this was of politics. There was a woman who sat in the seat opposite to me who opened up a conversation. I was happy to join in and hoped to impress her with the fluency of my newly acquired German. To my disappointment, she said, "I think we would get along better in English." and went on talking to the others in German. Hurt and snubbed, I took up my book and read in high dudgeon. Then the carriage emptied for a short time and she asked me my opinion of Germany – the usual question – and where I had been staying and with what sort of people. I answered briefly before the carriage filled up, when she again became distant and isolated me from the general conversation. I felt mystified and aggravated and especially so when I found her climbing into the same carriage as myself at Karlsruhe. Without more ado, I settled down to read as we sped along the valley of the Rhine.

Then, at the frontier at Aachen, which the French call Aix-la-Chapelle, she invited me to take a walk along the platform out of earshot of anyone else. She was, she told me, engaged in an enterprise of helping Jews to escape from Germany. She promised that when we got to England she would tell me more.

In the train from Dover to Victoria we sipped and ate the extraordinary luxurious tea provided by railways in 1937. I listened with horror to her account of appalling treatment meted out to Jews and suspects, of the cruelly devious tricks played on the families of those already arrested – ashes returned in a match box and other hair-raising tales – so hair-raising that at first I found it difficult to credit. Although the régime had become suspect to me too, I, like so many in England and certainly in Germany, had no inkling of what was really happening.

Before we reached Victoria, she explained to me that I would be an ideal person to join her association. With my connection with high-standing Nazis, which the Böppels and their friends were, I could be of the utmost use in the service of getting Jews out. She gave me her card and hoped to hear from me. To my shame, she did not hear from me. Next spring I became pregnant instead.

I went to my mother's flat, where I found my actor cousin, Geoffrey. The next time I met him there, he was in army uniform. This was not the end of my connection with Nazi Germany but that came later. It was very good to be home.

Despite my failure to co-operate with the lady on the train to help evacuate Jews, we did manage to get one girl and her brother out of Austria, but it was not a happy enterprise. There are good and bad in all cultures and the venture created some chaos where we lived. "They're foreigners." said the village.

Incidentally, soon after my return, the Field-Marshal was deposed. The unstoppable war looming larger.

Interlude

"Give my regards to Plymouth Lil", said the police clerk, as I gave my address before I left court. Our burglar had been led away to the cells.

When I left Hillary Terrace, we deposited our belongings in our trailer in a lock-up garage in Devonport. Unfortunately, an ex-employee had a master key and for many nights, wheelbarrows trundled away filled with our wedding presents. The police, however, became suspicious of this traffic and eventually got in touch with me. From a little sketch I made of a very modest sherry glass we had, they traced the culprit who was brought to court and sentenced to three months in Exeter gaol. When he came out, I got to know him and he helped me trace a few of the things he had flogged – he was quite a nice young man. It was irritating to see, when I called at his house, that his wife was wearing an apron with an embroidered "L" on her bosom – one of our linen towels that my mother had decorated with our monogram. Years later we found, in a London bookshop, Volume 3 of a set of books we had had. I am convinced we bought back our own book, it being on its own and the only one of the set we had lost.

By the time of the court case, we were living in a flat on the Hoe. I had found it on my return from Germany. There were three flats. Ours was the top one where we lived amongst the dormer windows, pigeons and mice – families of them. Our landlady, Lil, lived on the ground floor. She had a disconcerting way of calling out, "Who's there?" to our friends on the stairs as they came to visit us. Another disconcerting habit she had was helping herself to our sherry early in the morning while I was driving Tom to the dockyard at 8 a.m. One day she cracked the decanter – "One of my heads, dear." she explained. Mice scampered, the telephone failed to function and the geyser, which we shared with the flat below, blew up. Nevertheless we were happy there and spent the only Christmas together on our own that we ever had.

Lil was of ample build with a comfortable middle-aged spread. Her hair was apricot colour and she had a liking for pink blouses. Despite all the annoyances she had a kind heart.

After Tom sailed away, he wrote to say that he had left a photograph of me hanging on the wall. I went to retrieve it and found that Lil had removed it to her own bedroom and there it hung. She promptly took it down and gave it to me, "You look so young, dear, I loved showing it off – let's have a cup of tea." We had long ago realised that Lil's was a house of ill repute.

Our flat had character and was extremely snug, especially by candlelight. So much so that some rather grander friends, of whom we were very fond, took it for the next leave and were a bit astonished to discover the truth.

Deutschland Über Alles, Part II

Tom and I spent the Christmas leave of 1937 in Lil's flat on Plymouth Hoe – our second Christmas and one of the best, despite the mice and Lil's eccentricities. In the spring of 1938, Aunt Elsa invited me and my mother to stay with her and Uncle Charles at Cagnes-sur-Mer in the South of France where they had built a house for retirement. This I felt bound to do having deserted my mother in hospital on my way to Germany. I wanted time to digest the experiment of Herrenalp. I did not feel like going back at once and if I did do so, I wanted a different environment. The whole problem was perplexing.

It was a funny old time with the gentle pleasant routine, car drives and picnics, all thoughtfully planned for the elderly. Very comfortable and splendid for my mother and for me a chance to see Provence. One day, on my own in a bus from Nice to Cagnes, I learnt from the general tumult among the passengers that Germany had marched into Austria: the Anschluss (joining) had taken place, as threatened. I felt very depressed. A German boy who sat next to me said that it would be the greatest thing that had ever happened to Austria. I wondered.

At Easter, Tom and I went to ski in Austria. The Böppels had kindly offered us their hut somewhere where skiing was good, but Tom wanted to visit his friends who kept a Gasthaus in Gargellen in Vorarlberg, where he had a calf named after him. He wanted to see his calf, as well as the Thony family. We found that Gargellen was absolutely packed out with Germans now able to visit Austria on their own terms. Like people so often are when on a high, they were very macho. They let all their ideas boom through the Gasthaus and up the mountains: all the arguments I had already heard. While we were there, the plebiscite was held with the object of showing the world how pleased Austrians were with the Anschluss. It was an unpleasant time – the village returned a 99 per cent vote in favour of Hitler against their Chancellor Schuschnigg. Knowing our friends as we did, we wondered how the count could have been so high.

We were too disenchanted to join the drinking bouts in the Gaststube in the evenings, when Schuschnigg was denigrated as a traitor and Heil Hitler enthusiastically prevailed. We read our books upstairs and I became pregnant.

After that, all thought of my going back to Germany was abandoned – my family would not hear of it. I divided my time that summer between the farm at Plympton and Bushey with my mother. It was ideal for early pregnancy. There was one week which I spent camping on a common at Galmpton in Devon while HMS Newcastle was visiting south coast resorts – a sort of publicity stunt for the Navy. They had come to Torbay. Camping was very economical and enormous fun – I took the family tent: this was known as the Crusade's tent because of its special form, called a Bell Tent. The weather was perfect and Daisy took Tom to and from the ship. During the hours that he was away I ambled around an attractive common and cooked on a Primus stove. I missed my dog, Jock.

Back at the farm in Devon, where this time I stayed alone, I received a letter from Lilli, the German girl from the Embassy. The German Ambassador was coming down to Torbay and was giving a grand ball in celebration of a visit to Torquay of the German Pocket-Battleship, The Deutschland. Lilli invited Tom and me to the ball. I explained that he was at sea, so could not come, but she insisted that I should do so. Daisy and I trundled over Dartmoor with my evening frock in a suitcase and still get-in-able. Lilli had offered to get a room for me in the Hotel Ambassador, where the Embassy contingent were staying, but I found a more modest one for myself.

She very kindly took me out to have tea on board the battleship in the afternoon. The young officers were very courteous and the ship seemed to me to be much homelier and less functional than our own ships – in fact gemütlich and colourful inside. It was a thoughtful idea of Lilli's to ensure that I should know a few people at the dance.

The dance was extremely grand and glittering. Lilli contrived to present me first to her Admiral Vasner, who then presented me to the Ambassador Herr Von Ribbentrop. I gazed into his cold blue eyes. I also shook hands with Frau Ribbentrop, who seemed rather nice and easy. A lot of flattery took place – the Admiral had fought opposite a cousin of Tom's at Jutland. "One day", said the Admiral, "we shall be saluting your husband's flag." At that point I thought it was time to move away.

Next morning Lilli made some ridiculous excuse or pretence that the embassy staff had muddled her return ticket and that it was booked from Plymouth. She asked if I would drive her over there. I took her to the farm which she hated and she asked me to take her on to Plymouth, which I did. I began to show her the Hoe but "no", she wanted to go into the dockyard. This, of course, was quite impossible without a pass or an escort so I put a very disgruntled Lilli on to the train for London. What, I wondered, did she hope to learn from the dockyard?

There was one more coincidence. Admiral Vasner asked, as is an attaché's right, to visit one of the new British cruisers. The one chosen turned out to be HMS Newcastle, then in Devonport. When he arrived he made it known to the captain that he knew of Lieutenant Larken and so was placed next to Tom at lunchtime. The only result of this was that it boosted my social standing in the Captain's mind who, ever after, thought that I hopped in and out of Embassies when the ship was away. I kept the "au pair" version quiet.

The Germans were simple in their thoroughness. I imagine that we were definitely labelled for use – possibly as fifth columnists – in the future struggle. Perhaps we were registered on a card index. If so, it must have been destroyed by the Allies with a mass of other documents at the end of the war. We did, however, play a part from England but the scheme backfired on us. In any case, I failed to stop a war.

Dartmoor

When our baby was on the way, we found a house to rent at Horndean, near Portsmouth. It was a grotty house but had charm and was adequate with a very happy atmosphere and quite a large garden. Its name was Armadale and it cost us £60 a year. We were terribly excited. Mushrooms grew on the lawn. Tom in his dressing gown collected a basketful for our first breakfast – we felt real landowners.

So Armadale won our hearts. We loved it but were unable to do it justice by living in it for any length of time – the war came to disrupt any chance the Navy might have given us to do so. Portsmouth seemed as good a bet as anywhere: Tom hoped his next job would be there, so I was holding the fort until this happened, but we spent the duty part of the leave from the ship Newcastle at the farm in Plympton.

It was during this time that we made efforts to get a Jewish girl out of Austria and found one very willing to come, Helena Kupfermann. She was to live with us and to help in the house. At the same time her brother, Willie, also came and was to live locally and go to school. It was not a happy arrangement – we had left her in the house while we went down to Devon with sad results. The poor girl took over the house and entertained the neighbourhood, upsetting the milkman's wife and causing much trouble and gossip. She had the cheek to do all this wearing my clothes. Willie, her brother, disappeared. Eventually, after we ourselves had left, she married a village boy the day before war finally broke out. How we got into such a situation was, I think, due to my guilty conscience at not having co-operated with the lady in the train on my return from Germany in 1937. Nevertheless, we were particularly unlucky.

Tom was at sea during most of my pregnancy, so my mother came to stay. She revelled in the garden, which was large for so small a house and so slight a woman as my mother. The Münich crisis occurred in the autumn of 1938. Our son was born in January 1939.

We had spent that Christmas at the farm in Plympton during one of the coldest snaps I can remember. We drove Daisy across Salisbury Plain and up to Bushey amid snow. The maternity hospitals on our route were carefully marked with a circle on the Ordnance map.

However, all was well. Tom left me with his mother in the cottage in Bushey. My brother now lived in our old house across the road. On the great day, a Saturday, while I was battling in a nursing home in Watford, Tom was driving up from Plymouth in Daisy. He arrived to hear that he had a son. He left the next day, as the ship was to sail for Gibraltar on the Monday. I felt he hardly qualified as a father.

How times have changed. The nurse in charge brought the baby in to be breast-fed and to our astonishment insisted that Tom must wait outside. I expostulated. "I expect," she said "he thinks the baby is fed from a bottle." Poor nurse – I wondered if she knew how babies start on their curious journey into the world.

Tom left HMS Newcastle and was appointed to the Gunnery School at Devonport. This was a blow after hoping for Portsmouth, hence Armadale. I was becoming inured to the vague caprices of naval life, so we packed up and let the house.

July found us on the road again with an overloaded trailer which, once again, decided that enough was enough and parted company at midnight at Postbridge, close to Dartmoor Prison. We had already tried to relieve the trailer of weight by dropping off various things – such as a sack of our home-grown potatoes – at various railway stations on the route, also my trunk, which caused me some embarrassment in weeks to come. Even in the golden days of rail, mistakes did happen.

A friend had found us a delightful house at Crapstone near Yelverton. It had a wonderful view overlooking fields and woodlands sloping down to Bere Alston and the bridge over the Tavy and further on to Saltash. In fact, when the lights of Saltash went out on 3rd September, it was my fervent hope that I should be there to see them go up again when the wretched war was over. Of course I was not there and much water had flowed under the bridge by then.

Pat, my brother, Eileen and their daughter Desna, known always as Muff, came to stay with us on the last fateful days of August 1939 and early September.

Both Pat and I thought, like everyone else, that London would be bombed flat from the very beginning: Warsaw was already laid flat, so we persuaded my mother and my aunt to leave London. Pat met them and conducted them to my house – two very reluctant refugees. In my un-tutored youth, I put them to sleep in a room over the garage with three outside walls. It being a lightly built house they nearly died of cold. I also did not realise that sharing a room when you are old is difficult. The sisters became a little disgruntled. My aunt liked to go to bed early, so my mother's rustling of the Times newspaper at night was irritating. However, Auntie, who woke early, would get out of bed and start reading it at a time that my mother considered was still night.

I was adamant that the baby would not share a room, which was absurd of me. My mother made one of her devastating remarks on arrival. When shown upstairs, having been told she was to share a room: "There seem to be plenty of doors in this house, are there no rooms behind them?"

The trouble was that we were crowded. Not only was there Charles, Tom's naval relief – he was now to go to sea – but there was Charles' wife and baby and a nanny who seemed to have come too.

Then a great friend who lived fairly near had two French Bretons working in her house, an aunt and niece, and wondered if we would employ the niece. Into our lives walked Yvonne, bringing a life-long friendship and a very attractive insight into country ways in France.

An uncertain cook, Yvonne would borrow my bicycle to rush over to Tante Jeanne to get advice while our meals were cooking. Noises to which we grew accustomed emerged from the kitchen. "Zut – le soufflé ne gonfle pas." (This soufflé does not rise). "Quelle horreur – le fourneau ne marche pas."

Pat took the family home and we settled down to what might come. Neville Chamberlain made his famous speech and we dug up the garden for vegetables. On the second day of the war, we bought my bicycle, made in Elsick of best British steel, at a cost of £3. It is still rideable today and lives in my garage.

My aunt and mother made the black-out curtains for us. Tom was very fussy about their absolute perfection, so that my Aunt, who had a dry wit, wrote to Pat saying "We are making black-out under naval discipline."

It turned out that Tom did not go to sea until the following June, by which time our household had changed. Auntie went back to London, where she was proud to be an air-raid warden, and then to my brother's. Charles, the Relief, moved into the barracks and we made a new friend, Marjery Penton, who moved in with her baby son, David. Her husband, Mike, was at sea in HMS Vanguard. She and I, my mother and Yvonne continued for some time together after Tom had left. Marjery and I also established a life-long friendship.

Then my mother-in-law joined us. She had been the victim of a bomb dropped on Bushey, killing a soldier billeted in our old house. It also destroyed the Lych Gate to the church and the First World War Memorial. The bomb had blown Tom's mother back into her house breaking both her wrists. In actual fact, she had gone out to see if Miss Dack, two cottages away, was all right, but that redoubtable old lady had swept up the glass and gone back to her little truckle bed.

The first few months while the world waited to see where aggression would break out was known as the "phoney war" This ended and Dunkirk brought thousands of soldiers back from France who lay out on the moor recovering, luckily in splendid weather – our defeated army. Plymouth filled up with sailors from countries in Europe – some Free French which delighted Yvonne. The sight of the red pom-pom in their caps gave her renewed confidence in her country.

It was an exciting time. One lived from day to day and we gathered news from friends and family. Our house in Bushey was commandeered by the Army and suffered a cruel blow. Soldiers who were billeted there cut down the wisteria for firewood – the house never recovered. "An invading army", said my mother, "could not have done worse." Instead of the Army, as Pat had expected, he went to Basingstoke as Anaesthetist to Sir Harold Gillies, the founder of plastic surgery. He was in the Emergency Medical Service. The unit became the centre which taught Sir Harold's art to other surgeons around the world, including his nephew MacIndoe. All this coming and going and change was digested as best we could. Naval life flowed around us and every day there seemed to be new experiences, some very funny. One of the things Marjery Penton had to endure, she told me later, was that Tom's love affair with pianos had begun. A lady from Looe was willing to rent him an upright piano. To Marjery's consternation, while devastating news tumbled out of our old wireless: Norway had fallen, Holland had fallen, Belgium had fallen, the Maginot Line had collapsed etc., etc. – whenever Tom was at home, he and I played duets. As the German advance pursued its relentless way, strains of The Blue Danube drifted up to Marjery's room above, as she fed her baby. We did not play very well and, for her, the whole experience was excruciating. Marjery was sensitive, a painter by occupation. To her great credit, our friendship survived. I think the duets relieved our own feelings of despair.

Camp Follower

The telephone rang as I came in from the garden. It was June 1940, Dunkirk was over, England was a shambles filling up with Free French, Free Dutch and Free Norwegians, our defeated army was being re-established.

"Can you come over and cook for us?" said Tom's voice at some distant end.

"I expect so, but where are you?" I heard myself reply.

"In Cornwall."

"It's a long county, how shall I find you?"

"Get in the car and come to Millbrook. Don't forget when you get there to immobilise the car."

"How on earth do I do that?"

"Just take out the distributor arm."

"Where shall I find it?"

"Oh for heaven's sake, just come. Make for the Cremyll Ferry and drive to Millbrook. We have no feeding facilities here, so find somewhere where you can cook a meal, then telephone this number and we'll join you this evening."

"All right." But was it? I laid the telephone down with misgivings of a major nature. I could leave the house with my mother, Marjery and Yvonne – the little boys would be as safe as possible. But would I ever get back to see them again? Cornwall was divided from Devon by the Hamoaze, a wide stretch of water. France was, we learnt, suffering a nightmare on the roads as people fled for safety from the Nazis with what they could take. The enemy aircraft machine-gunned these exhausted winding trails of refugees as they travelled.

Tom had finished his commission at the Gunnery School in Devonport. He had to wait for suitable transport to his new ship, HMS Ark Royal. His restless nature could not settle to take his leave at home at such a moment in the world's history. Instead, he persuaded the authorities to let him have three naval lorries. These were fitted out with anti-aircraft guns. He was intending to ambush this mobile battery each night, in the hope of shooting down German planes which were now able to cross from Brittany and drop mines around Plymouth Sound.

I reached Millbrook in the gloaming. It proved to be a small town with a market square. Here there was a van from which the Ministry of Information was issuing instructions on what to do in the event of Invasion. This must have been one of Harold Nicolson's ideas. I forgot about the car while listening to a speaker. A soldier kindly showed me how to remove the distributor arm. I put it in my handbag. I bought some chops at a butcher who was still open and then, diffidently wishing I was not inside me, I went into the bar of the Commercial Arms.

The pub was full, mostly with soldiers, and doing a fine trade. At last I caught the eye of the publican's wife and explained to her what I needed. She consulted with her husband who took a look at me and nodded. "Yes, dear," she said, "you can have the kitchen while the bar is open. Help yourself – we've got runner beans in the garden. By the time we close they'll be over and your boys will be out." I left a message for Tom at the mysterious number he had given me.

I found the gas stove was large enough for my saucepans, or rather hers, and set to work. There was a long kitchen table which I set for as many as I thought would come and soon the men (the boys) turned up. They wore brand new battle dress in dark blue, the first I had seen, and each had a large torch in a pocket and carried a tin hat, I can't remember how many came – about six, I think. Tom looked pleased at the arrangements and introduced us all. They ate heartily, then smoked and soon were off. It was dark outside. I washed up and helped with glasses in the Bar. Mrs. King scrubbed the floor.

Before she had finished the noise began. Planes swooped down on to the Sound and our guns began to fire. I felt proud, but unable to distinguish between enemy bombs and our own gunfire. Mr. King stood in the street doorway and reported down to us, inaccurately, I am sure. Mrs. King explained that they ended up machine-gunning the street, so that it was not safe to sleep upstairs as bullets could penetrate the bedrooms.

Together we sat between two enormous barrels of beer in the cellar. Worse deaths than drowning, I thought, infinitely better than facing the black beetles in the kitchen. These emerged and swarmed for about two feet around the kitchen range at nights – DDT had not been invented and there was no remedy for such an invasion. Equally revolting later, when daylight dawned and the raiders left and I stretched thankfully in the bed upstairs, was the discovery that the disgusting smell that came from the water jug in the basin was that the last occupant had relieved himself in the jug. He must have been as frightened as I was.

At about 6 a.m. the boys arrived back and were ravenous for bacon and eggs. I heard about the night's adventures and then they went off to sleep. Tom went to report before he slept. In the afternoons he went around the district choosing places for the next night's ambush and I drove him while he looked. One day we toured the Mount Edgcombe estate and old Lord Mount Edgcombe came with us. His estate bordered the Sound and he offered to cut down any trees that hindered the sites for the guns even, he said, some trees that his brother had brought back from the Himalayas. This was handsome of him, but such was the feeling of anxiety and dedication. Anyway he was a very genial man. We sat in his dust-sheeted house and drank sherry. Later the house was destroyed by enemy action.

While Tom slept, I meandered about rather aimlessly. I was writing a letter to my mother beneath a hedge, when a German plane came over my shoulder – hedge-hopping as it was called. I swear I saw the colour of the pilot's eyes – blue of course – but perhaps that is a trick of memory. Ridiculously, I gathered up my letter and fled downhill into a barn – but my enemy was miles away by then.

We had one day off. We drove to a bay and climbed down a tortuous path to a stony beach by the sea. At this point, Tom remembered that he had left his revolver in the car at the top of the cliff – a heinous offence with invasion expected any moment, or so we thought. We climbed painfully back and one of us sat beside the bloody thing on the beach, while the other swam.

Keating spoilt it all. He joined as Tom's relief, as the battery had become a permanency. It continued to the end of the war, with several planes to its credit. Keating was greedy and unscrupulous. His worst offence in my mind was that he always got into the bathroom with Tom to shave in the morning, thus depriving us of time together. I hated Keating – he made a fuss on our day out about who would cook his supper.

Tom's date of departure was fixed and we went home. Feeling rather a heroine, I was nonplussed to find that Mother regarded me as a deserter – having a good time with the Navy. "There have been air-raids," she told me. In fact, the war had really begun for all of us.

Which brings me to the postscript. Years later, when all was over, we went back to Millbrook and visited the Commercial Arms. Mr. and Mrs. King were still there and they looked curiously at us for a minute as we came in, then the penny dropped. Drinks all round and we nattered away happily, exchanging further experiences of the war. Then came the astonishing revelation: I had always carried with me the impression that it was my forced calm that had steadied Mrs. King as things crashed around the little town – once a mine had hit the land and I have a piece of its parachute. "Do you remember how nervous you were?" said Mrs. King, "I never thought you'd get through." Well – how we deceive ourselves.

When closing time came, we were invited to linger. I glanced at the dirty glasses on the counter and Mrs. King laughed. However, danger suddenly intervened, the constable put his head round the door, probably for his regular, but Mr. King looked apprehensive. We took the hint and slipped out into the silent night.

Back to 1940. In July Tom left home and I went with him to London, where we visited St Paul's Cathedral. We climbed up into the Whispering Gallery in the dome. Here, if you whisper into the wall, a person directly opposite on the far side can hear you by putting his ear to the wall. It is uncanny. Unplanned, we said good-bye to each other, high up there in the dome of St Paul's.

Outside a tube station we parted, I to go back to Devon and Tom to some unknown destination and thence to join his ship. The last thing he did was to produce the revolver from his case and hang it round my neck. He had forgotten to hand it in but gave me minute instructions to do so. I think that perhaps he was a better sailor than a soldier.

My train journey back to Plymouth was very stark.

Dartmoor II

So Tom had gone. My mother, Marjery, Yvonne, I and the two little boys, Marjery's David and my Jeremy, settled down to Devon in wartime. In many ways it was not unpleasant. The country was deeply lovely, the view from the house was superb. Yvonne provided plenty of robust Breton surprises, which kept us from getting into a rut. My bicycle was continually travelling between our house and Tante Jeanne when Yvonne was not pushing Jeremy in his pram round the lanes. Tante Jeanne's employer was an Italian, Bigi Beverley, married to a British Naval Officer, who was a great source of friendship. Her house was shared with a cosmopolitan family, the Monacos : Italian restaurateurs in London, now stranded in England.

As well as the revolver to return, there were, at one end in our pretty sitting room, two life-sized seated models of Ordinary Seamen. These had been made by Tom with a frame and plaster of Paris and were finally painted by Marjery. They were intended to enliven some educational course in gun emplacements at the Gunnery school in Devonport and were known as Larken's Folly. One day a car arrived with two naval officers and they were driven away, sitting impressively side by side on the back seat. Their highly coloured cheeks gave them a rather tubercular look.

We worried about many things that arose, chiefly bright ideas from some authorities. One we intended to disregard, I remember, was an instruction that in the event of invasion we were to put all our furniture into the roadway to impede enemy tanks. We were riveted to the Radio as the Battle of Britain raged over Kent and the Home Counties.

Marjery and I had an agreement that if either of our husbands came home on leave, the other wife would do all the work, leaving the couple on leave in comparative luxury. This worked out in both cases: Marjery's son David was christened when her husband, Michael, came on leave. I went up to Liverpool when the Ark Royal came in there, but we came back home for a few days' leave.

We were always alert for the Invasion. Riders rode out every day over Dartmoor searching for paratroopers being dropped from the sky. One night Marjery and I were concerned by a human cough on the other side of the garden wall. When investigated, an old sheep shambled away. We discussed what to do if a German soldier came to the house. We decided to administer a meal laced with castor oil – that would keep him from raping us, we thought. And so we drifted on into the days of the Plymouth Blitz. Each night we watched the blazing skyline as the town burnt. During a night of blitz in a nursing home, which had evacuated itself from Plymouth, amidst the crash of falling bombs nearby, my daughter was born.

By the spring of 1941, an airfield had been built at Yelverton, which spread into Crapstone, our village. In fact, some of the accommodation buildings were in a field adjacent to our garden. One night during an air raid, this field was ablaze with incendiary bombs, which had been dropped. We reckoned that we had ten minutes or so before bombers came over with the big stuff. We organised ourselves to use our stirrup pump, a Government Issue. I thought that the two mothers would be well employed, one pumping from the bath and the other with the end ready to put out any further burning bombs that might arrive. This took our minds off the danger, but no bombs fell. The whole operation may have been a decoy, but the stirrup pump, after having an airlock, suddenly unblocked itself and soused my mother-in-law.

It was at this point we decided that, with two small children, enough was enough, and it was time to leave. My mother remembered that we had a cousin in mid Wales and wrote to her, asking for shelter. Marjery left to share a house elsewhere with a friend. Tom's mother went home and Yvonne and Tante Jeanne left for some stately home.

So it was that in May, just at the time when the Ark Royal was chasing the Bismarck at sea, we – my mother, Jeremy and my three-week-old daughter, Juliet – climbed into a pantechnicon with our worldly goods and left for Carno in Wales.

The Plas

The question was – how to get away with our belongings. The station at Plymouth had been badly bombed and was out of action. A friend of mine had lost all her luggage when the railway marshalling yard had been hit. I can't remember how I found a man with a pantechnicon who would drive us up to Wales. This was strictly not permitted – he was engaged only to move people whose homes had been bombed. However, he was willing to take the risk, being, as he said, sick of the dust and fumes in his lungs – twenty-four hours off would be bliss. With a mild feeling of guilt I thankfully accepted his offer.

He arrived the evening before our departure with the pantechnicon and the news that he had completely run out of packing cases. We had about two, which were quickly filled, after which we all set to filling the van as best we could. When every item we possessed was somehow stowed we went to bed, hoping that our worldly goods and we would have a safe journey.

He put an old sofa in the back for my mother and Jeremy to sit on. He was a courteous man. For me, he had fixed up a little curtain in his cab so that I could feed the baby in privacy while he drove. It worked for about two feeds after which we lost our way and abandoned this refinement. The trouble was we had no maps and all the signposts in the country had been taken down in order to confuse the enemy, should he land.

We left our house at 8 am, amidst tears of farewell to my mother in-law, Yvonne and our dear neighbours with whom we shared the air-raid shelter we had all built.

Somehow, by guess and good luck, we wound our way through England stopping for sandwiches and chats with my mother and Jeremy in the back. At last we surmised that we had got into Wales, when boys with singsong Welsh voices surrounded the van. It was beginning to get dark. We drove on and on and on, into the night. My poor mother thought that we must be climbing Snowdon – in fact we nearly were, but we managed to recover the mistakes we so frequently made. Finally we came to a village with a pub called "The Merchant of Aleppo". The time was two in the morning. Could this be Carno? I got out and knocked on the door. Immediately a head came out of a top window and a voice said,

"They were expecting you for tea up at the Plas." Carno at last. Following the head's instructions we turned into a drive. Our dim lights picked out the flowers of rhododrendons, ordinary ones but what an omen of joy and arrival. The dawn was not far away.

We found a somewhat distraught and weary gathering in the house that had assembled to help us unload. This, to my consternation, we were forced to do at once. Our poor driver revealed that it was as much as his life was worth to absent himself for another day, as the van was needed in Plymouth. Mrs Dai, the cook, was able to revive the poor chap with a good breakfast, before he took off on the road again. Mrs. Dai in the house and Dai outside reigned over the Plas.

Mid Wales was far away from the war zone. My cousin never quite understood how we had got ourselves into such a situation – perhaps rightly, she regarded me as a mild lunatic from that day on. Our luggage, which she so kindly housed, may have contributed to this idea – that Plymouth could produce 'no packing cases' she never could visualise. When I finally sorted things, I had a case labelled 'skates and banjos' containing Tom's father's fen runner skates and various musical instruments. Another case held my grandfather's Masonic regalia, which my mother seemed to be travelling about with – we could never remember why.

My cousin, another Marjory, had married the hereditary owner of the Plas, a Manor House, but he had recently died of a sad illness when in his prime. She took on managing the estate as best she could in wartime. She was from Ireland and was another sister of Geoffrey, the actor, now a soldier, whom I had joined some years back in Switzerland.

The house was beautiful, though a little dark, being panelled downstairs with linenfold carved oak. Outside, it looked onto a lawned garden, beyond which was a river running parallel with the house. Across the east end of the garden was a brick wall in the middle of which a large double doorway led into the farmyard. The other end was open to the west, where the valley spread out over agricultural land as the mountains drew apart. The setting sun in mid-winter turned the valley and the sky into a celestial glory of gold and crimson. A group of seven elms – the magic number – stood sentinel to the valley beside the river, casting shade over the garden on hot days in summer. Here the baby could be put to sleep in her pram. How secure we were and how happy was our valley.

I wandered with the children along lanes bordered by wild flowers in such profusion, against oak hedgerows entwined with honeysuckle. In the house, the flowers we picked shone like stars against the panelling. As I always had a pram to push, I could only go up the Aberdovey road or down the Aberdovey road.

There was a one-track railway line with a station ruled over by Mr. Joneses Station. The Welsh love for children opened all doors to us. Mr. Jones' small daughter became a friend to Jeremy. He also had the run of the farm and would trot behind Dai to watch a litter of little pigs, the sheep being sheared or the great thresher on the day it arrived, filling the yard with husks and dust.

There were a great many Jones in the village – Jones Sarn, Jones Shoes and Jones Aleppo as well as Thomases and Richards, all distinguished by their occupations.

Sheep governed the life of the valley. The bleating of the lambs calling for their mothers was a continuous sound in early summer, except on Sundays when drowned by the singing from the various chapels. I would stop with my pram outside, to listen in awe.

There were fields of oats, which gave a good yield that year, but few men to harvest it. While some long hot days persisted it was decided to go ahead with any help that could be found. One of the happiest experiences that I can remember was spent in line next to my mother, gathering the corn and binding it into sheaves in the oldest manner in the world. A line behind us stacked the sheaves into stooks. The children played in the shade in the care of some old ladies who minded them while we worked.

About once a month the village turned up at the Plas for an evening's entertainment. The chapels sank their denominational rivalry and sang like angels. Dai and Steven Jones-Sarn, both tenors, were much in evidence but never forgiven for singing in the open while ploughing: it was thought bad for a tenor to sing in the open. The effect on passers-by of the ploughed furrows, the swirl of the following gulls and the young men's voices was another overwhelming experience, never to be forgotten. As well as songs at the Plas, there were recitations and uproarious humour, everyone unselfconsciously able to contribute, followed by tea and scones and a collection for comforts for "our lads". The evening concluded with "Bring Back my Bonnie to me" and "God Bless this House" – very evocative in wartime.

"So they've sunk the Cossack." called out Steven Jones-Sarn, as darkness began to fall one day in November, as I was walking home with the children. A coldness wrapped itself round my heart as we plodded on. Casualties at sea were almost a daily occurrence at that time, but this made me more than usually uneasy. Many evenings the BBC news opened with "The Admiralty regrets to announce....." and one waited in suspense for the name of the ship that had been sunk. In the house I sat unhappily before the fire.

A few days later, I was half way upstairs, going to put the children to bed. My mother was at the telephone in the hall.

"She doesn't know anything about it." said my mother into the telephone, glancing as she spoke over her spectacles at me.

"What don't I know?" I turned and came down. She confessed that the Radio had announced earlier that the Ark Royal had been torpedoed early that morning.

This was no ordinary sinking – an enormous amount of information was given out, due to the fact that the Germans had been claiming that she had been sunk some weeks before. It had been a sort of game to unnerve the British. Lord Haw-Haw, an Irishman named Joyce who was employed to broadcast from Berlin to the British, continually began his broadcasts by asking, "Where is the Ark Royal?" implying that she was beneath the waves. However, letters from our husbands proved this to be wrong.

Well, now she was sinking. We were lucky in that we were actually told as much. We were also told that the ship, though damaged, was being taken into port, fairly encouraging it seemed, though worrying. Alas, this plan failed and after about a day and a half she went down.

During the next two days, the telephone rang continually. Chirpy, relieved wives rang to say they had had telegrams from their husbands, who were safe. I had none. Things of course went differently for Tom. As well as being Gunnery Officer, he was Officer of Anchor and Cables and so it was, that with six others, he was cut off in the bow when the order to Abandon Ship was given. Eventually, the seven decided that the time had come to swim, they tossed up to see who would be last off – Tom third from the end – and then they plunged over the side of the steeply listing ship.

They had a long swim. A Dutch tug turned away, thinking that there were no more survivors. Fortunately, however, after some time they did happen to notice Tom, who was picked up. "Take me to your captain." he said and fell flat on his face and passed out, but not before he managed to explain that there were others in the water.

After some days, the tug took them back to Gibraltar and I got a telegram from a friend at the Admiralty saying 'Tom, thank God, safe'. Tom's own cable followed, asking me to order him a new uniform.

Weeks later, after many cancellations, he reached Milford Haven on a Sunday, when no trains ran. The next day he reached us, still wearing the suit he had swum in. As the seawater had rotted the stitching, there were bits of flesh showing through the gaps, to the astonishment of Mr. Jones Station. Jeremy, who had come with me, looked searchingly into the carriage to see if there was not a little Daddy for his sister Juliet.

A curious addition came on my ninetieth birthday. Percy Gick, who had been serving in the Ark Royal at the time of the sinking, came to my party. He told us that the Tannoy was out of action and his task was to inform the ship's company to "Abandon Ship". He confessed to Jeremy that he had forgotten the party on the fo'c'sle. He felt mortified, but relieved at the outcome.

Bath

Tom's return was a few days before Christmas 1941. Terrible things were happening in the war: the battleships, The Prince of Wales and Repulse, were sunk. Malaya, Singapore and Hong Kong fell to the Japanese and the future looked very black. The American fleet had been destroyed at Pearl Harbour. This, however, brought us an ally – the United States declared war on Japan and Germany.

Myself feeling very torn between families, we took Jeremy down to Bushey to see Tom's mother, sister and husband for Christmas, leaving Juliet the only child at the Plas. We spent a day and a night in London. We went to a theatre, but I have forgotten what we saw. We then returned to Carno.

We started to enjoy our leave. I had fallen in love with our mountain retreat, never had I loved a place so much – the simple farming life in the mountains with the children had been wonderful. There was nothing to blitz here. We planned to climb Plynlimmon. This never came off, as Tom had another job thrust on him – this was at the Admiralty, which had decentralised itself into Bath. It was a difficult decision to leave the Plas and all that went with it, to bring the children back into the war zone. I was ashamed of my divided loyalties and I even toyed with the idea of leaving the children with my mother in Wales. In the end, family life triumphed – the children had need of a father and there might not be one at the end of the war. So down we went to join him while he lived ashore.

The winter of 1941/2 was a cold one. Tom had found a flat in the beautiful Circus. I travelled back from Bath in a blizzard to fetch the children. At midnight, the engine driver decided that it was impossible to go further, owing to snowdrifts, and he turned us out of the train at Shrewsbury. All hotels were filled with service men of all nationalities. After a paralysingly cold night, I can remember the enchantment next day of the Welsh countryside under deep snow.

The train took us down to Bath with all the paraphernalia that travels with babies. My mother, the two babies and my cousin Marjorie all packed into a crowded carriage. My kind cousin was storing all the miscellaneous stuff we had brought from Devon. We took up residence in No. 15 The Circus. When settled, my mother and Marjorie left us.

It was February when we arrived at our very grand flat in a very grand house. A plaque on the wall said that the house had once belonged to a Duke of Bedford. It was owned now by a doctor who was away serving in the army. We occupied the "L" shaped drawing room on the first floor and slept in the back part of the "L." separated by two great doors from the front. We slept in two beds and two cots in a row, dormitory fashion. In the day, we lived in the front part where we played, ate and bathed in a hipbath before the fire, surrounded by priceless possessions. These, to my horror, the caretaker was reluctant to remove for safety. From the huge windows looking down Gay Street, the winter sky through the bare branches of the plane trees in the Circus beguiled us into winter fantasies.

Life was, however, uneasy in No 15. The caretaker and his daughter looked after the house and bullied the lodgers – us. The Admiralty's arrival in their town was very unpopular among the elderly citizens of Bath. They failed to appreciate that peace had deserted all of us and were apt to blame the poor service people for the discomforts of war. We enlivened our forced stay in their town by exchanging stories of their hostility. One naval officer billeted on an elderly gentleman ate, by agreement, at his host's table. The old man never addressed a word to him in a six months' stay. We just managed to rub along but it was difficult – the caretaker and his daughter lived on the floor below us; the sound of little feet overhead was a continual annoyance to them, which maybe I understood. I managed to wash all our clothes in a tiny housemaid's pantry on the fourth floor, while the baby slept under the plane trees.

But I was lucky in having the caretaker's daughter, who was willing to look after the children between 9 and 9.30 in the morning, so that I could shop. On that hangs one of my most ridiculous but entertaining wartime stories.

The fishmonger in Milsom Street used to display, before a long queue, a slab full of delicious fresh fish. I joined the queue on my first morning, then became aware of a notice on the slab – "Not selling until 10 o'clock." He worked at the back of the shop, packing up orders which were handed, even in those war days, to chauffeurs in uniform. Innocently, I accosted him and appealed for clemency, as I had to be back for my children by 9.30. His answer, "What's that to me?" was discouraging and his implacability continued throughout our stay in the Circus.

However, years later I enjoyed vicarious revenge: the war was over when I found a paragraph in a national newspaper with the joke of the day. It reported a fishmonger who had put out a notice in front of a long queue saying, "Not selling until 10 o'clock." To his dismay the queue broke up, seized raw fish from the slab and pelted him, belabouring him over the head with whole codfish and finally hurling the day's stock at him or at the door, through which he just managed to escape. The members of the queue were taken to court and fined £10. They said they would pay £10 to do it again. It was of course none other than my old enemy in Bath.

Fraught though life was in Bath, there were never-to-be forgotten colourful moments. There had to be, to offset the bad times. We were there for quite a long time and had five moves of house in a year and a month. Despite these inconveniences, it was a very vital time in my life. Tom's life was eventful in any case, but daily life for civilians could be dull and onerous with all its incredible setbacks. One of Evelyn Waugh's characters summed it up saying, "If one thing goes right in war-time, the day is made." Memory divides our time up into the various homes we crammed into, each up a different hill with a different environment.

The tiny feet proved too much for the caretaker. He gave me notice to leave. I was angry and asked him if we were fighting the same war? His curious reply was that he could easily find a successor to us, to which I replied, "Make sure he will not be from the German occupying army." As so often happens in adversity, we were much happier in No. 5 Catherine's Place just behind the Circus. We got a trolley-cart and moved one evening into a ground floor flat. All seemed set fair – it was a pretty square near to the Royal Crescent with its delightful park below. It was April the weather was perfect and Bath was in bloom with flowering shrubs everywhere. I found it all enchanting. Every day I pushed the children in their pram through squares bathed in seventeenth century serenity – striped sun-blinds suggested decorous shaded drawing rooms where the new habit of tea drinking was indulged. We found houses where Jane Austen had lived.

On 25th April Tom returned home late. I wallowed in the bath while he ate his supper. The joy of the new flat was that the bath was at the end of the kitchen, ideal for a young family. As I soaked happily, there was an enormous explosion followed by another. Then silence. Tom rose from the table and in measured tones said, "I think they are bombing Bath." They were. Wet as I was, I wrapped a towel round me, seized a child, Tom the other, and we descended to the basement. Here we found our landlady and other tenants from the flats above crowding down the stairs. There we sat huddled together while the Luftwaffe rained bombs into the hollow that was Bath. The Circus just beside us presented a perfect target, which the young German pilots must have enjoyed because they dive-bombed it, sliding off our roofs as they rose again.

There was no defence. A new strategy for Bristol was put into action that night – all planes were grounded in favour of anti-aircraft gunfire. This did not protect us in Bath.

After an interminable time, the "All Clear" sounded, but the respite was short. Either in the first raid or the second, the Circus Tavern beside us was hit for a second time. Voices above called down to know if Tom was there – would he come out – and out he went. So now, I thought, we would not all be killed together. This must never happen anywhere, I told myself – the bombing of defenceless people with children. The bargain I made with the Almighty – that I would fight to prevent such things happening to others – was one-sided: I survived, but bombs still rain down on the innocent. I was never able to make up my mind as to whether five bombs fell within seventy yards or seven within fifty yards. I have since discovered that the former was right.

With daylight, the Lufwaffe disappeared. Catherine Place was a shambles. A friend came down from Sion Hill and collected the children and me – Tom was out, still digging. He told me how his party had moved on when he saw a hand waving from the rubble. He called them back and a man was extricated who by chance might otherwise have been left.

Our flat was intact, but in utter disarray with plaster and soot etc. One extraordinary feature of the blast was that the shutters of the window of our room were blown in onto the children's cots, but the empty milk bottle was left on the windowsill. The house itself was unsafe.

Outside, there were fire engines with hoses every few yards and the children greatly enjoyed being tipped up and down over them in the pram. Houses were on fire on all sides, as we pushed on up the hill.

I left the children for the day with the Husseys, who rescued us, and took Tom's bicycle and pedalled out into the country, determined to find a better place to spend the next night. I was somewhat confused, and at one house I knocked at I said that I had been bombed out of Plymouth, to which the householder replied, "Well don't come here – Bath's burning," which indeed it was.

Unable to find anywhere else, we spent the next night up on Sion Hill but in the shelter of another friend, Jack Boord. The alarm sounded and we took cover. Jack courteously inquired if the children and I were all right – I lay on the children to protect them and I thought that with two naval officers my fears would disperse. Not a bit of it. They spent a lot of time reporting from the open doorway of the shelter, as the raid got under way. After repeatedly saying "Get back old man." they slammed the door. "Do you think that's my house?" asked Jack. "Well, you can't do anything if it is." replied Tom.

The bombs seemed to whine past us and to fall on the beleaguered town below. Relief that they had passed was tinged with our anxiety for those down there. We knew, of course, that the one that is for you, you don't hear. Daylight brought the "All Clear." Jack's house stood; it had no windows. He went out and gathered people in who were wandering on the Common between Sion Hill and the town. They were in nightclothes and had lost their houses. One poor old lady I knew from the famous fish queue. We had christened her "Chicken-Pheasant" owing to her having complained to me as I stood behind her, "Since the Admiralty came there is no choice at all – it's chicken-pheasant every other day." Well, here she was, her house gone and the only thing the firemen had saved was the mangle. "What shall I do with a mangle?" she asked indignantly. I could do with it for nappies, but she was induced into giving Juliet her breakfast while I cooked bacon and eggs for the odd bewildered company.

Catherine Place, to which we went, was in a far worse state than before: the whole of one end comprising Julian Road had gone, so had No 1 on our side, with thirteen of the occupants, and the other two sides were on fire. Our house was uninhabitable and covered in dust, soot and plaster, but still standing. We began to gather things together.

Tom was sitting on an upturned linen basket in the middle of our sitting room, surrounded by chaos, when my brother Pat walked in. Tom's greeting was typical – "Remarkable to see you, Pat. I wonder if you would tie up that bundle of music over there."

Pat had got into the city with a doctor's certificate on the windscreen and had managed to find us. Being Pat, he had a drama imagining that our No 5 was Julian Road's No 5.

To his enquiries, the answer was "Well, we're getting them out now." but it did not look very hopeful, so he was relieved to be asked to tie up the music. It took us all day to get packed up. Activity was intense. The day before a large tank had been put in the centre of our square for such an emergency and the fire hoses roared away, with firemen up huge extended ladders pouring water into the burning houses. An old lady accosted Pat as he stood packing his car. She pointed questioningly to a kettle she was carrying – it was impossible to hear what people said. Pat looked up and managed to catch the eye of the fireman up a high ladder. He pointed to the kettle and the little old lady. Down came the fireman and filled the kettle and climbed up again. She bowed her thanks and trotted off.

Sometime during that day, I went to The Circus to see how our erstwhile landlord had fared. To my amusement, I found an avenging angel had struck but, at the last minute, had spared him. Three of the bombs dropped by the dive-bombers into the Circus were too low and did not explode. One had travelled along from the centre of the Circus and had stopped just short of the coalhole in which he and his daughter were sheltering. He had been evacuated into the inferno, but was luckily spared. With tears in his eyes, he thanked me for calling. I felt smug and knew that he knew he had been mean.

Our side of the square, with the exception of No 1 and half of No 2, still stood. We were No 5. Julian Road was flat. The other three sides were burning and an acrid smell pervaded everywhere. Life had erupted onto the street, the contents of No 1 were spewed in all directions and people brought possessions out on to the pavement to sort in front of the unsafe houses. Everyone who could, made and offered cups of tea. Late in the evening, a cart with drinking water stopped nearby and people ran with buckets – a service that lasted for many weeks to follow.

That night we left in Pat's car for Basingstoke. As we drove along, we passed lines of exhausted people, carrying what they could, overdressed and wearing even fur coats to save what they could, trudging along anywhere to avoid another night of bombing. We reached Pat's cottage at Upper Wootton late that night where Eileen had prepared a most comforting reception into which we thankfully sank. Incidentally, I upset a candle and nearly burnt their cottage down.

Civilisation

It is a moment in eternity:
It is a moment in spring.

The day lingers lovingly, caressing the town
Which rises above and around us.
Crescent rises upon crescent,
Square opens out of square,
The whole crowned by the tufted trees and hills that abound us
Lit by the dying light
Of a complete and perfect April day.

In the Park, nurses and mothers linger
For the children have been caught up
And are indistinguishable from the spring,
Savouring as only children can
The full mystery of unfolding life to which they themselves belong.
A boy of three kneels unselfconsciously to pay
Homage to a tulip: the first his memory allows.
A tiny girl laughingly points to the colours of the crocus
Then runs with outstretched hands to catch
The snow petals falling from the almond tree.
Yet withal it is the grown-up,
Condemned now to be spectator,
Who can capture and set aside such a moment in eternity.

Reluctantly we go our ways,
Gay Street rises to the stately Circus,
Whose plane trees cast a dappled shade.
At another turn a sunblind's splash of colour makes us
Wander back to capture in imagination
The chink of slender china, smell an aromatic smell,
Hear gay chatter enjoyed in shaded sunshine,
Familiar to an age now gone.

We passed beneath St Andrew's spire,
Whose clock told mockingly the lateness of the hour;
Yet unreproached we amble on
To reach our own untroubled square.

Today the plum tree's flowers had reached this year's maturity
Her petals drift and fluttered slowly down
To join the carpet spread below
And in doing so piled gently on a baby's hand
Who sleeps below and breathes
This essence that still hangs warm and pungent in the air.
The setting sun holds promise:
Sleep will pass the night and, waking
We shall meet another day long since begun.

When morning came, the living thanked their Gods for life,
The dying prayed only for release.
The town and all her beauty lay
A prostrate, acrid smoking ruin.
The stench of rubble filled the air,
The dust the eyes and lungs.
Smoke choked and hoses hissed,
As people scrambled over bricks and stucco
Old craftsmanship trampled under dust
By feet that could not care.
Only one thought lay uppermost,
Profound relief that the monstrous night had turned again to day.

Gone was the spring and the blossom:
The trees stood naked and torn, tragically raped and bereft,
All trace of the flowers now gone.
Endlessly slowly we climbed,
We turned at the top and looked down.
A thick grey pall hung over the city,
Swollen from smouldering remains that were left.
We looked at the crescents of houses
Crowns of their architect's skill.
But houses no longer smiled back.
Instead, crescent still rose upon crescent,
Lines of skulls with sightless eyes,
With jagged yawning gaps we dared not contemplate.

St. Andrews's spire, still smouldering, raised a skeleton to the skies
With one blind socket where
But twelve hours sooner,
A clock had marked a moment in Eternity.

Bath II – Broken crockery, pianos and hens

It took several weeks before I could get back to Bath with the children. They stayed at Pat's cottage and then their two grandmothers joined forces and looked after them in Bushey.

I bicycled around Somerset in one of the wettest Junes ever known. But there were no houses to be found. In the end, some naval friends, working with Tom, offered us the top floor of their house. We had two rooms and a bathroom. A third small room was made into a kitchen. Cooking here on a Primus stove with an oven over it for four people throughout the summer was a feat in itself. We washed up in an enamel bowl on a wooden table. One was in mortal danger: the installation of electricity in this damp Bath house gave me electric shocks from the water in the basin. However, I was never electrocuted. It was bliss to have the family together.

I must explain the oddity of the house. It was built on Bathwick Hill and there were two storeys on the roadside. We were one floor up from the hall and entrance but, clinging to the contours of the hill, the house descended on the garden side another three floors, so that the garden was five floors down from us.

Early in our stay, on the first Sunday I think, I was invited to bring our tea down into the garden. I prepared a tray but my small daughter managed to reach up to the table and pulled the tray off, breaking all the china of any prettiness that remained to us. Dispirited, I shut the children in the bedroom, placed a bucket in the middle of the kitchen and threw all the pieces of broken china into it. People swear on occasions like this, I thought, and I wondered what effect that would have on me. My vocabulary was small in this respect, smaller than today, but I found myself repeating fuck, balls and, of course, bloody hell – a term which all sailors use. Finally all was collected and I straightened up to feel that not much relief had come from swearing. On the contrary, there was a strange curious feeling of silence in the house, which I found discomforting. Then, to my horror, from the hall on the floor below came, in very cultured tones, a female voice saying, "That was a delicious lunch, we have enjoyed it. Thank you very much."

I sank into the only armchair to consider the situation. A rather bad start. Down in the garden it was hard to explain, especially as they had just given us a good character to their friends.

Despite this, we were endured. There were, however, reasons why we moved during the next winter. A very promising advertisement appeared in the evening paper – a house to let. Instead of going to inspect it, Tom went direct to the agents and took it there and then, before other people came back from viewing it. It was a beautiful house owned by a German lady, who wanted to get away to avoid the awkward hostility against her that emerged after the blitz. The efficient German hausfrau had exquisite taste and took great pleasure in comfort. It was amazing. We settled in most happily, so much so that Tom once more began to think about his piano playing.

One night the local evening paper carried an advert – 'Naval Officer temporarily based in Bath would like to hire a piano on a monthly basis'... etc. He had several answers and used to call to inspect the instruments on his way home from work, but he made no final decision. Instead, he wanted me to try them. This was an odd illusion, with my lack of talent my only achievement had been thumping through the bass of "The Blue Danube" and annoying poor Marjery. I was also reluctant to spend our afternoon walks struggling with the pram up the various hills of Bath to assess a piano.

However, one day when Tom was away on one of his visits to a shipyard in the North, I was drearily doing housework. Absent-mindedly I was pondering over Jeremy's fourth birthday party due in a week's time. What games to have for a four year old? Musical bumps were always popular but how to provide music? The penny dropped. I rushed to the kitchen scales, where the answers to Tom's advert were lying, and perused them carefully. I selected one, a Mrs. Gravel, 24 Hyde Park Mansions. She was not, apparently, on the telephone.

My mind galloped. Speed was required, also a miracle, as I knew transport would be difficult. I decided to take the bull by the horns – however one does that – and telephoned to a firm, Green and Marsh, in the piano trade. A very kind voice re-echoed my suspicions – it would be very hard to transport a piano in so short a time. I decided that the best thing to do was to give them Mrs. Gravel's address and at the same time to write her a letter to explain and to arrange the whole matter. When the children were in bed that night, I wrote the letter. I ended asking her to let me know when it would be convenient to remove the piano, should there be any choice.

The weather next day was of typical West Country variety – blinding rain. It cleared a little after lunch and I decided to take the children out and to post my letter. Dressing small children up in such circumstances is a performance, as everyone knows: mackintoshes, boots and hats. Finally we were ready and I set out, bumping the pushchair down the steep steps from the house to the road. There, to my astonishment stood a huge furniture van bearing the name of Green & Marsh in large letters on its side.

"Got a piano for you." said one of the men cheerfully. They were already unloading it with a slow shuffle.

"The people consented?" I asked in amazement.

"No one in," came the reply, "but the key was in the door all right."

"You mean, you went in and took the piano?" I found myself saying. Crikey. I set off at a spanking pace for the nearest post box, while the men began to shuffle the piano up the steps to the house. I got back to find they were already crossing the doormat in the hall.

"Where do you want it, Missus?" "Oh, anywhere." I answered in panic "No, here." indicating the dining room. Without wasting any more time, the men uncovered and placed the piano and departed, without further word or even waiting for a cup of tea.

I felt extremely uneasy. There was nothing I could do, except hope that Mrs. Gravel would not be offended. I comforted myself that the letter would arrive in the morning.

"What do you want to see her for?"

I could hear my son's little boy's voice from the open front door. He was playing outside and I was in the kitchen. I hastily cast aside my apron, patted my hair and somewhat apprehensively set forth. A large man dressed in thick Harris Tweeds stood in the hall. In his hand was a heavy ash walking stick with an enormous knob for a handle.

"Are you Mrs. Larken, may I ask?"

"I am."

"Do I understand that you have authorised Green and Marsh to break into my house and to remove my piano?"

For one ghastly moment I struggled to repress an hysterical desire to giggle. The enormity of what had happened became even clearer. I led him into the dining room and, after a few moments of inspection, he agreed that this was his piano. I found a bottle with some sherry in it and got him to sit down. Slowly, he managed to thaw and he and I pieced the story together.

Mr. Gravel, for he it was, had no knowledge of Tom's advertisement, nor of his wife's reply. She was away visiting relations. Mr. Gravel had come home on the previous day and had put the kettle on to boil, as was his custom. Also, as was his daily habit (he was a racing man), he had gone out to the newsagent to buy the afternoon paper, leaving the key in the lock. He returned and made his tea and took it to his favourite chair and turned, before opening the paper, to put the cup down on the piano. To his astonishment, the piano was not there.

Neighbours were able to report on the strange arrival of Green and Marsh's van, of the quick removal of the piano and the disappearance of the van, all within a quarter of an hour. "My wife must have taken leave of her senses." But I found out from him that she never played – in fact, the piano was only used for Mr. Gravel's teacup.

The bottle of sherry neared its end and we both laughed immoderately. That night, Tom returned from the north of England and was delighted to find a piano. He sat down at once and started to play "Hark, hark the Lark" and "Who is Sylvia? What is she?", his favourite songs. He thought the handling of the affair had been a bit clumsy, but the fourth birthday party was a huge success, especially Musical Bumps. Mr Gravel wrote charming letters each month when the rent was due and allowed us to take the piano with us to our next and last house in Bath.

Hens. When some friends who were leaving Bath asked if we would take on three hens, we were delighted. The hens endeared themselves to us at once by laying an egg during transit. We settled down to look after them in a nice little back garden we had in our new house, up another hill. The German Hausfrau had come back in order to send her son to a special school nearby. This last house was our best from the point of view that it was equipped adequately, but it was shabby and semi-detached, with a garden for vegetables and altogether suitable for children – we could not harm it. In this house we started our venerable long line of cats. I nervously got a kitten and that was it.

Next door, our semi-detached neighbours were kind enough to put scraps over the fence for the hens – occasionally they got an egg back. It became obvious from the quality of the scraps that in the third year of the war they were rather choosy eaters. For example, they had parcels from South Africa as we had, but the mould on the cheese and fruitcake we scraped off and guzzled with pleasure. Not so next door. A speck of mould and chunks of cheese or fruitcake came over the fence. One evening, Tom's mother was staying with us when Tom asked, "What's for supper?" The old lady, who was tall and had great dignity, rose majestically from her chair, laying aside the ubiquitous knitting for some grandchild and made her way to the back door, saying, "I will see what the Hamiltons have put over the fence." She returned triumphantly with cheese that gave us Welsh rarebit for three nights. The hens lived with us for many years, even on board our Thames Sailing Barge after the war was over.

There is still an epilogue to pianos and our stay in Bath. I bought a spinet or really a square piano as it turned out to be, dated 1810.

I had gone to a joiner for some small job and saw it there. I asked the joiner what he intending to do with it. His answer was, to break it up next day for the timber. I asked what he would take for it. "Fifty shillings." was his reply. Fifty shillings amounted to £2.50 today but was then a small amount, though enough to make a hole in the house keeping which was £3 a week. Next day I produced the sum and our old friends, Green & Marsh, fetched it for us and were extremely enthusiastic. My mother played Scarlatti on it and it lives with me to this day. It is possible that Jane Austen may have played on it during her stay in Bath.

Time was running out but before it did, fate struck a devastating blow. A man had killed a pig. To breed a pig or pigs meant that you had to declare the fact and later share the meat. The man did not wish to do that and was hiding the carcass in his shed. One morning his wife telephoned him at work in Bath to tell him that the Inspector of Food was in the vicinity and would he hurry home and bury the pig.

He drove as fast as he could in his van to beat the Inspector. From a group of children who were walking beside the road, one ran out. She was a big child for her age, but she was unused to traffic, as with petrol rationing there were few cars on the roads – which made life more serene. The van knocked her over and fractured her skull. She was our daughter.

It was Christmas Eve. We took her in the van to the nearest hospital, where by extraordinary good luck a famous neurologist was visiting. This was comforting, but, alas, finally of no avail. Penicillin had just been discovered but it was only available for the Armed Forces. After leaving hospital in triumph, she developed meningitis and she died, after much anxiety and surgery, on Good Friday in the Radcliffe Hospital in Oxford.

The Banned Area

The end of my time in Bath was spent between our home and Oxford, where I lived in lodgings visiting the Radcliffe Infirmary several times a day and often during the night. Tom's mother took over the house while Tom remained ashore. After that, my Italian friend, Bigi Beverley, Juliet's godmother, took Jeremy and Mona, the Welsh girl who had come to help, to her house in Silverstone.

Then a very dreary thing happened. There was a law at that time disallowing one to stay for more than three nights as a visitor in a hotel. This was to frustrate enemy spying. In order to be near the Radcliffe Infirmary I had found undergraduate digs in which I could stay. Landladies were short of undergraduates – they were at the war. For a few weeks this became my headquarters in Oxford – I used to rush home to see Tom and his mother in Bath when I felt I could. Two things happened – the landlady became impatient as Juliet, and therefore I, lingered. Then her son got mumps. He was in the habit of having long telephone conversations to help pass the time. We used the same telephone, which resulted in my catching mumps too.

Tom had come home on compassionate leave during the last days of Juliet's life. He went shopping to find food that I could swallow, but there was no disguising the fact: I could not visit the Radcliffe Hospital. There was nothing for it but that I must go the Isolation Hospital. My landlady too was adamant. So off I went.

To my astonishment, I was received with the utmost hostility. A small hard-faced woman, the matron, interviewed me. All books, my only comfort, she insisted, were to be burnt if I unpacked them. Tom was not allowed near me, although he had looked after me most efficiently for a day or two. "Rules", said the matron, "were rules." I myself was fairly certain that mumps was not spread by books, like scarlet fever or measles, so that the book-burning was absurd. They were my only comfort. I was then given a sausage roll for breakfast. Try eating one when you have mumps. In my despair I danced on my bed refusing to eat it, groaning with pain after the first mouthful. This remains the only time in my life that I have met quite such inflexible stupidity and unkindness. It was, I am sure, an exception and today I mourn the loss of the position of Matron now banished from hospitals. There must have been something very odd in that Isolation Hospital, because when the Night Sister came to say goodbye to me she said, "I would not like you to leave this hospital without knowing that the staff here are deeply sorry for the way you have been treated."

Tom brought the sad, final, inevitable news to me, standing on a balcony outside my window. Despite all the wonderful efforts we had received from surgeons and nurses, we were defeated. The accident was on Christmas Eve and Juliet died on Good Friday.

I had learnt a great deal during my vigil in Oxford. One was the valour that comes to people in real trouble. We would sit in a small waiting-room, waiting with resigned patience for news of the vital operations on our nearest relations. Juliet was in a little ward for two patients. Eight others passed through as time went by – only one recovered. When we were alone, I used to converse with them. It was a very sad and thoughtful time.

After this we went our ways, staying first in Bushey where we buried our little daughter – her uncles, aunts and grannies around her, supporting us all. That night, Tom went to Portsmouth where preparations for the Invasion were in full swing. I went with Pat to the cottage at Basingstoke, once more a refuge. In Bath, my mother-in-law and Bigi packed up the house.

The war had taken on a new complexion. But secrecy was paramount. I went to visit Tom in what had become a 'Banned Area', the country that surrounded Portsmouth. This meant restricted entry: one could come into the area with a day return railway ticket only. Tom was incarcerated in a tunnel beneath Port Southwick on Portsdown Hill. He was able to come out and have lunch with me. Before going back, I met some people who had bought a house and wanted it lived in, so that it would not be commandeered by the Military.

I did not use my return ticket. I stayed the night with friends and next day arranged to take on the house. Soon Jeremy and Mona joined me.

The house had been owned by an old lady who would have nothing to do with mod cons – we existed on a pump for water, candles for light and an earth closet for a lavatory.

Lots of people helped to furnish the house in a haphazard way, with any bits and pieces from people who had evacuated from London and had stored furniture nearby and most generously offered pieces to our new friends, Colonel and Mrs Crump from Bedales School. Inside, our living quarters varied from grandeur to bare necessities, while outside we enjoyed a wonderful garden looked after by a full-time gardener. It had a lily pond, beautiful lawns and acres of woodland. We lived off lush vegetables grown by Curnoe, the Cornish gardener. His first job every morning was to withdraw the lavatory pan through a trap door in the yard in order to empty it. If the occasion found you seated there, the shock was apt to cause constipation: I continually suffered it while there.

We were also happy to send Jeremy to the junior school for Bedales, Dunhurst, where he was welcomed by the loving headmistress, Tarky, (Miss Clarke) which was balm to all our distressed feelings.

However, after a week or so, peace, one morning, was shattered. A furniture van drew up and out got a very angry lady, thin and brittle. She was accompanied by her gentle and quiet mother, dressed in grey. Unbidden, she rushed into our house, claiming that the carpet in the dining room was hers. It had in fact been loaned by Paul Maze, the painter living nearby, who had mistakenly directed Barbara to the wrong part of a furniture store, saying, “Help yourself, my dear”, and she had – she had also patched places. In London the carpet had covered a room with pillars. “These looked like postage stamps.” said the angry lady, with the utmost contempt.

Her piercing voice exclaiming “My carpet is ruined.” brought down the master of the house. About twice a week, Tom came home to sleep and eat after being on duty for thirty consecutive hours; this happened to be one such time. He appeared in his dressing gown in the midst of this affray. Then Jeremy, with a child's power of imitation, echoed the lady’s strident voice, “Daddy, the dining room carpet is ruined, ruined.”

“Madam, I must ask you to leave my house.” said its master, whose well-earned sleep he felt had been so suddenly interrupted. Tom insisted that she went out on to the lawn where she had the driver spread out the carpet and its underlay. It was a most embarrassing situation, chiefly for the poor gentle mother and for our friends, the Crumps. However, war was war and there was little to be done. We lost our carpet and the van drove away – our footsteps echoing on the bare board from that day on.

It was early June 1944. On about the 4th I received a message from Tom from his dungeon under Fort Southwick. He suggested that we should come down on the next Sunday to picnic on Portsdown Hill. A good idea and we would catch a glimpse of him, I thought. Sunday turned out to be a miserable day, entirely unsuitable for picnics, so at about lunch time I rang up and explained that we would not set out but might do so the next day, weather permitting. A great friend of Tom's answered and sounded amused. He translated my message to Tom into more official language, indicating that I would put the whole thing into operation the following day. I agreed.

Next day, 6th June, was still gloomy but a shade better, so we set out, taking the bus from Petersfield. On Portsdown Hill the cold wind blew keenly. We found a haystack to shelter behind and spread out our tea hoping that Tom would soon emerge. To pass the time we played a guessing game, "I spy with my little eye..." At one time the letter of the object to be guessed turned out to be 'S' – "sea?" No. "Ships?" we said "Oh yes – lots down there in Fareham Creek." was the satisfactory answer. And so we went on. At 6 o'clock we were tired of waiting for Tom. We were chilly. We gathered up our things and went for the bus.

Tired though I felt on the top of the bus as we journeyed home, I noticed that, instead of the usual long lines of camouflaged tanks beside the woods along the road, with soldiers camping in the woods, there were empty spaces. "An army has passed this way." I thought.

Next morning I woke up and listened, as usual, to the radio for any news and found that the invasion had taken place during the night – that our troops were fighting at that very moment on the beaches of France. At last the penny dropped. Our friend's words on the telephone, as I postponed our picnic, turned out to be Eisenhower's words in his signal that postponed the invasion of Europe on 5th June 1944. It had come through a few hours before mine. Incidentally, the windows of our house shook for some days as the bombardment continued across the water on the coast of France.

Next time I saw Tom I had to confess that we had sat behind a haystack and eaten our tea. "Do you mean to say that when the greatest invasion fleet that the world has ever known started to move that you never even looked? And I had arranged for you to be there"…. "You are a bloody fool, Peg." So I knew I was forgiven.

But, oh dear. Well, it is true – I am the woman who did not see it. It does however show how complete was the secrecy at that time and, as we all now know, the Germans themselves were fooled, to our great credit.

My heart said "Is this road inevitably mine?"
"Yours to the end " beat in my ears
An inexorable reply.
To which in anguish from my heart rose "Why,
When some pass gently down the years,
Must grief bespatter mine with tears until I die?"

"Mine to the end" Oh well – I looked and saw
Richness, suddenly in such profusion
I'd not seen before.
There walked with me a motley band who bore
Life's trouble, sorrow and confusion
But transferred with deep compassion all they saw.

My heart cried "These are the free, the debonair"
They see beauty, know friendship and in laughter's quick release
Have found life's measure,
They grow strong, walking as if in leisure,
No barriers, no explanation, no belief
But in the medium of deep compassion they find life's treasure.

Written after the loss of our second daughter Harriett, who died as a baby in 1948.

The Last Dreary Years

Somewhere amongst the boxes hoarded in my attic, I hope there is a photograph of the "Morning After." It was taken in the Tunnel under Fort Southwick, the "Ops Room" for the Invasion. The staff are standing in front of the PLAN, which is on the wall behind them. It meant that the Royal Navy ships had landed the Invasion Force on French soil during the night – the first step towards the liberation of Europe had been carried out. The company look like actors in front of the final curtain, when an immense drama has been enacted. They are triumphant, exhausted, dazed but also very humble, as they should be: the future is in the balance, fighting across the Channel must now be horrific.

Our house at Steep shook from the bombardment for several days. As well as our shabby windows we had other signs of the invasion – a happier omen – a friend returned from France with a Camembert cheese – like the dove with the olive branch for Noah, we felt. We began to adapt to the new prospect.

There were unexpected casualties from the Tunnel. Tom would come home with a high fever and toss and turn all night. This became a recurring event until he was sent to attend a Medical Board. This resulted in sick leave. It was very unlike Tom.

At the same time, our house, Armadale, which had been let since 1938, became vacant. We decided to go home. Alas, the last tenants had been disastrous – frightened drunks who, with flying bombs, had given up, leaving chaos behind, broken bottles and uncared for furniture, heaped up to keep out the doodlebugs.

We cut our way through a hayfield of the garden to get in at the front door and face the worst. So the sick leave was spent trying to retrieve the house with spasmodic days of fever and bed for Tom. He was granted a further period of leave.

It was a funny time, but not unpleasant, as we were happy to be back after the whole war away. Perhaps our grief began to ease.

Then suddenly a signal (command) arrived from the Admiralty: Tom was to go abroad on his next commission. We both assumed that he was supposed to be cured and very soon off he went.

A week later another signal arrived: he was to appear at another Medical Board in Portsmouth. In fury I rang up the Admiralty to say that by this time Tom was in Trincamalee in Ceylon. To add to my dismay, reports from friends in the Navy came back stressing his very poor condition.

My spirits were not very high as I tried to come to terms with our misfortunes. Alas, a miscarriage for me did not help. My mother, who loved Armadale and its garden, came to stay and this was an enormous benefit.

At about the beginning of the next year, Tom became gunnery officer to the British Pacific Fleet and moved with Admiral Sir Bruce Fraser to Australia. Australia saved him. The trouble was Tuberculosis, which had become rife in the Tunnel. Tom was one of the lucky ones. One or two died. It did occur to me that possibly Tom may have been the carrier. In Bath he used to work very late and even came home to eat his dinner as late as 3 am. He confessed that he had had to lie down sometimes on the roadside on his way home. All this now changed. The fleet that arrived in Australia was greeted with enormous hospitality and generosity which, added to the sun, good food and the temporary relief from war had an amazing effect. Basically, Tom was a very strong man. Ever after, when pulmagraphs were invented, the medical world would never believe that such a big scar had cured itself. Once, when an X-ray negative got smudged, he was rushed to hospital.

In England, beyond becoming very envious as letters arrived, we settled down to a new aspect of the war. Our planes went over in thousands, it seemed, to bomb Germany. A sight one shuddered at, remembering what it was like to be on the receiving end of the bombs.

Several threads ran through our lives for the next two years. The most continuous one consisted of the evacuees from London and Portsmouth who abounded in the village. Jeremy did not lack companionship. Mrs Newman came in to help clean and her evacuees – two girls and a boy – were constantly in our garden with, of course, friends. Jeremy became bilingual, to my pleasure. One evening he was having a bath, his evacuee friend Dennis was helping. At the airing cupboard outside the bathroom, I heard his remark – "Cor, this bath ain't harf bloddy 'ot." I put my head round the door. With complete composure, he said "Mummy, the water's too hot." That's a lesson learnt, I thought.

We were occupied with making rations go round, helped by queuing for Woolton Pies once a week (pies made, it was said, from squirrels) and listening to Tommy Handley, "Much Binding in the Marsh", the Brains Trust and other diversions on the wireless. Friendships blossomed and were very valuable.

Very soon, I found a couple who came to share the house with me. A young naval doctor had married a nurse and they were expecting a baby. It seemed a happy solution to family life. At the same time, I was able to get enough petrol to take Jeremy to school at Dunhurst, where he had already started. He brought himself home by bus, with a change in Petersfield. In those days, one was confident of little boys being safe.

It was agreed that Meg, the nurse, would cope with the house and that I would grow vegetables in the garden, which I managed fairly successfully. Cooking was shared. My mother remained happily, on and off.

Bosanquet deserves a section for himself. He came into our lives at some time when I was alone in the house one afternoon. I was just ready to go out, when there was a knock at the back door and there stood a man of the road – in fact a tramp. He had a nice face and seemed a reasonable person. I explained that I was due to leave the house. He showed immediate signs of taking himself off until I asked if he was hungry. "Well..." he began. I said that the only thing I could offer was one or two sausages, but that if he could cook them he was welcome to them. He brightened up, I gave him a pan and showed him the stove and then went off. I had a feeling I was right and I was. When I returned, the coal hod was filled, wood was chopped up and stacked in the garden, his plate was washed up and there was a note of thanks on the kitchen table.

Of course he came again. I even passed him on to Pat at Upper Wootton. He made a gate for them. Eileen asked about bathing but he preferred a bucket. He slept in the greenhouse and then put a cup of tea on the stairs for me. So we fell into a rather charming routine. He did little jobs before taking off towards Portsmouth.

He was well read. He could quote freely from classical literature. He told me that the parson in the village in which he had spent his childhood gave him lessons in reading and arithmetic. From his name I gathered that he was an illegitimate son of a family of that name in Cumberland. From his earliest days he had slept rough, in spite of his mother's despair. He loved all things belonging to the country. His visits were very bright interludes.

The war in the East came into our lives with letters, not too frequent but very long and full. Several chaps got together and took a flat in Woolamoloo, Sydney. They were vitally engaged on planning the invasion of Japan. Tom travelled about between the islands of the Pacific and ships at sea and became engaged in a Japanese suicide raid on some battleship. He also came down in the Pacific, when the plane carrying him had engine failure.

His description of the event: they were progressing quite normally when the pilot regretted there was some trouble, no cause for anxiety, but would the passengers be alert. Then a further message – would they lie down with their feet towards the propeller? Then, as Tom said, the sea seemed to be rushing towards them. But "still no cause for anxiety." They were on the surface of the sea. Now, "no anxiety", but would they step out very quickly into inflatable dinghies which were awaiting them ? This they did and the plane sank. They got out charts and survival kits. A bubble came up and in it was, among other things, Tom's suitcase. He rescued it and waited for a further bubble with a second case, but it never came. Unfortunately, he had packed all his trousers in the second case.

They began to adapt to the new circumstances and had got out the charts and survival kits when an American plane flew over. Soon after that, an American destroyer arrived to pick them up. On board they were treated to survival brandy and taken back to their place of departure. Tom sat down while waiting and wrote to me. It turned out to be the anniversary of our wedding day, he added, I hoped, with satisfaction.

VE-Day came and I took Jeremy up to London, as my mother had done with us in 1918. The reception of the event was tremendous but very wisely contained. No "War to end wars" this time, instead thankfulness that it was ended. We stood outside Buckingham Palace with my mother, but were glad to get back to our home in Horndean. Saying goodnight to Jeremy I explained that we did not have to worry about the Blackout any more. "But how shall we keep the black out?" he asked me anxiously. It had never occurred to me that it could have been another sort of comfort.

Then on 6th August 1945 the Atomic Bomb fell on Hiroshima. Mrs. Newman made the remark that summed up all our confused feelings. "Oh my – it's dreadful for those who think, isn't it?" and wasn't it?

Part III Reaping the Whirlwind

The Sailor's Return from the Wars

The earth is dead
and the sky is lead
And the wind that blows Is bitter and shrill.
Old bones ache
But hold for the sake
Of what memory knows
Of the Spring.
But my heart sings
Like a lark who wings
His way to the sun above.
And all I see is the tan on your face
And all I hear is my heart's wild race
As each day brings
As if borne on wings
You nearer to me, my love.

The earth is dead
And the sky is lead
And the wind that blows Is bitter and chill
The young are numb
And minds are dumb
And life is confined in a rut.
But my heart fills with a pleasure that stills
The winter's death and fear.
And all I see is the tan on your face
And all I hear is my heart's wild race
As each day brings
As if borne on wings
Me nearer to you, my Dear.

Written in the spring of 1947. The war was over but food was short. Our home, a wartime house shared with another family. My mother was ill from a stroke. Tom was returning in a slow boat from China.

All sorts of unexpected things arose with the re-establishment of Tom. Nothing is what you imagine it will be before it actually happens. While the slow boat from China ambled its way back to England, we spent our time trying to improve the shabby wartime house. It was two years since Tom had left. Early one morning in May we went down to the dockyard in Portsmouth. A friend bicycled down to see that we were put on board a tender that took us out to SS Reaper at Spithead. We climbed on board and there was Tom – very fit and sunburnt from Australia and Hong Kong. After drinks in the wardroom surrounded by happy returning sailors we went ashore – the bicycling friend, Michael Le Fanu, had married the daughter of the Admiral Superintendent of the Dockyard and we celebrated further in his father-in-law's house before going home to Armadale.

During the two years' absence we had kept up a good communication between father and son – I had written letters at Jeremy's dictation. However, during our first lunch together I realised that both males in my life would have to adapt as wife and mother had to be shared. Of course this was common with all returning fathers – mothers were no longer the children's property and to the fathers, yes – marvellous to see them but when do they go to bed? Fortunately this did not last too long. I, too, had to adapt.

Our first days were madly happy – the weather was good, the garden engrossed us and we enlivened the evenings with champagne from Australia. Time seemed unlimited.

Our pattern of life had changed: the evacuees had returned to London, sadly some to a broken home. We lost touch. We ourselves gained a most happy addition to our family – a boy of seven whose parents had to return to Kuala Lumpur in Malay to pick up their livelihood after escaping from the Japanese in 1941. John Warren was to go to a prep school and to spend holidays with us. It was heartbreaking to witness the philosophical courage of this splendid little boy whom we all loved – he and Jeremy became good playmates.

Tom driving back from Petersfield one day picked up a vagrant who said he was going to see a lady in Horndean. "So am I." said Tom and he and Bosanquet arrived at Armadale. His visit was even more successful than his previous ones. He and Tom got on very well. Bosanquet stayed for a week as usual. Being summer, he was well accommodated in the summer house, put our tea each morning on the stairs, worked all day and finally drank his wages and left. He enriched our lives with his literary and philosophical quotations.

It was another matter when he arrived in mid-winter. He slept in the hall. For Jeremy's birthday party, when we hired a conjuror to amuse the company, Bosanquet entertained the company as much as the conjuror. But that was all much later in the following January.

During the summer Tom was appointed to his next commission – he was to command a destroyer, HMS Sluys. He was overjoyed and I with him until he rather guiltily informed me that the ship was building at Birkenhead, was to work from Portland and to be based at Devonport. Really he might have stayed in China for all his family would see of him. As a first step we packed up and went and spent a cold August in rooms (lodgings) on the Wirral in Cheshire. Here I spent my time preventing two small boys being drowned in the treacherous tide on the sands of Dee across which "Mary called the cattle home" with such dire results.

"Well you ought to do what I am going to do – live in a Thames Sailing Barge – then you wouldn't have all these worries". This innocent remark was made to me by the man sitting next to me, the captain of the sister ship of HMS Sluys. We were having lunch on board in Camel Laird's Yard in Birkenhead.

Readers may have noticed that both Tom and I were subject to impulses but not usually at the same time. This time, it was mine. The trouble at the end of the war was that husbands who were in it for "hostilities only" came home, were demobbed returning to the bosom of their families so that it seemed doubly hard to be separated again and so soon. I simply had to find a way to escape from the situation.

The immediate result that day was tea in this man's cabin poring over prospectuses, which he had accumulated from firms advertising craft no longer wanted by the Admiralty. We left that evening with our pockets stuffed with information and, most important of all – a copy of Arthur Bennett's book "June of Rochester". This might be said to have been our undoing – the author described his early married life aboard a Thames Sailing Barge in the 1930s. Arthur was a wonderful seaman, though an amateur he ranked as a Sailorman, which professional barge skippers are called. He became a most valued friend. He did however see barging through rose coloured spectacles, as I was to find out. At that time however it all seemed crystal clear to me – what could be easier – Tom a sailor by profession could see to all the seafaring side of it and we would have a movable home. Paradoxically, it was because Tom was a sailor that it fell to me to find a Thames Barge to live in.

The winter of 1946/7 was one of the worst of the century including 1963 – one of those lurches that the Arctic suddenly does. The new paint applied to HMS Sluys froze while being put on. She accompanied the Vanguard carrying the King and the Royal family down the Channel on their way to

South Africa. At the same time, I was making frequent journeys between blizzards and a measles epidemic at home to see what frequently turned out to be unsuitable barges. They were to be found in all sorts of creeks and one even at Reading. This one was lived in by the wife of a shipmate of Tom's from the Far East. They and their family became life long friends, Bryan and Lavender Westwood.

Finally it was at Sittingbourne that the managing director of a shipbuilding yard and I scraped the snow off the hatch covers of a barge laid up at the yard and descended the ladder into the dark, damp, dank, empty unwelcoming hold of Five Sisters. Never having seen a converted barge, I had nothing to go on as I looked at the dismal scene below. What came over me when we climbed back on to the bank was pure poetry. Her sails were brailed up and neatly stowed after her final trip to her present berth. She looked business-like and elegant under her cloak of snow. Her appeal was irresistible. She had been left in perfect order by her late crew. Then there was Mr. Harvey. Mr. Harvey was an enthusiast: he loved barges. Like so many East Coast countrymen, he had lived amongst them all his life. The barge world had endured over several centuries, reaching its zenith in the nineteenth and twentieth centuries and holding its position until the end of the Second World War. The Thames Sailing Barge was developed from a flat-bottomed river craft with one sail steered by one oar or a sweep in Tudor days. As it developed it could navigate the shoals and sandbanks of the North Sea coasts. Being flat-bottomed, they could penetrate far up estuaries, thus farmers from the East Coast could get their cargoes of grain and farming produce including hay to towns and mills, particularly up the London River where they fed the horses who pulled London's traffic. And so the breed of farmer-sailors sprang up known as Sailormen, a sturdy breed with much ingenuity about whom it has been said that "the diversity of their lives enriched their characters" From early trading with Holland they developed the spar known as the sprit invaluable for a cargo boat in every way. These farmer-sailors went further and brought stone from Portland and coal from the North to build and heat eighteenth-century and Victorian London. Sailormen, as they were always called were talented men. So simple is the structure of a Thames sailing Barge that one man and a boy can sail it. Our experience was : "Some boy!".

Another feature which came via Holland – brought there by the Spaniards who in their turn brought it from the Pacific – was the lee board which prevents a flat-bottomed boat from drifting sideways.

This great industrial fleet as indeed it was, was maintained ashore by shipyards, repair yards, sail makers, timber yards as well as trading companies whose cargoes the barges carried. This was the world of the East Coast of England until after the Second World War. The barges' length was anything from 76 feet to 120 with a beam of 18 – 25 feet. They carried a great deal more than is carried today by the juggernauts on our roads.

There she lay under a cloak of snow, abandoned by her previous owner but in seamanlike order, her sails brailed up, her ropes coiled and belayed, hung in listful readiness, so that she managed to convey hopeful expectation. Her tall mast and sprit gave her elegance that warmed my heart and I took courage. Impulse got me.

I left the yard and retraced my steps uphill (I was pregnant and very tubby) to the house of Mr. Harvey who was recommended to me as an expert. To me he was advisor, longstop and even guardian angel in this unknown world and somewhat hazardous enterprise.

He was a great ally and continued to be so after Tom had come back for Easter leave. Proudly at Sittingbourne I showed him what I had found – our barge-to-be. It was a slight awkwardness that the night before the survey Tom noticed that Mr. Harvey's name was on the writing paper as a director of the firm selling Five Sisters. I had unwittingly asked him to do the survey. This was a most disturbing discovery. However we got round it with Arthur Bennett's help. We were staying at Rochester. We found him living in Whitstable and rushed for his advice, which he readily gave over tea and fruitcake made by his wife, Dorothy. In the end we had two surveyors, Mr. Bailey, a friend of Arthur's, for Tom and Mr. Harvey for me. Together they got us our barge for £640.

The buying proved to be the easiest part. Anything done in the immediate postwar days was extraordinarily difficult. Already having a house to live in meant that we were not eligible for any permits without which it was impossible to buy anything. There was a general directive from the Ministry of Supply that there was no timber in the country and nothing would alter this. A firm in Whitstable informed the Ministry that their yard was stacked with timber and they were very sensibly hoping to revive the oyster trade by getting ahead building oyster harvesting craft, but they got the same answer – there is no timber in the country – so no permit. They were as glad to meet us as we were to meet them. We sailed round to Whitstable and were put on a slip on the beach against the Sea Wall, upon which were the offices and workshops belonging to the firm of R.J. Perkins.

We spent the most happy summer holidays staying in a small pub, also on the Sea Wall. All along the beach were other slipways on which shipwrights worked. Lying in bed in the early morning, I listened to the hammering on wooden hulls on the beach. For hundreds of years these echoing blows must have been familiar sounds in that part of the town. The squeal of electric drills had not yet arrived.

It was a paradise for small boys. They lived among the boats and climbed all over Five Sisters. We swam from the Five Sisters when the tide was up and when it was out, we dug for cockles on the beach.

Fitting out our home proved a very difficult job; it was done by fair means and foul. As Mrs. Peraton at the farm in Plympton once remarked, "The war has made rogues of us all". We did not actually break the law but we had to do with defective things. We had no bath, then we acquired two and had to get rid of one before the Ministry of Supply discovered our good luck. The glory of our barge was the Rayburn stove in the kitchen (we decided to use household names for the interior at this point). One day in Petersfield, I saw in a shop window a cooking stove, a Rayburn, advertised at £60 – "No Permit". Overjoyed, I sent Tom a cable – "Have found a Raeburn – shall I buy it?" Tom was in the Mediterranean somewhere. That evening an answering cable came back. "Are you sure it is genuine – stop – Where do you propose to hang it?" Mystified, I studied the blurb and found of course it was Ray (rays of heat) and not the same name as the portrait painter. Naval officers love that sort of joke, especially by cable. The next thing I bought was a cracked hand basin for the bathroom and I did not consult Tom.

Early in January 1948 Jeremy and I, two cats and three hens took up residence in a far from ready Five Sisters. We had been deprived of Tom, who was in hospital in Stonehouse, Devonport. It was one of our TB crises due, it was later discovered, to a smudged X ray. The shipyard was not expecting us, despite our having warned them that our house was let from 5th January. There were troubles all round (the chief carpenter had a row with his girl on the ice) and other troubles added to a lack of communication, but there we were alongside with a pantechnicon containing our furniture. Fortunately, the roof was not on, so it could be lowered into the hull by use of the sprit, my first use of it.

By nightfall we had managed to get everything undercover and to fix up beds. As I sank gratefully between the sheets I found them to be full of concrete. "This", I told myself, "is rock bottom."

From the next day on, we lived amongst wood shavings, sawdust and cement, making tea for the men countless times a day and trying to equip ourselves further with Tilly lamps and a hundred and one things for our seafaring life to be. Days passed quickly enough until it was time for Jeremy to go school. As it was to be his first term at a boarding school, my chief worry was how to get his trunk off in a suitable state to impress the school matron, a terrifying figment of my imagination. I must eliminate all traces of shavings, cement and general dirt.

Tom was suddenly let out of hospital and came to join us for a few days (the faulty X ray had been discovered). He decided in true naval style that it was time to give a shipyard party. Somewhat dismayed at the prospect of getting the trunk ready and trying to entertain the workforce, the party turned out to be my salvation: wives, sweethearts and girl friends helped me stitch on name tapes while the men sang bawdy songs and we all drank dry a barrel of beer. Next morning we trundled the trunk to the station and it was dispatched with complete confidence on my part. Matron turned out to be charming and, of all things, her name was Miss Hunter-Dunn.

Despite Tom's reprieve, he was not allowed to stay, so I and the two cats and hens lived alone in the barge, rising and falling with the tide. The Harbour Master and his wife were very friendly and kind and Joe, the sail rigger for the firm, came daily to keep an eye on the bilges and other troubles that might arise. Other barges came in with cargoes of grain and there was plenty of company by day. There was a certain wry humour about my being prepared to live on a barge, especially on the part of wives. In the evenings, when I went to telephone to Tom, Joe would come and wait in the barge while I wove my way through the deserted harbour between railway trucks to and from the telephone box. If the tide was out, I had to climb down thirty feet of rusty ladder to get back home. Joe was always warning me against someone he called "the one-eyed sailor" who might tie up alongside. I made sure the strong back was made fast on the hatch cover. Then one night Joe said "He's here, so watch out." and true enough, there was a boat alongside with someone bending over what I presumed was the evening's catch. Oh well – this was life afloat but how unpredictable it could be.

Even more unpredictable than I thought was the whole of the next day. I woke up to find Tom on the quayside on a lovely fine morning. The first thing after breakfasting was that Tom met our neighbour, the "one-eyed" who turned out to be an old shipmate from the war, so I left them deep in shared memories, chatting affably on the quay-side.

In those days of rationing there came a time when you were no longer allowed to get a temporary ration card: it was compulsory to register in the town where you were at that moment. This now applied to myself. At the harbour gate was a small grocery and I went in and began negotiations. The grocer was very co-operative; shops were beginning to value customers.

“Can I send the goods?”, he asked and I was just about to comply when the door burst open and in came the Harbour Master.

“Hurry”, he cried “Five Sisters is half way across the harbour. Run and you'll catch her as she goes about. Without another word he picked up the shopping, stuffed it into the baskets and ran from the shop. Unable to excuse my behaviour I could only shout over my shoulder as I scrambled after him “No address, we're leaving now.”

And there in the middle of the harbour, a most graceful sight, foresail and mizzen-sails already set and filling, as the south-easterly breeze bore her majestically towards the harbour entrance was Five Sisters. The Harbour Master had not stopped, the longshoremen closed in round us, chuckling and giving advice. “You've cut it rather fine, Missus, haven't you? We'll see you aboard, never fear.” and so on as I trotted along after the Harbour Master. At the western jetty, Five Sisters advanced slowly towards us. I recognised Skipper Albert Friar's stalwart figure at the wheel, Joe by the mast coiling ropes.

“I'll have to jump”, I remember saying, a little resentfully. Everyone around me laughed, apparently this was obvious and common practice. Albert's large form bent to the wheel, the sails flapped as the barge's bow slowly turned towards the middle of the harbour again, her side slid within a foot or two of the jetty. “Now's your moment, Missus. Jump.” Frantically I did, landing as I learnt later, on the port quarter. Tom caught me and Joe caught the shopping baskets that followed. It was only later that I learnt that the original intention had been to wait for me at the western jetty. However, everyone was anxious to catch the tide without further delay. I felt approbation, not articulated, by Albert. The explanation of the sudden decision was explained to me as we wound our way with an east wind behind us into the estuary – in fact into the London River and joined the mass of intricate traffic that surged up on the flood tide.

The London River

I sat on deck in the warm winter sunshine and watched the coasts of Kent and Essex draw together while Tom worked attentively with Joe on sails. I was recovering from the shock of my departure and wondering where I was to come in – this was a totally new world. Anxiously remembering those skippers' wives in Whitstable who, when on board, were "so handy at the wheel" I enquired shyly of Albert how he knew when he was right. "Why, by the feel." he replied in his rich, slow, rolling crescendo, which we quote to this day – "Always," he added, "let your bob lay along your topsail."

The bob is the equivalent of the yachtsman's burgee, but it is permanently fixed to the truck or knob at the head of the topmast and is generally the flag of the firm owning the barge. This golden piece of advice became the first to be passed on rather smugly by me to any new and nervous helmsman who might be visiting us. Nevertheless, I was never a good helmsman being a better deck hand also, I might add, I was cook which I coupled with engine watching below.

That was all in the future. That morning in February 1948 I was absorbed watching the shipping, which began to close in as we approached Sea Reach. Poring over the chart, I noted the names of the channels, the hazards and the shoreline. Who for instance were Jenkins and Chapman to give their very English names to those Norse-sounding words 'swatchways'? Swansmead conjured up delectable water meadows where Plantagenet swans raised royal cygnets – which had little to do with the dreary waterside of today. Further up, the comings and goings of the Tudor and Stuart citizens still hung in the names of Galleon's Reach and King's Reach.

Cups of tea were called for. I went below and found the kitchen was full of smoke. Thankful to be in a boat with the right sort of people – competent sailors instead of just me – I calmly put my head up the hatch and informed them on deck that the barge was on fire. Somewhat dismayed (rather to my satisfaction), down they came to investigate: a small piece of the new roofing of stuff call Gyplith was burning round the Rayburn chimney. "Must have been smouldering for days." remarked Albert cheerfully as he plodded back to the hatchway. I remembered rather ruefully how I had secured myself against the One-eyed Sailor with such confidence on my nights alone. The fire was extinguished by the aid of a child's enema syringe which we happened to have.

Back on deck, I experienced for the first time the amazing sight of the Thames Estuary on the flood tide when every conceivable craft seemed in those days to converge on London: cargo ships from all parts the world, coasters, colliers, ships loaded with timber from the Baltic, pleasure boats and yachts. The most extraordinary thing was the intricate weaving of Five Sisters with sail power alone cutting her course miraculously through this jungle of traffic, passing within feet of large ships' sterns with complete ease under Albert's hand. At the ebb, the reverse would take place with a sailing barge, I learnt later, when the traffic surges down river with equal intensity. All this is in the past – container ships changed the whole system. Today, with the barrage, the river sleeps rather sadly with an occasional pleasure steamer to rouse interest.

We got as far as Erith before the tide defeated us. Albert and Joe slept on board, after a supper from the goods the grocer had supplied. Next morning, with an entire change of climate from spring to cold cloudy weather, we pushed on the flood to Greenwich and dropped anchor exactly opposite the King Charles steps from which Tom and I had left so many years ago to be arrested at Woolwich Arsenal, at the start of our married life.

This was as far as Albert and Joe were coming. Tom and I would wait here. We had installed an engine, an Atlantic it was called, dating from the beginning of the century, but some part was apparently missing. We had booked ourselves a berth in Chelsea but this seemed a good place to lie at anchor for a short time, to collect ourselves and await the missing part for the engine. Tom could commute from here to the Admiralty where he was now working. As I would be alone on board, by day at least, I would have the Naval Collage at hand, should I be in trouble.

Albert told me before he left that if ever I heard a rattling of the anchor cable I must let out more cable. This I would do by throwing cable stowed on deck over a huge barrel beneath the winch and out it would run. During the next few weeks I heard nothing but a rattling of the cable, as river traffic surged up and down. I never actually let out cable, being fearful of what I would do if I expended it all. In spite of my anxiety, the Barge was always there when Tom called from the bank on his return from work in the evening.

The time at Greenwich was the most perplexing of my life. Apart from the old cable, there were other complications. Every morning we rowed ashore to the landing stage on the same bank as the College. Tom, rather incongruously wearing a bowler hat and clutching a brief case, was bound for the Admiralty. It was my job to get myself, the dinghy and any shopping I might have done back on board. On the first morning, it was discovered that I had never mastered rowing in a strong tide. The ebb on the London River flows at about 6 knots. As a child, I had learnt to row on a lake in Wales and naïvely thought I could row. Consequently, after a few hasty instructions on Greenwich pier, I realised that there was no other way. I set out a near nervous wreck. Following those instructions, I kept close to the shore until well above the barge. Then I struck out, pointing into the ebb tide and "crabbed" out until I met the barge, to my great surprise striking her in the bow. The blow nearly drove me out again but I clung on, fastened the painter round my waist holding the dinghy's bow in with my feet, myself stiff as a ramrod, and clambered onboard. I was so overcome with my success that I forgot to wave to my anxious husband but lay looking up at the sky for some time.

[Extract from "Five Sisters" written in 1970]. I pulled myself together at last and applied myself to the first painting. Everything inside, having been scrubbed with caustic soda, now had to be painted five times. Nothing short of this number would produce a satisfactory finish. At some time tar had penetrated to the two-inch-thick pitch pine lining or inner skin, as well as to the deck heads and hatches overhead. After a period of trial and error, we discovered that the first coat must be of knotting, a thick sealing liquid. This was followed by priming, then two coats of undercoating and one of gloss. After this, sulphuric acid smuts would rain down upon us from the power stations, but this discovery was yet to come.

My painting was interrupted to correct the sheer of the ship to the changing tide. This was done by setting the wheel so that the tide swung her away from the traffic. I used to gaze at one power station upstream and another down until I judged she would 'do' for the next six hours. Before going below I always had a good listen to that old cable after Albert's warning, as it growled and bumped with the passing traffic. The high tide was a crescendo of noise and activity – all hell let loose, in fact – as the traffic surged up past me: big ships for the Pool, tankers and colliers for the power stations, tugs towing six or eight lighters laden with timber, all hooting as they changed course, leaving a wash to lap and rock the barge. The effect of the motion, added to the smell of the paint, was very apt, I found to produce seasickness.

Although life surged around me, I was isolated and lonely, except for the cats who were beginning to settle down like the hens in their coop on deck. On Wednesday afternoon, friends of Tom's came from the College to help paint. In contrast to my isolation on board, my shopping expeditions became delirious delight. Since then, I have always thought that dwellers along the

London River, especially those at Greenwich and Deptford, also World's End, are some of the nicest people that there are.

At dusk I had to climb on deck with an enormous, disgusting, old, old lamp. This had to be hoisted on the forestay, lest we were run down in the dark. It always blew out as hoisted. Eventually I got it to stay alight. From then on I strained my ears, listening for a shout from the shore which would herald the return of the Master. I would set out once more in the dinghy. This time there was a difference: I could not fail to hit the shore at some point, and, thank God, I would not have to row back.

[End of extract].

From this quote it is clear that my world had entirely changed – my status as housewife seemed to be abandoned – I was a simple deck hand – in training at that. This discovery was a bit depressing but it was my own fault – I had started the whole thing. Having a sailor for a husband meant that I was, it seemed, alone on board, looking after his ship.

Chelsea Reach

Life in Chelsea Reach was very pleasant indeed. The King's Road simply flowed with milk and honey. We could have bought baths galore; there were sheets and sheets of asbestos to be brought home in taxis, ourselves sitting in front with the driver. 'Utility' clothes, as well as 'utility' china, could be had at Peter Jones in Sloane Square, while lower down at World's End pots and pots of paint, stains and varnish were stacked out on the pavement. There was also a daily ration of philosophy to be picked up from 'Grandad' at the paint shop. He sat perched on the boss's counter, smoking his terrible tobacco, swinging his old rheumaticky legs as he put the world to rights.

Today, the moorings on Cheyne Walk are extremely popular. The large mud bank on the north side of the river is crowded with craft of all kinds, including converted landing craft from the war. These had begun to arrive in our day. Neat little homes sprang up on their decks with gardens on the roofs, tended by neat little wives in gingham aprons. They all cluster round the old lighter, Pamela Hope (The Pam), which served as a boatyard workshop.

Our own mooring was further up, tucked in under Lott's Road Power Station, beyond which was the Kensington 'Tip'. Rubbish from dustcarts and lorries was poured into barges alongside. These in turn were towed away and the contents dumped on the Maplin Sands, from whence, I read in a newspaper, it was all washed back up the Thames again.

The great enemy was the dirt. The Power Station and Wandsworth Gas Works were like rival volcanoes, one or other was always active and the little tugs on the river also did their best to add to our despair.

We were the last boat but one on a trot of eight. Five of these were old barges, but for the most part their sea-going days were over. Next to us, on the inside, was an enormous barge called The Ash. She was inhabited by a large family with numerous branches, all of whose members claimed to be communists, provoking thereby much 'tut-tutting' in the neighbourhood. They worked very hard converting their home around them and seemed extremely happy.

On our outside was a steel Dutch boyer, the Hendreka, where Francis Baines, a musician, lived. Francis played the double bass in the London Philharmonic Orchestra and later transferred to the Hallé. He spent much of the day composing and a symphony of his was played later that year in Berlin. When the evening concert was in London, members of the orchestra would come back with him for supper on board: omelettes and his wonderful draft

Perrier – pear cider – sent up from carefully chosen growers in Somerset. It was extremely good. After supper they used to play far into the night; the rule was they never played their 'bread-and-butter' instruments but enjoyed themselves playing each other's. We would lie awake in bed, listening or, as summer advanced, we would be on deck gazing into the rich London sky above our masts.

As the days grew longer, we worked late into the night ourselves. I used to cherish the thought that "night must fall" and work cease. Then, one day, Tom found that he could rig an arc light to the mast, thus enabling us to wire brush, putty up or even caulk seams far into the small hours.

During the school term, we painted endlessly, both inside and out: I during the day, helped by Tom in the evenings, unless he had work to do on the rigging.

It was a hot summer, given to thunder showers when rain poured through the dry shrunken wooden decks. The damage caused below by these deluges drove me frantic until we decided to scrape and re-caulk the seams as well. Our little oil cooking stove smelt of tar ever after.

Moored to a pontoon at the head of our trot was a large craft called a Minca, which letters stood for 'Made in Canada'. She was built of wood during the war, a 'dumb' barge used for carrying supplies. She therefore had no engine nor any other means of propulsion and was very roomy inside as a result: ideal for conversion into a houseboat. She was being worked on by a very clever carpenter, called Ted Jones, who later came to help us as well. I was envious of the large windows that could be cut in the ship's side close to the water line without endangering the safety of a ship that was not going to move. The owners and Ted could exercise a glorious freedom of design.

Ted was a find. He was employed at a high rate by the day, but his day began at 8 a.m. and ended about 10 p.m. In that time he contrived the most wonderful builtin furniture made from what material we could find. At the end of the week, when everybody went shopping, Ted's string bag was full of the luxuries that were beginning to creep back on to the market, whereas those who had spent their money on his carpentry were content enough with a herring or two. Ted spent the weekend jiving.

The Minca was inhabited by a major in the Grenadier Guards and his very attractive wife. They raised the standard of our grubby community from time to time by appearing splendidly dressed, threading their way through the mud and debris of the boatyard and driving in a taxi to Buckingham Palace to dine with the King and Queen.

We were all rebels. The river naturally harbours rogues and this may have been contagious. With so many hands against us, it naturally tended to bind us into a rather tight-knit community. We all suffered the dirt and shortages of materials. Our rents were high for few amenities, the Port of London Authority, the P.L.A., did not like people living on the river and still do nothing to encourage them.

It therefore became all the fun in the world, if some planks slipped from a passing lighter, for us to put out in our fleet of dinghies to collect all we could before the river police arrived on the scene. It was a point of honour that anything we did not want ourselves went to the Ash. We once spent a whole afternoon salvaging a large door for them. (Times now, I understand, have changed : anyone taking timber from the river would be considered a benefactor.)

Once a police boat was sent to capture a black cygnet just in front of our mooring. The cygnet managed, whenever the boat was close enough for a stout policeman to lean over the side ready for a pounce, to dart away along the surface of the water, squawking loudly as it did so. Time and again it managed to evade capture. At each escape the boating population cheered, spectators from the embankment joining in, until finally the cygnet won and the game had to abandoned.

It was perhaps this episode that produced a nice conversation, which the Minca wife reported after dinner at the Palace. The King said, "I hope you are looking after my swans down on the River." To which she replied, "Oh your swans – when one had a damaged wing the other day we had the entire Kensington Police out in a boat, but when my bicycle was stolen no one took the slightest notice."

Our sympathies, so easily roused for the underdog or by underprivileged cygnets on the river, were not required for immediate shore dwellers, despite what Dickens tells us about them. All Thames-side inhabitants are sturdy and independent, but those who live around the World's End at Chelsea are known to be a race apart: a singular people, lively, kindly and extremely sharp-witted. They are said to have lived there for generations, indeed, since Chelsea was a small village with a bun shop. Their great-grandparents would have known the notorious Cremorne Gardens.

Dirty and bustling as the river now was, there remained a few tiny reminders of its past beauty. True, the gardens had been done away with – it was said to satisfy the prim Victorian morals of the City merchants, who pushed out into the pleasant suburb of Chelsea. London has got Lott's Road Power Station in their place. But below us, the river swept in a large curve under four exceptional bridges. At low tide, the diminished stream with mud flats on either side had a peculiar peace which contrasted with the bedlam of high tide. On the opposite side further down was Battersea Gardens and one afternoon, as I sat sewing on deck, the scent from the flowering trees was carried to me on the gentle south-easterly breeze.

There was one event, which seriously darkened my life at Chelsea. It might have extinguished the flame altogether. It was in early June, and we were painting in full spate. Our ambition was to take the barge to sea for a short cruise during the summer leave in August. There was a great deal to be done. Friends and acquaintances came to see what it was like to live on the river. We either pressed paintbrushes into their hands or worked around them as best we could.

Then, one day at breakfast, I learnt that a man was coming to look at the engine. Certain preparations had to be made to enable him to get at the part concealed beneath our entrance. I helped Tom dismantle the ladder of the main hatch. We laid it carefully on deck. Tom then left for work. He climbed over the other boats and barges and walked along the Embankment. He waved his straw boater as he re-passed the barge. I did one or two jobs on deck, then filled a little old kettle with paraffin from a tank, and glanced at the view under the four bridges before swinging my leg over the coaming, preparatory to descending by the ladder. There was, of course, none and I jumped straight down the hatchway – an eleven-foot drop!

When the man arrived, apparently, I was wandering about and asked him if he could see why my head was so damp. He took one look and disappeared. He returned with Ted, who also disappeared and returned with an ambulance. There was an ambulance driver and a woman, who turned out to be a keen tea maker. She asked me how to make it on the barge, while the driver bandaged my head. Later I found the matches and lit the oil stove. By now it seemed simpler to go on and make the tea, which came in very handy, I remember, because a few minutes later the fire brigade arrived. They had come, not as you might imagine because I had managed to set the barge on fire with all the paraffin, but because the ambulance man said getting me out was "an awkward sort of a job". The fact that I could walk hurt his professional pride. By now I was fully conscious, feeling light-headed as if intoxicated. I began to enjoy the party very much, until a big burly fireman swung me over his shoulder. We proceeded bumpily up the fore hatch, crossed the deck and went down a ladder into the incoming tide. We waded to the beach where I was laid on a stretcher. I gazed up to the Embankment, where I saw, to my horror, a large crowd had gathered. I closed my eyes at once and assumed unconsciousness while hoisted up over the railings and into the ambulance.

Then a terrible deceit took place. Once inside, the doors closed and we set off. A man I did not remember seeing before sat beside me. He had a hospital entry form in his hand and, sensibly enough, I thought, suggested that time and trouble would be saved by my answering its questions as we drove along. By past experience I knew that hospitals will not take so much as a foreign body out of your eye without knowing if you are a Catholic, Muslim, Seventh Day Adventist, or just C. of E. (Heaven knows what happens to the 'don't knows'.) Unhesitatingly, therefore, I gave him my name, the name of my husband and his profession, my religion and my age. We had just exhausted the whole dreary questionnaire when we reached St. Stephen's Hospital. I then became extremely hazy until late that afternoon.

That evening there was a 'Visitors' Hour'. "We're in", said Tom cheerfully as he threw the Evening News and the Evening Standard on to my bed. He pointed to headlines, and I could just focus. Each paper had a paragraph of about an inch and a half – a tit-bit for weary commuters on the front page. Each had discovered the same joke and had headed it: "COMMANDER'S WIFE 'DOWN THE HATCH'."

There followed all the details I had so innocently given to the horrible man in the ambulance, mentioning that the Fire Brigade had been called in to assist, but, worst of all, in brackets was my exact age. Mortified as I was at having brought ridicule on my husband's name, I am sorry to say that I was more distressed at the publication of the figure in brackets at that moment than of anything else in the world. I had just arrived at the stage in life when one imagines that one looks a great deal younger than one is. I was 40.

A porter who came to move my bed one day told me that the newspapers constantly rang up to ask if I had got any worse. So in the end I had the satisfaction of defeating their morbidity by getting better.

Tom called every evening on his way home. He always had a parcel of herrings in his Burberry pocket. He marinated them and turned the quantities of milk that his permits ordered him, which now went sour, into cream cheese. "Rather slow cooking." I pointed out, but he said he understood the methods and could work while the meal was slowly preparing. "Tom amongst the fish bones." said my sister-in-law, who had dropped in to see how he was getting on and described a macabre scene in Five Sisters: kittens, undisciplined in my absence, everywhere (both cats had families simultaneously), a pungent smell of herrings by the light of a spluttering Tilley lamp, cooking in vinegar, and Tom reading "Plays Unpleasant" by Bernard Shaw.

Five Sisters puts to sea

I returned from my stay in hospital and at once was caught up in preparations as we had planned to take Five Sisters to sea on her first cruise. In every spare minute, Tom worked to finish various jobs, working on the rigging, collecting charts etc. and of course, crew. Our great friends, Bryan and Lavender Westwood, who converted the Barge Atlas at the same time as we were doing Five Sisters, were, of course, coming. We were greatly honoured that Arthur Bennett was to join us – a king of amateur bargees. I was stretched provisioning the ship under strict rationing. Everyone who could, painted.

I do not intend to write fully, blow by blow, of our seafaring life on the Barge Five Sisters because, I have already written a book on that alone. Suffice it now to be a précis of our experiences as a guide through these years, hoping that perhaps readers will catch up with the book itself.

On Chelsea river front we attracted many visitors – Tom's were glamorous Wrens demobbed from the War in the Pacific, whereas mine were decrepit ladies, convalescents from the Women's Accident Ward out on parole. They had to be revived with brandy from the effort of crossing the floating craft of neighbouring boats and then, after much hospitality, helped perilously ashore by Tom, especially if the tide was high.

The school summer holidays were on us and were complicated. Jeremy arrived and John too, but his parents had returned on leave from Malaya and so he departed. His place was filled by Tom's two nieces, who had sadly lost their mother during the last winter. Their father was abroad and so it was agreed they would come to us on the Barge. We ourselves had also suffered a major tragedy that winter, when we lost through jaundice our new-born, and much looked forward to, second baby daughter, who had helped to replace our former loss. So we were all a bit rough, but the young were marvellous, at thirteen years old and eleven, in their resilience and spirit. Somehow, we got by. Their spirits and sense of humour have remained with them throughout their lives and mine.

So we went to sea with six adults and three children and an auxiliary engine which cut out at intervals on our way down the Thames. Our adult crew, though experienced sailors, were unaccustomed to Thames Sailing Barges, especially one that would have been better without our engine. To explain, I include an extract from the ship's log meticulously kept by Tom down the years : -

FRIDAY ~ 6th August. All finished painting. At lunchtime the hens were moved onto the Dalraida (neighbouring barge) with the help of Horace Law and John Holmes.

16:00. Said goodbye to the neighbours. Fred and his mate warped us out to the buoy alongside the Tug Scottie. Very heavy rain. Tom still occupied at work.

06:00 Tom fetched the Turpins (friends from another barge), in the Dinghy, also fetched Ann Holmes. Waited for the ebb before starting.

08:45. Started engine, slipped and turned opposite Lotts Road Power Station. Friends in the colony waved goodbye and Francis blew his foghorn from the Hendreka. Engine stopped very hot in Chelsea Reach just below Albert Bridge. After clearing pump and filling up, engine started but was jammed ahead. Anchor was foul of a mooring but we got it clear and set off again.

10:00 Engine cut just under Westminster Bridge. Anchored off County Hall. Attempted to "drudge" through the temporary bridge but had to be helped by a kindly official. Secured to . . . lighters where we spent the night. roused every quarter of an hour by Big Ben."

The engine cut out twice the following day, but we reached Greenwich towed by a tug. There, close to our mooring at the buoy opposite the Naval College, was a large notice on the roof of a building which read "Jacubait – Marine Engineer." Well, here was our salvation. We heaved out the innards of the Engine, which had earned the name under which it went during the rest of its long life with us – the Great Bastard. We sailed away happily, having engaged the services of a Barge Mate for the weekend. It was a good exchange. He was a good teacher if you understood him – the unfortunate chap had no roof to his mouth, which was complicated with the unfamiliarity of barge terms. Nevertheless, we all survived.

I had two shocks: the first as the weather deteriorated and we split our foresail in a squall crossing the Buxey Sandbank. I discovered that when heeled over in a flat-bottomed barge, the bilge water came up into our living quarters. This not only caused despair to me but was frightening to the children.

The other shock was the Mate's remark on the meal which I had proudly produced that evening. After a stormy passage, we had reached an anchorage with other barges at Brightlingsea in Essex. Beef Bolognese was my intention, made with corn beef and wartime spaghetti, cheese and tomatoes. He rose majestically from the table, having consumed a plateful, with words I could just decipher – "I don't want to be rude or anything, but my wife gives better food to the fowls." Luckily he left next day. After that, it was a great joy for me to exchange him for Arthur Bennett.

Having come to terms after my many shocks and discoveries and the children's seasickness, we settled down into our new life. It was very new. We journeyed on in comparative tranquillity with Arthur, Bryan and Lavender. We settled down to life on the estuaries of the Thames in Essex and Suffolk.

Spreading out our huge foresail in a sail-maker's yard – Taylor's of Maldon (I had proudly repaired it, learning to use a padded palm and a thimble) was enormous fun. The family dressed our sail, using household brooms with some ghastly mixture of red ochre and linseed oil, plus some ingredient I have now forgotten. We discovered the joys of sitting outside a pub with tankards of beer in our hands and looking at our beautiful ship. We swam, we walked and we sailed the dinghy. The children became reconciled to the life as I did, especially when listening to Arthur's stories of the sea. Finally, we returned in due course to Chelsea.

There was one episode, which was alarming. We were anchored on our way up the Thames at Greenhithe, while Tom returned from a day's work at the Admiralty. He was standing on a jetty waiting to come aboard; some other men were also waiting. Quixotically I jumped into the dinghy and Angela cast me off. I had not experienced an ebb tide at this part of the river and had to learn very quickly, as I was immediately swept down-stream at knots towards the mouth. Ashore, the men who ware all waiting for an expected craft noted with dismay a dinghy putting out. One muttered "and it's a woman too." "Yes, "said Tom, "it's my wife." Soon I was picked up by the launch. "Don't you ever go out," they solemnly told me, "in the ebb tide at Hythe."

Back at Chelsea, we found the colony in uproar. The rents had been put up, the services cut and in any case the anchorage was not up to Tom's standard and so on. There was nothing for it but to find a new mooring. A supply of fresh water is always the trouble in finding a mooring. On a very wet Sunday we tramped along the towpath of the Thames. Late in the evening, drenched to the skin we fell into Cubitt's Yacht Basin at Chiswick. Our son charmed the lady commodore of the establishment into giving us tea and offering a berth, which we instantly accepted. So it was that another phase of life afloat started. For some years we lived very happily at

Chiswick, in a boat yard between Chiswick Mall and Kew. We had found a home.

The Yacht Basin was a very special place run by the formidable but extremely kind elderly lady, Miss Prys, who lived in a Thames Barge, the Hibernia. She reigned supreme. She had been sunk in another barge by enemy action during the war. We put our hens ashore; we had a garden and many friends in boats around us. We were joined by Peter and Mary Milburn and their family, old naval friends, who lived in another barge next door for sometime. It was very satisfactory for our two families who played happily in boats. In the autumn of 1949 Tom was made a Captain and our lives changed. Tom returned one day from seeing the authorities at the Admiralty. "How would you like to live in Paris?" he asked on his return.

Paris

We had invited my mother and my aunt to spend Christmas with us on board in Chiswick, a very cosy project for us all. Instead, Christmas was spent at Gravesend in the Barge Builders' and Owners Yard belonging to Woods. In late December having lowered the mast and signed on a crew, we set out for the always exciting journey under the bridges of London at night. It was undertaken on an ebb tide.

The bridges sparkled above us in a million lights, each had its eccentricities of tide as we whirled between the supporting uprights. Past Tower Bridge everything changed, we were free to navigate the broad river, the stars took over which in December are twice as large as usual. We reached Gravesend in the early morning. It was a day or two before Christmas.

The only berth available at the short notice they were able to give looked very adequate until the tide went out, when Five Sisters settled herself happily in the mud but at an angle of some 30 degrees. This situation of course repeated itself every six hours as the ebb set in. I made a cake for Christmas, which came out of the oven looking like the Leaning Tower of Pisa. Despite this peculiar defect and several others, we coped as best we could to reassure my mother and my aunt that there was nothing too odd about our Christmas spent on a slope. They, for their part, showed remarkable fortitude. It was, however, I had to admit, the most peculiar Christmas I have ever spent. Down on the lonely river opposite to Tilbury nothing moved. The world stood still as, perhaps at Christmas, it should do.

The holiday over, the men returned and work to prepare the boat for her new diplomatic role in Paris began.

Tom's day of departure dawned on 2nd January 1950. He was so involved in work on the barge that the taxi was actually alongside on the waterside while he began to pack. He was to leave for London, where he would meet his fellow foundation members of NATO and travel overnight to Paris. At his first conference, he told me that he kept his tar-stained hands beneath the table, lest they astonished his neighbours.

After some essential work was completed on the rigging and hull, Arthur Bennett helped move the Five Sisters to Hoo in Kent where we would be safer from the Southeast winter gales and where he himself and his family lived in his Barge Henry. At Hoo we indulged in various refinements to the interior which up until now had been fairly adequate, but basic. The easiest of these innovations was the installation of a generator to provide us with electricity for lighting, instead of relying on hanging Tilly lights. The generator was placed beside the Great Bastard in the engine room, where she became known as the Little Bitch. Together they decided down the years how to confuse us afresh. However, the chief complication which plagued my life at Hoo involved the installation of a new Siesta Stove from which central heating was to be run. Tom had drawn plans for this. These, however, did not coincide with those proposed by the plumber. It fell to me to explain each to the other. At first I attempted to do so as politely as possible, masking the unflattering things each attributed to the other. The only effect of my solicitude was that each thought, as with all go-betweens, that it was my fault. The plumber avoided me and sulked, while Tom raged by letter or down the telephone from Paris. I rebelled and put the plumber on the line to Paris. This had the effect of bringing Tom back the next weekend. To my astonishment, when they met, each of them became utterly mild and polite, though still suspicious of me. Best of all, our central heating went in without further ado and worked to everyone's satisfaction ever after.

January to March of 1950 was a season of high winds and storms. Improving our interior involved my returning one day from Rochester on a bicycle, with a roll of linoleum under one arm. Supply conditions in shops were still stringent and one was always on the hunt for bargains.

One bargain I had to achieve was to secure a certificate from HM Customs to assure the French authorities of our seaworthiness, before we could enter French waters. One morning, I found my way to a small terrace house in Rochester. Over the door was a board on which was written "HM Customs and Excise". Inside, the equivalent of the front room of the house was bare, except for a table in the middle of the room. There was a hatchway into a back room, which seemed to be full of people talking. I could distinctly hear the chink of cups. At the hatchway a seaman was having a conversation with someone I could not see on the other side. He had to bend to speak. I waited expectantly for my turn, but when it came, a large man with a beady eye looked at me through the hatch and closed it down.

I knocked. After what seemed a long time, the hatch was opened. A girl gave me a malevolent look. I explained what I wanted. She replied that the gentleman I had to see was engaged. She shut the hatch. Cups continued to clink.

Presently, the hatch slid rather stealthily up again and Beady Eye looked out. I explained again what I wanted. He regarded me carefully before telling me what an impossible thing it was that I asked.

“To begin with,” he said, “you have to satisfy us over one or two things. First of all, you have to have a Master to skipper your ship.” Painstakingly, I explained that there was one already. “Certificated?” he asked penetratingly. “Well, no, Navy.” I replied. He looked unimpressed and said “Uncertificated”. Then I would have to show that we had a reliable engine. Indeed we had, I lied. There would have to be adequate security in case the ship caught fire – the list was endless. Then, worst of all – the barge would have to re-measured.

Finally I agreed to call back next day. Meanwhile he would telephone to London to the Ministry of Transport to see if they could possible spare the time to re-measure Five Sisters.

In the end the man did come and I held the end of the measure while he performed these unnecessary calculations. He had forgotten his lunch so he ate my Woolton Pie – a wartime weekly issue but tasty.

Days of further frustration followed over the delay of papers etc. until I suddenly saw red and the futility of the whole thing. I was being taken in. I refused to surrender the original barge papers of 1891 on which I appeared as the last owner.

I set off once more and banged loudly on Beady-Eye's hatch. “Surely,” I said, “ships can just leave England without all this fuss. What happens if they do?” He gave me a cunning look and closed the hatch. I waited and could hear him fumbling with papers. Twenty minutes later, the hatch cautiously opened again. “You'll have to sign this.” he said, passing a form out to me. I signed and the hatch closed. When it next opened, he handed me a bluish paper which bore an official stamp. He suddenly looked benign as I began to read:

“To all to whom these presents may come, I the undersigned Officer of His Majesty King George in the port of Rochester in the city of Rochester send greeting.

Whereas the Vessel called the Five Sisters of Rochester, whose Master is Edmund Thomas Larken, is about to sail from the said port of Rochester on this 17th day of March in the year of our Lord one thousand nine hundred and fifty and from thence for Calais and other places beyond the Seas, with seven persons on board including the said Master. Now, know ye that I, the said Officer, do hereby make known to all men, and pledge my faith thereto, that at the time of granting these presents, no Plague, Epidemic, Cholera nor any dangerous or contagious disorders exists in the above Port or Neighbourhood.

In testimony whereof I have hereunto set my Name and Seal of Office on the day and year aforesaid”.

Alas, the ink has faded and I can no longer read Beady-eye's name, but it has an accent on the second letter signifying French derivation. This document is kept next to the document dated 1891 which I had refused to surrender to the re-measuring man. Both are kept in a most treasured file belonging to Five Sisters.

"To Calais and beyond the seas". How simple. But was it? As I said, that year was full of momentous gales and on 17th March Tom arrived from France, as well as our crew. We would be six in all – four strong men: Colin McMullen from Sheerness with a young Irish cousin of mine Brooke Webb, doing National Service under Colin, Bryan Westwood, Frankie Howey and Arthur Bennett. The Barometer had dropped while everyone was in the train and so we ate supper hoping for better luck next day. It was worse, so the weekend passed with Colin playing our piano and everyone singing and eating up the provisions for the voyage. Sunday night brought the miserable decision that all must go their ways and Tom return to Paris. We would have to wait a fortnight before conditions and everyone's time again fitted. As they left, the wind died down and backed into the East. The sky became clear and gentle: ideal weather for a Channel crossing. Worse still, it looked settled for a long period but would that last over a fortnight and beyond? As a parent, I was mortified. The Easter holidays were upon us and I particularly wanted to spend them in France on the Seine. The children available at that moment were our son Jeremy and Philippa Milburn, whose parents had shared barge life in Chiswick and were crewing for us. After some anxious thought, I rang up Woods' Yard in Gravesend and asked if they knew of a skipper who would sail Five Sisters round to Dover. We would then be well placed to take off as soon as Tom could return. They knew of one, a single-handed skipper. I waited, watching the weather while he took a barge to Ipswich. Then one day there was a firm tread on deck above me and a very neat seaman descended below in a confident manner and shook me by the hand. "Hewson is the name – H silent as in Rhubarb." After a tantalising delay with the wind still easterly, we set off. One of the delays had been that on the morning of our intended departure we were 'neaped' – that is to say there was not enough tide to float the barge. We sat on the mud for yet another day. However, by fastening a rope round an adjacent tree the next morning, we warped our way afloat and got off. I had managed to raise one other member of the crew, Frankie Howey, another Naval friend, who somehow coped with the Great Bastard, thereby giving himself lumbago for which we later used to iron him in days on the Seine.

I had managed to divert our next crew to join us at Dover, all except Tom who missed the message in Paris but transferred joyfully from Hoo to

Dover. Rhubarb left us after doing a magnificent job, while I made him tea and Frankie battled with the G.B. for our entry into Dover Harbour. We then made last minute preparations before setting out to cross the Channel. I had somehow obtained, for a very short time, an aura of sanctity. Being always the least maritime member, I was now asked how Rhubarb would have done this or that and was listened to avidly. It lasted for a few days and then I reverted to my usual more humble status.

Our first landfall was Boulogne – not Calais and beyond the Seas. Boulogne was a very post-war town with booths for shopping but we had arrived on French soil. Our real arrival in style was in Honfleur on the mouth of the Seine, having collected the children at Dieppe. After a magnificent night sail down the Channel, we reached Honfleur on Good Friday in perfect weather. We were received as only the French can do, with the Customs on board drinking strong coffee and red wine, presenting us with a further document "In the Name of the President of the Republic..." to take its place with Beady-Eye's. We were locked into the famous basin and it was heaven: all the sounds of France around us like a big bell being tolled across the water, wonderful food in the market, primroses to be gathered, 'moules' to be eaten and a climb up to the stone church of Ste Marie de la Garde, the sailors' and fishermen's church overlooking the Baie de la Seine. Inside, the church was filled with little memorials to survivors from danger, commemorated by small hand-made models of ships. It was also high up here that painters in the days of Impressionism sat smoking and drinking at a nearby café. Our visit to Honfleur, bathed in Easter sunshine, was a never-to-be forgotten respite. We made great friends in Honfleur. The maritime town was extremely interested in our craft, many remembering the days when Thames Barges frequently traded with the town. Old salts discussed the rigging, explaining it to each other. . We reached Rouen after a two-day sail and here everything changed. To begin with, we lost the fine weather and then our original crew, who had to get back to England. Only the children remained. Before the crew left, we lowered the mast and from now on had to depend on the Great Bastard. Tom's leave was up and he returned to Paris. He would return the following weekend with a crew from NATO (not yet called NATO but EMMO). The children and I would look after the ship until Friday. The greater part of our journey was now behind us, at least on the map, but under the aegis of the Great Bastard the major part still lay ahead.

The Seine

I was very nervous meeting the new crew from Paris next weekend. They were all from Tom's office and were keen to see Five Sisters. They were charming and brought their wives and children. We settled down as the trip spread out into weeks into a harmonious party. Two strong men became adept at swinging the G.B. into action which then ran for a few hours before heating up and by Sunday night had put itself out of action. So the children and I spent from Monday to Friday at various small towns along the Seine. Most memorable was our stay at Mantes-la-Jolie. The river front had been demolished during the war as the Allies had crossed the Seine at the very point where we lay. The lovely old bridges had been destroyed by the retreating Germans and piles of debris led up to the Cathedral above. The liberation had claimed eight hundred victims in a twenty-minute bombardment. In spite of this terrible and avoidable accident of war, we never experienced anything but friendly good manners while there. Monday morning of that week found everyone busy getting off to return to the office in Les Invalides where they worked. They dressed in their town clothes. As Tom was preparing to leave for the station, he placed the punctured G.B's exhaust on the deck in the engine room. "You will have to find someone to mend the silencer," he said, as he jumped ashore.

"What is it called?" I shouted after his retreating form scrambling up the debris.

"Tuyau d'échappement." he shouted back, as he ran to join the others. Dumbfounded at my situation, I gathered my mental resources together. I was driven by necessity to achieve our project I wanted to get to Paris above all else. No one seemed inclined to come and look at our Tuyau d'echappement. They all had better things to do. There was nothing for it but the Tuyau must go to them. We fitted it into a suitcase and I set out again, this time for a little atelier (workshop) on the far side of the river. I left the children behind, as I had a sneaking feeling that they spoke better French than I did. I crossed by one of the army temporary bridges and tramped for some way. I could just carry the suitcase.

I found a little shack of a workshop. The proprietor, in blue overalls and wearing steel-rimmed spectacles, was preoccupied, bending over his work. He was talking to a friend. I stood and waited for a good moment to speak. Feeling very much a fish out of water or a woman in a man's world, I at last began to speak as politely and proficiently as I could. He listened impatiently to my halting French and soon began to shrug and “aw”' at the same time. “If I had the time, Madame, and if I could get to the river, which you understand is some way off (I did understand that point).. . . but without seeing your tuyau ... it is impossible, you understand ....”

“Mais, Monsieur,” I cried, triumphantly opening the suitcase, “voici le tuyau d'échappement!”

He was astonished and was tricked into giving me his attention. First he took off his spectacles and cleaned them, then he put them on again and peered at the enormous rent in the silencer. He became very kind and confidential. The outcome was that if I went to the Renault works and asked for Monsieur Healy, an Englishman (H silent as in Rhubarb) he, with all his equipment, would be able to help me.

Well, that's what I did. Mr. Healy, who had married a French girl after the war, proved a great asset. When Friday evening came I was able to display a mended Tuyau. Mr. Healy came on board to meet the Master and drink wine with us and, of course, to discuss the engine. The patched up tuyau took us as far as Maisons Lafitte, where the French Navy installed a flexible tuyau that lasted us for some years. From here, Tom took the children back to England for school once more, while I looked after the barge and listened to the nightingales, which sang all night.

The Quai d'Orsay

At last, on Saturday 16th May, with the new pneumatic exhaust installed, we chuffed our way triumphantly into Paris and tied up in the very centre at the Quai d'Orsay. This was due to the auspices of Jacques du Gareau, Tom's opposite number in the French Navy and a great friend and ally of Five Sisters.

We had picked up friends at Vincennes. From then on, the ship was packed with members from the Office and their offspring. Children of all nationalities managed to understand each other and to encourage each other in mischief. However, it was such a moment of triumph that such things mattered very little as long as they did not fall overboard. I was so occupied that the special trousers from Lillywhite's, bought with this very occasion in mind, remained hanging in the cupboard. We both looked our part – bargees. Various people came to call on us which was a little embarrassing as supplies of champagne began to fail, but we soon discovered that vin ordinaire was the equivalent of only two shillings a bottle.

Very early next morning, I put a drowsy head up the hatch. A city of trees and open spaces greeted me.

The quay itself was wide and gravelled. Against the high wall on the landside grew large plane trees and trees grew in the street above its stone balustrade. Across the Seine, row upon row of chestnut trees had just broken into leaf and their fat embryonic pink and white flower buds were thrusting out into the sun.

Exactly opposite to us on the far bank was moored a long houseboat, an old péniche newly painted white. Along her deck, between festoons of geraniums, were written in large letters the words 'Touring Club de France'. A few small boats nuzzled against her side.

To the right and above the Touring Club, the early morning traffic was beginning to weave its intricate pattern on the Place de la Concorde. It moved with the deftness of a ballet and windscreens sparkled in the sunlight.

The stone quays glistened in the clear morning air and the reflected bridges shimmered in the moving water. The gold of the Pont Alexandre III had been cleaned that year. Above the bridge, four sparkling horses grouped on the arched roof of the exhibition building, the Grand Palais, reared high into the sky, in salutation, it seemed, to a gilded morning in May.

Five Sisters lay at one with her surroundings. Her tall mast reached the tips of the trees that grew in the street above. Her brown sails hung neatly brailed: her black and blue hull looked the acme of good taste. She accepted her new circumstance with undisturbed dignity and perfect grace, mistress of her situation.

Our own first few days were less tranquil and more bewildering. To get down to earth – or more appropriately to water – on that first morning, our tanks were completely empty. The sink was piled high with every piece of glass or crockery that we possessed and not a drop could be squeezed from the taps.

We gave ourselves coffee at a small tabac and each ate a brioche. Tom went to his office to tackle the water problem by telephone, while I went back to Five Sisters and viewed the shambles with distaste. After some time a black car drew up on the quayside and two men got out. They peered incredulously at Five Sisters, and then finally, somewhat uneasily, they stepped on board.

One was Monsieur Chauvin, a small lightly built man, wearing a grey suit. The other, large and middle aged, spoke little but was constantly appealed to and shrugged at by Monsieur Chauvin. Monsieur Chauvin shrugged a great deal during the next half-hour, making deprecatory noises around the words "Mais, Madame ....." The truth was that Monsieur Chauvin did not want to give us water.

He asked how long we expected to stay in Paris. "Anything up to two years, Monsieur." produced such exchanges of horror between the two men that I might have given up all hope of water and therefore remaining at this quay. However, I somehow got the impression that Monsieur Chauvin had only to strike the stones of the Quai d'Orsay and water would gush out. It was only after his second visit that morning that this proved to be more or less the case.

There was a flap in the wall across the quay opposite our mooring. When opened, this revealed the most enormous tap, fed from a gigantic system of pipes beneath the road above. Below the bridge, the Pont Alexandre III, was a door behind which a suitable enormous hose was kept. That afternoon two men trundled the hose out on a trolley and in a twinkling our tanks were filled.

During the whole time we spent in Paris this performance was repeated each time we needed water. Monsieur Chauvin would arrive and wring his hands, refusing to co-operate with polite, if hopeless, expressions of regret. The 'Old Fruits', as they became known by Tom, waiting for the sign, would advance with their hose on the trolley as soon as resistance had been worn down. Shouts, gestures and gushing water would then intermingle, all in exchange for a bottle of wine – white in summer, red in winter. For full domestic use, as opposed to cruising, when we had to be careful, we filled our tanks every ten days. We got to know Monsieur Chauvin and those Old Fruits very well indeed before we left.

The reason for this extraordinary pantomime was, we discovered, an old administrative quarrel. Our quay was the possession of the French Navy. The Navigation de la Seine, of whom Monsieur Chauvin was a representative, resented the Navy's rights and liked to exercise control over the water supply. The French, however, are excellent hosts, and Monsieur Chauvin too kind a man to be capable of obstruction beyond a face-saving point. When he appeared in his official capacity at the various functions that took place on the Seine, of which there were many, he always waved from the committee boat with apparent enthusiasm. We in our turn used to wave back with warmth.

The Quai d'Orsay has meant to most people, particularly in time past, the French Foreign Office, romantic, remote and powerful. In our day it was still a hub of diplomatic activity with smart limousines coming and going. It managed to look imposing, withdrawn and delightfully cool behind its deep blue sunblinds.

Down on the quay we saw the reverse side of the coin. We lived between the police and the down-and-outs. Every morning when the Chamber of Deputies, situated next to the Foreign Office, was sitting, a neat blue van arrived and took up position on the ramp of the bridge under the shady trees. Inside, a dozen or so gendarmes would spend the day playing cards. If the debates in the House became heated, another van and occasionally a third would arrive. I do not know if our own MPs are so protected from savaging each other – perhaps our lack of Latin blood makes it unnecessary. Anyway, there they sat, day after day, playing poker and occasionally rushing into the Chamber to separate the Deputies. When evening came they would pack it up and drive off, leaving us with our nearest residential neighbours, les clochards who camped permanently beneath the Pont Alexander III – they were always friendly, but the stench was powerful.

The hell of living down on the quay was the long trudge to the shops. Most people in France contrive to live close to shops. This is not difficult as a rule, so no one minds carrying back milk, wine and long loaves of delicious bread as well as everything else. For me, down on the quay, with a long flight of steps to climb to the administrative centre and with avenues of fast flowing traffic to cross, it was not so easy. Nor was it possible to shop twice a day as the French do, in the morning and again before the evening meal.

At first negotiating the tremendously fast traffic was a hair-raising ordeal. Finally I took courage from a blind lady who asked me to see her across the four avenues in the Esplanade des Invalides. Appalled by the responsibility but determined to take no risk, I waited my chance until finally she pushed me into the traffic with a firm pressure on my arm and the words "Maintenant, Madame." and somehow we whirled through! She released my arm with touching thanks, but a whimsical smile and the advice: "Madame, jamais reculer." After this I took my bicycle and hung massive baskets on the handlebars. All too often, the food was consumed immediately after my return to the barge by visitors who happened to have dropped in while I was out foraging. The weather that summer was very hot and I soon devised a plan for storing the food: each morning a man and cart arrived on the quayside calling, "Glace, glace." One of us would rush out with an old vest and wrap up a large chunk of ice to put in the firebox of the Rayburn; the oven then became a perfect refrigerator. Hot meals were cooked on an oil stove.

One day, as I came down the steps of the Pont Alexandre III in the early afternoon, I noticed that a larger crowd than usual had gathered by Five Sisters I realised that something unusual was going on. In fact someone was clearly giving a party on board: there were people sitting, standing and lounging about on deck. Furious as I became at this intrusion, I was particularly piqued to notice that no one appeared to be enjoying themselves; and small wonder, for as I looked more closely I noticed another peculiar thing was that everyone had come most inappropriately dressed: although the day was exceptionally cool and overcast, no one had very much on.

On the quay a middle-aged, thin, dragonish woman, wearing the inevitable black, tailormade suit of the day, was shrieking to the girls on board. I pushed through the crowd and addressed myself to her. Without pausing she waved a hand in the direction of the crowd behind her, and there I saw a fat man who was fussing round a camera on a tripod. I accosted him, but managed to make little impression until I announced, with as much dignity as I could muster, trembling with rage, "Monsieur, moi, je suis la propriétaire."

His manner changed at once to smooth and conciliatory. He infinitely regretted that no one had been at home for him to ask permission, and so he had taken the liberty. He felt sure that we would not object when I heard his was the house of the grand couturier – Balmain. He added slyly that he had read in the Honfleur Courier that we were very amiable.

Neither this information nor the strident voice from the edge of the quay to the disdainful girls soothed me. A prolonged argument was avoided, as I believe they must have taken all the photographs they needed, but we never saw them in print. The poor freezing girls drooped off Five Sisters, whose mast and sprit seemed to look down on the whole affair with amusement. The girls wrapped themselves up and, followed by the dragon lady, got into a taxi and drove off. Monsieur packed his tripod and camera and the rest of the company into another taxi – I must indeed be an egoist, he threw at me through the window as a parting shot, to keep such a fine ship to myself. It would not be the same if I called at his house of haute couture. I hesitated, tempted, but thought of the dragon lady in attendance and preferred indignation to compensation.

It cannot be denied that Five Sisters had a most distinguished address: the Quai d'Orsay. But she laid claim to much deeper snobbery: she was on the Left Bank. The Right Bank, be it expensive, smart or tawdry, always looks to the Left for thought and inspiration. The Right visits the Left almost as a duty, but the Left stays quietly on the left, just living and sometimes thinking. Five Sisters enjoyed her status of the Left Bank, which brought great benefits with it. The first of these was the students.

The painting was a very happy institution, which became established by a casual meeting on a Saturday early in June. We had been down to the Latin Quarter discovering some churches, which had been old when Abelard had lived, older than Notre Dame and built in clearings in the forest. As we sauntered down the ramp from the bridge, we noticed two young people sitting on the quay beside Five Sisters. One was a fair, pretty English girl with the kind of looks that one is pleased to know are considered English on the Continent. The other was a good-looking, tall, slim young Scotsman. They had spied Five Sisters of Rochester and had decided to wait until her owners returned.

We invited them on board and they stayed to lunch. After lunch they begged for some job on deck, which we for our part readily found, and so the afternoon wore pleasantly on. When leaving they promised to return the following Saturday with other recruits, and so the habit began which lasted throughout our time at the Quai d'Orsay. In exchange for the work we provided tea and an evening meal of omelette, wine and cheese. Five Sisters was maintained at a high level by young people of many different nationalities and for many years the quay bore marks of our particular blue paint. Later, our niece Muff brought further contingents of students from Trinity College, Dublin.

The maintenance of Five Sisters brought us face to face with an acute difficulty: one that the whole delegation faced after the first few dazzling weeks. When we came to France we left Austerity England behind and found ourselves in Europe flourishing under Marshall Aid. Shops were full of food that had not been known in England for several years. Butchers' shops displayed rows of succulent, beautifully prepared joints of meat; we drooled past delicatessen shops, charcuteries, with a bewildering variety of cold meat and delectable cooked food; the markets were stacked high with vegetables, fruits and cheese with which France is peculiarly blessed. Our gastric juices became out of control during the first few glorious weeks – until we discovered the awful truth: there was to be no allowance for our delegation to buy what shops offered nor to meet the inflation current in France – England had run out of money. Sir Stafford Cripps, the Chancellor, was adamant.

In any case to maintain a Thames barge is always costly and, of course, we could not afford to buy materials in France, even if all the things we needed had been obtainable. It became the custom for people who had to return to London from the office to ask Tom if they could bring anything back. This was a great kindness, especially when a tin of Hercules Glue oozed its tarry mixture on to a carpet in the night ferry to Dunkirk. We also had friends at the Admiralty to whom these things could be delivered and then picked up from there.

I came back once with a barge's shackle among my underclothes. A yacht's shackle can be anything from one to, say, three or four inches of galvanized metal, but a barge shackle can be eight inches of one-and-a-half inch thick, cast iron. "What," said the astonished customs officer at Dieppe, who was suspicious of the weight of my suitcase, "does Madame do with this? Are you afraid of assassins in France?".

A wing commander off to London dropped into Tom's office to ask what, if anything, he could bring back. Tom was having trouble with the ship's batteries; they were becoming very elderly, and the Little Bitch worked daily to maintain a reasonable state of charge. We depended entirely upon them for our light each evening. Tom was anxious to obtain a hydrometer to take the density of the electrolyte.

"I would be grateful if you could bring back a hydrometer, Steve." he said.

Two days later Steve walked into the office. It was evening and Tom was working late.

"Well, I've got him," he said quietly, "he's washing. Shall I bring him in to see you or give him a drink first?"

"Who, for God's sake?"

"The hydrographer, don't you remember, you asked me to bring one back? I've brought one from the Air Ministry."

Tom's face went ashen as his accustomed invective burst forth with more than usual vigour.

"Bloody hell, Steve....." Steve put his hand in his pocket and quietly drew out a hydrometer.

My mother came to visit us. She arrived after a severe illness, but France was so much her spiritual home that my brother thought the benefits of a semi-convalescence with us would far outweigh the rigours and upheaval of the journey. And lo and behold, he was right. After only a week, she declared that she could not go another day without having her hair permanently waved. This was a splendid sign; my mother was what the French call "coquette."

So I made careful enquiries and settled on a hairdresser called (unromantically, I thought) Agg. Agg was in the Rue François Premier in a very superior quartier. The day I unwarily fixed on was 13th July.

Tom was away that day in Rome, but he was expected back about lunchtime, in order, he said, to go to the bank. I have already mentioned that we lived a rather hand to mouth existence. We ourselves lunched early so that my mother could cash a travellers cheque on the way to Agg. Alas, to our dismay at the Bureau de Change at the Aerogare there was a queue several hundred yards long.

"Oh well," I said, "let's take a taxi and Tom will be home soon. He is going to the bank so I shall have the housekeeping money when I come to fetch you. You can cash your cheque tomorrow." What simpler?

I deposited my mother at Agg's which proved to be a most sumptuous and apparently affluent place with a very expensive air. Having no more money myself, I plodded home in the heat of a blisteringly hot afternoon. On the top step, as I pushed back the hatch cover, was a note, which said "Captain Larken has been detained in Rome. He hopes to be back by midnight."

I sank down in consternation in the kitchen. How on earth was I to bail my mother out of Agg's, the exquisite Agg's, without ignominy, or worse, not at all?

After a time, I noticed a foul bluebottle fly had settled on an empty milk bottle. Of course – "La consigne!" In France then, and perhaps now, one paid a deposit for each milk bottle. This one was worth 30 francs (old money). Off I trotted with renewed vigour to the Epicerie, where Madame gave me my 30 francs. I crossed the road to the Tabac and bought a jeton, a sort of counter made to fit into public telephone boxes. I asked for the number of Tom's office at Les Invalides. Gilbert listened sympathetically. He agreed that the situation was grave but, he said, he would pass the hat round. Then, if he had any success, he would be at the window on the inner courtyard. To my infinite relief, Gilbert was waving something and leaning out of the window. The contents of the 'hat' contained, it turned out, 1000 francs extra because the next day was the great 14th July, the Fall of the Bastille and all banks would be shut, said Gilbert, for the next five days.

Relieved beyond measure, I set out to trace my weary way back to Agg's. The shop was in the process of closing: sunblinds were being furled, floors swept and the staff leaving. There sat my mother, exquisitely coiffured, on a pale pink satin studded sofa, idly turning the pages of an exotic fashion magazine.

"Do you know," she said, "I thought you were never coming!"

"I nearly wasn't." I replied.

Every August, Paris empties. The exodus begins as early as the end of June when the school year ends. Baccalauréat students by this time are prostrate with exhaustion and nervous tension. Children look pale and washed out. In the streets by the end of July, only the concierges and their families are seen scuttling along to the Epicerie, boulangerie and market. By August, the shopkeepers themselves begin to put up notices – "Fermeture Annuelle." and then the restaurants exchange "Fermeture Hebdomadaire" (which to the non-classical scholars means 'weekly') for "Annuelle." thus seeming to put dust sheets over the townsman's great preoccupation in life: eating, drinking and conversation. The unfortunate people who are left tramp the lonely streets to find the one remaining open shop in the quartier. Deserted buildings take on a menacing aspect, footsteps echo and the whole undertaking, once so pleasant, becomes a great bore.

Our French friends all left with their families at the end of July to join grandparents, uncles and aunts in 'properties' on the coast or in the mountains. We were as anxious as anyone to get out of Paris. With the long hot days the level of the Seine had sunk and the waters had become slow flowing and turgid. Decomposing drowned animals got lodged between the barge's side and the quay. They constantly had to be eased through upon their way with an oar – a most disagreeable occupation. We planned to get above Paris, towards the country near Fontainebleau. Here the water above the town would be clean for swimming and the air fresh for relaxation and recuperation for six whole weeks.

Two small friends of Jeremy's, Tim and Jo, and their mother, were coming to stay, and others were to follow. Feeling by now very reduced after the heat and tempo on the quay, I began to wonder how I would manage with the new influx and be able to carry the summer holidays, coping with new places and shops.

I need not have worried. We came in contact with a charming French girl, Jacqueline, who joined us in order to help me and to learn English. She already spoke it very well and applied herself and her humour to studying the English. Her help was simply beyond my dearest dreams. She and her entire family of all generations became great friends over the years down to the present day.

On an August evening, with some of our Irish students who came for the ride, we set off to explore the Seine above Paris. Next day we found our island: on an offshoot of the main river it lay. For some weeks Five Sisters was cocooned beneath heavenly willow-trees overhanging the water, caressing shade after the blistering heat of the Quai in Paris.

The Island became our home. It was inhabited by birds, butterflies and all the things that live close to the earth. It was a paradise for cats and small boys, who could squirm through the undergrowth and escape detection. We could swim on either side of the Island. Before breakfast it was pleasant to dive in off Five Sisters, swim about in the early morning sunshine and climb out by the half-lowered leeboard. Below in the kitchen stood a jug of steaming hot coffee.

On the other side of the Island was a little sandy beach, just large enough for sunbathing. The river had hollowed out the ground from beneath the trees and one could lie in the current of the main stream, holding on to a root and watch the little river animals who were un-suspecting of a human presence.

Soon we began to lose the desperate sense of urgency that city life generates. I can remember lying listlessly in the water and looking up into the sky. A foot suspension bridge crossed the Seine a little below the Island. It led to the village of Evry Petit Bourg and a boy on his bicycle was wobbling his way across to the village. What two brilliant inventions: the suspension bridge and the bicycle – as simple and effective as Five Sisters herself. There are moments when it is impossible not to mourn for that world without the internal combustion engine.

The boy was replaced on the bridge by the rotund curé in his flat hat, in conversation with a Dominican monk, wearing the white and black habit. Both crossed from the direction of the village.

Everything about Evry Petit Bourg was of a toylike quality. One felt that even the porter at the station hardly believed in its real existence as he sent up his cry, filling his lungs like an organ in crescendo and cadence – "E . . .vry Petit Bourg." as the train pulled in. The railway ran parallel to the river and the road crossed it at right angles. The station snuggled behind two neat rows of chestnuts, espalier and square cut. The town plan, in fact, resembled a hot cross bun. Beyond the station, under a tracery of trees trained to form an awning, lay the small market. Here we bought all we needed or could afford, which included little melons now in season, globe artichokes and grapes – modest but delectable fare. On each side of the main street were small cafes, with tables under their awnings, beside the sandy road.

Jacqueline tells me that the town I describe has gone forever, swallowed up in the sprawl of small houses for commuters from Paris. I shall hope never to destroy the picture of Evry Petit Bourg that is indelibly printed on my mind.

Our life flowed smoothly along. The boys made a camp, the cats went hunting and Jacqueline's family came to visit us, bringing a picnic and cousins. Jacqueline coped admirably with the schoolboys and helped them to catch swallowtail butterflies. She even endured our yacht piano, which was saying a good deal as she was in those days something of a pianist. Pat, my brother, and his family collected Muff and called on us as they went south for their holiday.

We were so delighted with the Island that we decided to stay on well into September. The weather was still perfect and Tom could commute to work from Evry Petit Bourg. He and Pierre, a French boy who had joined us, were rowed ashore every morning and collected in the evening. The early morning swim became a brisk affair and we lit the Rayburn. I can think of few things more satisfactory than drinking coffee from that steaming jug beside the kitchen stove's warm heat and dripping on to the deck on a crisp September morning.

Finally we returned to Paris, just in time for the children to get back to school. The days were shortening noticeably as we slipped into our berth on the Quai d'Orsay. Jacqueline's parents came to meet us. A great change had come over the quay in our absence: to begin with, we were glad we had lit the kitchen fire, and to our surprise we now had neighbours. To M. Chauvin's despair, three boats were moored alongside the quay and these were shortly joined by another. M. Chauvin seemed to think it was our fault for being there in the first place.

The Villa Betaana

Tom had occasion to go with others from Nato to Toulon and we decided that I should join them there, and that Tom and I would go on to Antibes to the hotel where Pat and family had stayed during the summer. With great excitement for a break I set off.

It so happened that an acquaintance was making the same journey at the same time and we agreed to travel together. This was a good idea except that at Avignon he persuaded me that it was ideal to get out of the train, cross the line to another platform and have a cup of tea. He knew the form and that there would be heaps of time. He did not know my anxious temperament when travelling. I could stand the strain no longer and persuaded him to return across the line to our own platform – just in time as the train began to move – I wondered if he was trying to abduct me as I sank, a nervous wreck, into my seat.

Tom met me at Toulon and informed me that we were invited to dine that night with the Prefect of Toulon. Luckily I had a frock that would be suitable and off we set from the hotel into the country and to a very grand house. To my dismay the fateful Mistral was blowing and my coiffure was demolished on the door step.

As a result I was shown upstairs into a beautiful bathroom to rearrange myself. Unfortunately, possibly because I was unaccustomed to houses and beautiful bathrooms, I decided to make the most of it and turned on a tap. Nothing came at first until suddenly a blockage cleared itself and I was soaked from head to foot – hair and all. I stood dumbfounded for a minute and thought. There was nothing I could do, I could not remain in the bathroom so I set forth downstairs and entered the Salon where everyone was drinking cocktails. Tom approached me "What the hell has happened?" "The tap had an air-lock", I explained. I was handed a drink.

The dinner table was a long one. I sat opposite the Prefect's wife. The warmth of the meal began to dry me off and towards the end I noticed that she was looking at me with some curiosity. My dress was 'shot' in colour of the blue/green variety, which really was rather fortunate; I comforted myself with hoping that I was thereby less conspicuous. Anyway I dried off before we were returned to the cars to be driven away to the hotel. "What on earth were you doing turning taps on when you only wanted to comb your hair?" asked my bewildered husband. "You are a bloody fool Peg" he remarked as he fell asleep. This was his favourite summing up of my character. Next day we took the train to Antibes and from there by bus a few days later to Cagnes-sur-mer.

It is time that Aunt Elsa came back into the story. First I have to go back to days before marriage when I was working in the architect's office. It started as a golden dream but it faded as dreams often in reality do.

By this time Uncle Charles had retired from Egypt and, in order to avoid the English winters, he and Aunt Elsa had built themselves a house in the south of France at Cagnes-sur-Mer. I have described how my mother and I visited them there in 1938.

Before I was married, or even thought seriously to do so, I came home one Saturday from London for the weekend. My mother told me that Aunt Elsa was in the garden and that the last Lady Herkomer, her second step-mother (the 'wicked' one), had died and was being buried in the churchyard just over the hedge from our garden. She stressed that Aunt Elsa was particularly anxious to see me as soon as possible so, with a certain amount of trepidation, down the garden path I went. And there she was looking very pensive and walking slowly up and down the path that ran parallel to the churchyard next door.

"Here you are," she began. "This is a solemn occasion in my life. You know that my stepmother Lady Herkomer has died and is being buried at this moment," to which I assented. "Well," she went on "I owe her nothing and do not wish to be present but I like to think my own thoughts in the peace of this garden." This I understood.

"Now you know that your mother was the nearest I ever had to a sister and that due to your grandmother's kindness my brother and I grew up – otherwise we would have starved". This I pondered about. "That being so," she went on, "I wish after Uncle Charles's death that you should be my heir." I was flummoxed. "Now my reason is this – your mother and I are of similar age so that we may die at about the same time – double death duties would impoverish any legacy I leave. You will never let your mother starve, that is for sure. So you will treat your mother as the owner of the villa until her death and after that it will be for you and your husband, if you have one, to enjoy. On this subject she became emphatic, "I beseech you to be careful – always make yourself comfortable in life." This filled me with alarm – I was already mixed up with Tom and doubted if comfort was on the menu should he and I ever marry – adventure was not in Aunt Elsa's vocabulary for living. However I managed to mumble my gratitude as best I could, feeling very unworthy, uneasy and self-conscious.

About a year later Tom and I did decide to marry. Aunt Elsa came for her annual visit and I took him to have lunch with her at Bushey Hall Hotel where, this time, she was staying. I was a little apprehensive: Tom was not a conventional person, but then nor was Aunt Elsa. We started rather shyly then suddenly he won hands down when the waiter placed a plate before her: the gravy sauce was in danger of overflowing but Tom took a knife and balanced the plate safely before the waiter returned to be admonished. "He is resourceful and I like that," said Aunt E, and I heaved a sigh of relief. After that she always referred to him as the Admiral.

As regards the Villa Betaana ever belonging to my mother and myself we somehow could not imagine it. The person who thoroughly enjoyed the idea was my brother , Pat, who foresaw many happy holidays for all of us down the years to come.

We married, and then in 1938 my mother and I, as I have said, paid a visit to the Villa. It was near to the sea, overlooked the Nice Golf Course on which the famous and notorious played, watched from the balcony by Aunt Elsa. It was a stone's throw from the sea where Aunt Elsa took her morning dip – it had a nice garden. It also had two Italian servants who kept the place immaculate. I still did not believe the dream.

In the summer of 1939 Aunt Elsa and Uncle Charles were on their usual visit to England and spent a night in Calais en route. An unexpected tragedy now struck. Poor Aunt Elsa was discovered sitting peacefully in front of an open window while Uncle Charles was below enjoying an evening sundown drink. He returned to find that she had suffered a heart attack and apparently died peacefully in the soft evening light.

Inconsolable, Uncle Charles came on alone. She was buried next to her father in Bushey Churchyard and, unavoidably and ironically, next to her stepmother. Uncle Charles never returned to France or to the villa at Cagnes.

He had nieces in Wales and remained with them and was there when war broke out. He missed a terrible ordeal for elderly compatriots who fled from the south of France in a collier in the utmost discomfort for the rather spoilt wealthy aged.

He used to write to me telling me where I would be able to find things when the time came. The war and family life engulfed me completely so it was still hard to take things in, and anyway Uncle Charles was alive.

In 1942 I was standing in the hall of a house where we were then living in Bath when I read a telegram telling me of Uncle Charles's death. One day later everything around me was reduced to rubble as the luftwaffe blitzed Bath and left us homeless.

The Villa lay submerged beneath a sea of troubles as the war wound its weary way through the next six years. Somehow news filtered through that the Italian servants had left, that the car had been commandeered, that the Italian army took over the house. They were careful and even made an inventory of the furniture. Then the Germans took over the whole of France and the villa fared badly. Little news then came through to us but the place was pillaged for lead, electrical wiring and all fittings, baths, basins etc. Fortunately the furniture had been removed by Uncle Charles's solicitor and was in store.

In the chaos that followed the end of the war travel was difficult, almost impossible, and expensive, if possible at all. Uncle Charles's solicitor wrestled with the French authorities. We were in arrears with the ordinary taxes, but I was fined for the delay and also not being a blood relation there was a further tax to pay. It became evident that the furniture in store must be sold then to meet some of these arrears: the French were out for anything they could get.

Tom took leave and we went by train to Antibes where we took a bus to Cagnes-sur-Mer. So much had changed but I was just able to find my way to the villa. It stood looking very down at heel, but in a garden overflowing with carnations and vegetables. The solicitor had warned us that the Germans had left a ruin, which the local people had raided further for anything useful. He also told us that it was now occupied by Italian squatters, in fact a poor family of market gardeners. We walked up to the front door, a solid door of good craftsmanship, as Aunt Elsa would have had it. We knocked loudly.

A small girl opened the door. We stood for a moment in mutual surprise. I pulled myself together and produced the speech I had prepared: "Bonjour. Moi Je suis la Proprietaire". The small girl instantly closed the door. We stood in uncertain silence. A few minutes passed and the door opened again and there stood a dark-haired, colourful Italian peasant who threw open his arms and welcomed us with a huge smile; his wife, a small thin woman, stood behind him and came forward with a confused smile on her face. Behind their parents stood two rows of offspring who were each called forward to be presented. It suddenly took on the flavour of medieval landlords returning to their estate after a long absence.

Amidst all this bonhomie we were invited in and taken round the poor shell of the house – how they managed to live in any comfort I don't know. There were a few beds, a cot, rather dirty covers, but not much else. We climbed to the top of the house and I looked as I had done with Aunt Elsa at the lovely view across the plain to the Alpes Maritimes with the winter sun beginning to set, a little snow already on their summits. The garden below was beautifully, neatly cultivated. The children were there picking carnations: it was clearly a market garden. I felt relief that at least someone was enjoying the place.

It became time to go for the bus and as we left with so much good will on their shining faces a huge armful of carnations was pushed into my arms – the ones the children had been picking.

Next day they were triumphantly got back to Paris – the only produce from our estate.

The end was that with Marshall Aid the French decided to make the whole place into the Nice Race Course and pulled down all the houses in their way, including the Villa Betaana and the golf course. Finally in 1956 we at last received our compensation. It was a shrunken sum but it made it possible to improve our Thames sailing barge and we bought a second-hand car. This was not the life of comfort that Aunt Elsa had envisaged. Sadly my mother had died before then so had no fun from the Villa Betaana.

Incidentally, to help finance the villa, Aunt Elsa had left us money in Russia – the Russian Imperial Loan of 1913 – Kiev Tramways and Railway shares. All useless until Gorbachev came over to England and paid something towards old debts. With £500 I took my grandchildren and great niece for a wonderful holiday in Ireland to meet their Irish cousins.

A friend of mine pointed out that without wars and revolutions down the years, the investments at compound interest would have been a lot, so I was a millionaire manqué – luckily Barge improvement, Ireland and a Ford Prefect car was blessing enough.

Paris Year II

Immediately ahead of Five Sisters was an old comfortable launch occupied by an elderly couple, the Choseneskis. Madame Choseneski had been an opera singer in Warsaw. She had golden hair, now fading, piled high on top of her head and her bust, like most opera singers, was well developed. She hankered after past glories and viewed her present life and her husband with scarcely concealed scorn. This was very sad as he was a nice man, but fortunately he understood no English, which she and I spoke together. Therefore, while she was complaining so bitterly about him, his snoring or other awkwardness, glancing as she spoke in his direction, he would courteously rise and bow as if acknowledging a compliment.

They had a friend, an old lady, who used to visit them and for whom it was essential that they had an upright chair. They used on these occasions to borrow one from us. Monsieur Choseneski would be sent to fetch it an hour before the old lady was due to arrive. The actual physical operation of removing the chair from our boat to theirs was as complicated as Trooping the Colour and it took nearly as long.

First of all, the formal request would be made by Monsieur and notice given that he would be arriving later to fetch the chair. I would then get it placed. At first I made the great mistake of thinking we could get it up the stairway together. Later I found it wiser to have the chair ready on deck. Monsieur would then arrive for the second time, would click his heels and bend to kiss my hand. Then he would bend down to pick up the chair. I learnt to allow plenty of room in order to avoid being struck as he clasped the seat to his stomach and straightened his back to the upright position. He would then click his heels and bow over the chair (head only) and, turning, would advance smartly to the ladder against the quay. Placing the chair on the quay, he would turn towards me, kiss my hand, click and climb up the ladder. Once up, he would pick up the chair as before, click and bow and be off to his own boat. Madame Choseneski would be watching anxiously from the deckhouse and one could hear her grumbling tone as the chair was unceremoniously somehow lowered into their boat. The whole proceeding was repeated in reverse order after the guest had departed.

An English fishing boat, the Gannet, arrived during the autumn. She was fine and sturdy, semi-converted but in need of maintenance and care. Her somewhat improvised living quarters were on what would now be called 'open plan'. This gave the impression of spaciousness within. She was lived in by Elisha and Sadie.

Elisha was a philosopher from Arizona. He was in Europe on a very advanced scholarship for further study. He was of Danish extraction and first-generation American. He was good looking in a way which was immature or boyish and which belied his intelligence. His slight build was of the DH Lawrence type with high cheekbones, beautiful skin and hair, and a reddish beard. Throughout the winter he was occupied writing a thesis for his doctorate.

Sadie was a remarkable young woman. Small and square, she was Canadian by birth with a Scottish mother, but something about her suggested Eskimo blood in her rugged character. Her wigwam life in Gannet was adorned with touches of excellent taste of traditional origin such as antique candelabra, which threw a bewitching light on to the untreated rough timbers of the interior. An artist who adored strong Mediterranean colour, she dabbled in design and at the same time was sentimentally attached to such things as Chilprufe for children and British-made goods. She was an excellent cook and, being fond of eating, could smell out good cheap restaurants anywhere. She was warm-hearted, uninhibited and undaunted.

Sadie spent a lot of time away from Gannet seeing friends in studios and also in Five Sisters, so that Elisha could work undisturbed. Sometimes she brought young philosophers to see us. They liked the old-world atmosphere – the great beams and timbers of the interior of the barge and spaciousness. Light too had an evocative quality in Five Sisters. The many scuttles round the coach roof and the dead lights overhead gave a charming suffusion of light, particularly when the sun shone – mornings being delightful. Whatever it was something made Five Sisters conducive to discussion and a door was opened for me on to a world that I had only observed as a curiosity. We had been down for odd evenings to 'La Bibliothèque', St. Germain des Prés, where one could drink liqueur brandy ('fines') amongst the philosophers of existentialism, all of whom seemed to be enormous men with great manes of hair like lions. Jean Paul Sartre was still the king round whom the 'lions' gathered. In the cellar below, people danced as they now do in London, colour and sex recognising no barrier. Of all this we'd been spectators, but now the discussion swayed to and fro in our own sitting room – albeit amongst lions of the new generation.

During the winter our Irish cousin, Kitty Shackleton, came to stay on her way to ski. She arrived with stitches in her upper lip, which she had torn on a bramble when hunting. A vet had stitched it up then and there, which was typical of her raffish, indomitable spirit.

I had invited Sadie and Elisha to meet her. During the evening Kitty produced a scrappy piece of paper from her pocket on which her uncle had written a few notes as to some possible family relationship that he wanted to make clear. Next day we put Kitty on a train and Sadie burst in excitedly. "What a privilege," she said, "to meet someone from the hunting shires with her family tree in her pocket."

Winter was so different from summer time down on the Quai that without our new neighbours we might have felt isolated at times. It was cold. Our French friends sometimes invited us to lunch on Sundays, which we enjoyed. We gave small parties on board for various friends and visiting NATO people. Paris looked lovely under a dusting of snow, but the snow did not lie. Five Sisters' rigging picked out in rime was always a beautiful sight.

Early in the New Year, General Eisenhower arrived to take up his post as Supreme Commander. The happy, informal days at Les Invalides were over. The headquarters now moved by stages to Marly, near Versailles, and everything changed. Thousands of U.S. servicemen arrived overnight, very long cars appeared for the first time in large numbers in the streets of Paris and Coca-Cola spread like a rash across France.

The whole pattern of the life we had just become accustomed to was basically changed and for the most part not for the better – with one exception. It was soon discovered that the U.S. corporal who typed the letters in the new office was paid more than the Europeans of Brigadier rank. The Treasury's hand was forced at last and we had a pay rise. Five Sisters no longer had parties eating sandwiches for lunch – the British delegation now lunched in the cafeteria at Marly and could well afford a 'hot dog'.

The flowering chestnuts came again and with them Sadie's baby, Jacob. After she got home from the impressive convent for poor mothers where her baby was born, Sadie would be found suckling him wherever she found it convenient. I felt nervous at times lest Maurice, the Embassy driver, would arrive with a car load of majors and colonels from S.H.A.P.E. as it was now called, who had a few minutes to spare before being delivered at the Aerogare for a flight back to England. The sight of suckling babies were not as usual in those days for senior military gentlemen as it is now.

With the return of summer, we had to face the problem of getting Five Sisters home again to England. Tom would be coming to the end of his appointment later that year, so the obvious thing was to take her back during the summer leave when we might hope for good weather and find crews able to help. The great difficulty was for Tom to find time to prepare her for sea.

We were discussing this difficulty with the two originators of the painting parties, the Scotsman and the pretty English girl, now engaged. The Sorbonne year and their course were now finished, and they were off home. However, they thought they had a solution. They knew a Cambridge undergraduate spending his vacation in Paris, who would like to come and work on Five Sisters. Next day the tall figure of the Scotsman was seen striding along the quay and beside him sauntered a short, thickset figure – a Chinaman, whose name was Shing.

Shing came from Burma but was Chinese. His father was a wealthy merchant, who wanted his son educated in England. So he had left Burma as a small boy to live with a guardian and go to school in England. He spoke English with a smooth Cambridge accent and at 20 his outlook was indistinguishable from that of any undergraduate of the day, with all their confidence and panache. Shing used to discuss poetry and philosophy and viewed his own country with detachment. He intended returning to Burma, he explained, when he would relearn the language and eventually become a judge. He had thick black hair under which laughing eyes looked out of his Oriental face. He had taken a flat near the Opera, but worked daily on Five Sisters, wearing bathing trunks and a straw hat, the weather being once more hot.

Back in England some months later, we met Arthur Bennett. "How do you account," he asked, "for this story." I shall here repeat it.

A friend of Arthur's, who was steeped in Thames barge lore and barge affection, went to Paris for a holiday. He climbed the Eiffel Tower, and from the top spied, amongst the trees along the Seine, what could only be the mast and sprit of a Thames sailing barge. Coming down, he at once set off to find her and at last he came to the Quai d'Orsay. He advanced slowly, taking in every detail and stood for some time watching her. There seemed to be nobody about on board, but ashore a Chinaman, wearing shorts and a sun hat was working on the upturned dinghy. Arthur's friend thought this over and decided to make a few enquiries. The question was, in what language to address the Chinaman – English or French. He decided to try pidgin English.

"Likee workee big junk?" he began ingenuously. Shing straightened himself up and stopped varnishing. "Yes, indeed, thank you," he replied. "It's as good a way as any other of passing the time." The over-smooth accent was exaggerated and unmistakable.

Abashed and puzzled, Arthur's friend returned to his hotel and reported the whole encounter to his wife. "I expect you dreamt it," she suggested.

"Certainly not, I will take you there myself and show you. We will go on Sunday."

And so they did, but the quay was empty. It was 13th August and we had left the day before.

At midday on the 12th August, the Great Bastard was lashed into activity. Very unostentatiously, the last line attaching Five Sisters to the Quai d'Orsay was let go. It ran softly along the cobbles on the edge of the quay, round the bollard and fell limply into the water to be gathered inboard. Five Sisters was already pulling gently out into the middle of the steam on the first leg of her journey home to England.

Looking back, we left the Choseneskis in solitary state, all other boats, including Gannet, being away. They were on deck: Monsieur bowed with his usual courtesy and Madame, in benign mood, waved and blew kisses as if taking a tumultuous final curtain at the opera. Familiar sights began rapidly to fall astern. In any case, only a glance could be spared as we were busy making up ropes and tidying up on deck as best we could with the mast lowered.

Our return to England was uneventful. We had fun coming down the Seine with a varied crew; Muff and some Irish students came with us, Jeremy and friends. We stopped for some days at Les Andelys, a small riverside town. Friends had a house here, high on a hill at the top of the town. The children established a system of signalling between the house and Five Sisters, which often ended in their shouting to each other over the rooftops.

Down on the quai, every action on board Five Sisters was observed by a family whose garden came down to the towpath. They had a gazebo of clematis in which they sat after lunch and in the evening. We could hear their laughter behind the clematis and, if they caught sight of us, they waved their glasses. The grandfather was a tremendous know-all who had an answer for everything. He kindly pressed his escargots on us, which we liked, but he also poured water into a cement mix that Tom was working with. This jeopardised the civilities a little but, fortunately, only temporarily.

At last the day dawned for the departure from Les Andelys and the gentle days of valediction were over. The last farewells were said, butterfly nets and killing jars were put away and the mast lowered. 'Grandpapa', bobbity as ever, was keen to let go our stern line too soon, but a member of the crew stood guard over it, gathering it up at the critical moment before jumping on board with it as Five Sisters pulled out into the stream.

At Rouen, we parted sadly with the river crew, except Shing, and met the Westwoods as crew for the crossing. We visited Honfleur once more and renewed our old acquaintances. Finally Jacqueline joined us at Newhaven and another English crew joined. From then on, we had nothing but gales and were delayed in Newhaven and Dover. Eventually we reached the London River and Five Sisters rejoiced visibly in her home waters.

Our difficulty now was to find a Barge Yard which would give her a refit. These were becoming rare and after visiting Oare Creek in Faversham and Hoo we found Bugsby's Hole at Woolwich.

Pinched between Dorman Long's, the black-ash towpath and the even blacker river water of the Thames at this point, was a barge repair yard, where business was conducted in Dickensian manner and with Dickensian humour by an outstanding extrovert, the 'Boss'.

A tall, lanky and rather gloomy figure, Alf, was looking out for us on Sunday night and took our line thrown to him. The Boss was away but would be down in the morning. Alf lived in the workshop on the edge of the towpath and had done so for years. He cooked his meals on the forge fire, which he blew up every morning with the blacksmith's bellows. Soon after, the smoke began to rise from the chimney and a most delicious smell of bacon and eggs floated over to Five Sisters.

Being a Sunday night and the last of Tom's leave, we were no sooner made fast than the Master was packing to take the night ferry back to Paris. Monday morning therefore found me in the old unenviable position with a list a yard long of things to be done, which had to be discussed with barge experts. In spite of my dislike of being the entrepreneur, it is only fair to say that there were few misunderstandings ever on what was required to be carried out in any yard. Both barge builders and the Master knew what they were talking about.

Soon after eight o'clock, Dick Norton, the Boss, arrived on board. His nickname, 'Whisper', stemmed from the fact that his conversation could be heard on the opposite bank of the Thames, half a mile wide at this point. Whisper was anxious to get details of all the work to be done at once, he shouted, as he was off next day on his holiday. My heart sank at this news – it had taken hours of telephoning to get an active barge yard to take us at short notice.

"Where are you going?" I asked him, as affably as I could at the top of my voice, supposing him to be deaf. "Paris," he yelled back. "Taking the Missus to Paris. Ever been there?"

Goodness, what a stroke of luck. Before long, it was all fixed up: he and the Master would meet and discuss all the details of the refit together in France, to their mutual satisfaction. And so we left it for the day, he to go home and pack and I to get accustomed to the strange new life at Bugsby's Hole.

That night, a telegram was delivered on board Five Sisters. I myself was to return without delay to Paris. Our pay had been increased to measure up with the Americans and, although backdated, it could not, under currency regulations, be transferred to England. Whether we liked it or not, what seemed to us a small fortune must be spent in France within a month! Jacqueline and I climbed on to the night ferry at Victoria Station, having left Five Sisters in the care and under the watchful eye of Alf.

So it was that we found ourselves one balmy autumn evening outside a restaurant on the Grand Boulevard, sipping cognac with Mr. and Mrs. Whisper, discussing Five Sisters. Whisper's fund of stories during the evening never ran out and his voice gathered even more than usual strength, but the details of our re-fit were fully gone over. Our hats, Mrs. Whisper's and mine, became a little more tippety as the evening wore on. Finally we parted outside the restaurant and Mr. and Mrs. Whisper crossed the boulevard and started home to their hotel. The empty street at one in the morning seemed nearly as wide as the Thames at Woolwich when Whisper's resonant voice reached us from several blocks away: “Trust me, she'll be water-tight and shipshape for you in October.”

Once more back in England, we set about getting the barge ready to leave her for, probably, two years. We were to go to Malta. We were once more safely in Cubitts Yacht Basin and were able to find a tenant, a very suitable one: an army officer who had just married a delightful girl and thought the Barge, as a first home, was most romantic. We found that he was very anxious to prove to another service that the Army could care for a boat as well as the Navy could. We felt very reassured and rightly, as it turned out.

Malta

On 9th December 1951 I left England for Malta. For the first time in my life I savoured the new development – the Navy was to move us with all our necessary belongings. The Army had had this service for years and the Air Force had automatically followed suit, but the proud Navy had done things the hard way which meant, unless your could pay for a passage, wives stayed at home. I also went by air for the first time in my life.

The age of technology had not reached Malta in the 1950s, as my arrival illustrates. Tom had gone a week or two before me. The Navy flew me out in early December. In England, since our return from France, it had rained and rained. Despite Whisper's assurances in Paris the caulking of the decks in his absence had been a bad job, so that it rained inside the barge as well as outside; this made packing difficult. Being sure that I would be fairly exhausted from this and from sadly bidding farewell to my mother, who was not well, I particularly requested that I should slip in quietly and sleep it off before bracing myself to face the new life ahead.

To my concern when I arrived at the Tinghe Court Hotel the hall seemed to be crowded with servants, some even peeped over the banisters. Hotel guests sauntered through too, all with a look of curiosity on their faces. A few days later I discovered the reason – a friend put me wise.

Tom had always been fussy about beds, even after we abandoned our own. He got the manager to remove two twin beds and to install, quite properly, a double. A week before, the hotel had put in a lift, a muchprized innovation. A high dignitary of the Church had been to bless it and send it on its first journey upwards. Then our large bed was squeezed in. Alas, not only did the load jam the lift, it put it out of action for a few days. When guests on the top floor complained to the manager as they struggled up the stairs he replied, "Oh, it is the wife coming from England for whom the bed is demanded." If they expected a beautiful Scandinavian or a Sophia Loren to arrive all they got was me, exhausted, dirty and very plain.

We were very lucky in finding a delightful house in Mdina, the walled city overlooking the north of the Island. The Milburns were living in a flat there, an attic flat above The Zara Palace Hotel. They were our oldest and dearest frends: our lives crossed so many times – one being in Cubitt's Yacht Basin Chiswick where they were in next door barge. We had hoped that my mother would be able to join us so we had this in mind. Alas this never materialised as she suffered a stroke and moved to Pat's. The following summer I paid a visit to England to see her. Meanwhile one of Tom's nieces,

Carol, came out to Malta; she was suffering from a hole in her heart and it was thought a good idea for her to spend time in the sun. She went to school at the Sacred Heart Convent. On my visit home a friend came to live in our house and Tom went to stay with Ian Inguanez

"When you get to the Second Crusader's armour, put your hand behind the helmet and you will find the light switch, then turn left and go on until you reach the Roman wine skin where the next switch is, then keep on." Tom was offered hospitality by Ian Inguanez in the Casa Inguanez in Mdina while I was summoned home by my mother's illness. Tom had warned Ian that he might have to work late and be returning after the Casa's main entrance was closed. Ian had two very holy sisters, who were highly nervous, quite necessarily at night. Tom's anxiety was lest he mistook their rooms and crashed in by accident.

Ian, a Northern Irelander, was serving in the British Army of Occupation in Germany at the end of the Second World War when he inherited the "most senior Noble Title in Malta." This came to him from his famous and notorious aunt: the Most Noble Mary Sceberras Trigona D'amico Inguanez, twentieth Baroness and sixteenth Baroness by descent of Diaril-Bnie and Bukana, the oldest territorial fief of the Maltese Islands. I have not gone mad on titles but there is such history behind this flow of unpronounceable names dating from the Knights of St. John. Despite the heavy heredity going back to 1330 Ian was the most delightful, inconsequential, gentle person with a fine sense of the ridiculous. Ian was our neighbour in Mdina. He turned the beautiful Casa Inguanez into a sort of museum with things the soldiers brought home from the days of the Crusades onwards. The Casa was stuffed with curios but it was also an hospitable home, which was housing Tom while I was away.

Living at the Quai d'Orsay had been glamorous, colourful and exciting. Living in Malta in the ancient town of Mdina, Notabile or Citta Vecchia, as it was variously known, was an experience of deep and moving depth. To me, until that time, the Mediterranean in spring had meant a dusty littoral where a chilling wind was apt to arrive and curdle the mimosa flowers into hard little balls in brittle sunshine. Despite a wind called a Gregale, which caused St. Paul's shipwreck as described in the Acts of the Apostles, blowing ferociously during my first few days I soon fell under the spell of the island's enchantment. Ulysses had dallied for seven years in these parts and no wonder.

There were two distinct compartments to our life in Malta. Up in the Silent City, as it was also known, there was the luxury of living within enclosed walls. The Arabs in planning their towns, I am told, used to see that they were not too big for the comfort of the citizens, which gave a wonderful quality of serenity. Within the walls the Cathedral presided over each hour of the day and over the seasons' festivals. Bells woke us at daybreak as well as a thousand sparrows living in an orange tree in our next door neighbours' garden. A solemn tolling recorded mid-day and the Angelus announced that the sun's relentless course (at any rate in summer) was nearing its end. Below, in the narrow streets behind deceptively plain walls, were large houses with inner courtyards, balconies and flowers where life worked out its day in privacy.

Down in the Grand Harbour and Sliema Creek the Royal Navy worked its daily round as methodically as the Catholic Church did in Mdina. 'Colours' took place morning and evening as the White Ensigns were raised or lowered with ceremony on the ships in harbour and everyone stood to attention. Purposeful sounds pervaded the dockyard: radio orders, bugle calls and pipings aboard, with ships going to sea or coming in from sea. Wives and families would gather on the Baracha Gardens to watch our husbands' ships make their stately exits or entries from the sea into the Grand Harbour or out again.

The Maltese and British cultures seemed complementary and made for smooth running days with time to explore. The simple daily turning of the earth on its axis in these happy latitudes may also have contributed to our feeling of well-being. Light varied enormously through the day: from the roof, from which we could see nearly all the North of the island down to the sea, the glorious clear early morning sunshine picked out the beautiful contours of fields and buildings, to be followed by the crescendo of heat towards mid-day when colour was drained out of everything until the natural gentlencss of afternoon returned the richness. Then the beginning of shadows presaged the sun's dramatic disappearance, a great crimson-orange to green ball which sank in glory over the Victorian Lines, old military fortifications to the West, watched by most of Mdina from their rooftops, no doubt a glass of gin or Milita in their hands. The island is of honey-coloured stone, soft to cut like cheese, they say. The Knights of St. John had used this stone to outstanding effect and satisfactory proportions when building their fortifications, harbours, aqueducts, churches and the auberges, also their love nests. There was always a beautiful building to be seen despite the uglification, which Malta has caught, from the rest of the commercial world. The honey-coloured stone reflects a luminous light far into the evening, absorbing the sun's rays during the day.

The summer is hot and dry, yet oleander trees continue to flower bravely throughout the long hot days. In Autumn the rain falls in torrents and one shuts veranda windows which were opened in the spring. After a day or so, a delicate green haze breaks over the land as the young grass pierces the iron hard soil. Winter is full of flowers that cover the cliffs, arum lilies grow against the Crusaders' castles, narcissi are brought by children to the door, acanthus, irises and crocus abound. For some reason, scarlet pimpernel is deep delphinium blue. Halcyon days. When I looked up the definition I found "Days of calm which the ancients believed occurred about the winter solstice." It was true. Enormous stars hung in the sky on Christmas Eve – every house had its crib in the window. With the little square stone houses, the donkeys and goats (Shoats in Malta being crossed with sheep) it was almost as if the Christmas story had taken place here.

Malta holds history in the palm of its hand. Neanderthal man has left the most spectacular remains of temples; a famous underground oracle, the Hypogeum, carved out of rock must have been a sacramental place, with many others, for thousands of years. Before man arrived, animals escaping from the Ice Age to warmer climes in Africa left their remains petrified in an underground river. The Maltese language came from the Phoenician traders and it is said today that it is the language nearest to that in which the Sermon on the Mount was probably given. The Romans established themselves, St. Paul hid from them in the catacombs after the shipwreck, the Knights of St. John driven from Rhodes established themselves in Malta and fought the Great Siege against Suleiman the Magnificent. Napoleon had his eye on the island. He stole many of the artefacts, now in the Louvre in Paris, belonging to the rich Knights. In the Cathedral in Mdina they managed to paint the silver gates black before Napoleon got there and so they remain today. It was after this that Malta asked to belong to England. Nelson had defeated Napoleon in the Battle of the Nile. Malta throve as a British Naval base and became a target for the Italian Air Force during the Second World War but the brave Maltese endured and defended their island with the Navy with unquestionable loyalty against the most savage attacks.

For two months after Christmas the weather could be horrible, the Gregale much to be feared. I can remember sitting listening to the announcement of George VI's death dressed in an old dejected fur coat, fur lined boots and an oil stove beside me. Nevertheless, I remember picking Seville oranges for marmalade in Bosquetto, the old Grand Master's summer residence in gentle spring weather. A gate in our walls led to a lovely valley with a bubbling stream alive with tadpoles, the banks were full of swallowtail butterflies. Periwinkle grew beside the gate and a huge old fig tree dropped juicy purple figs practically into our mouths in Autumn. One of the most attractive sights in April and May was fields of red clover. These were harvested with the greatest care as summer feed for animals.

Our honey-coloured house was built into the ramparts of Mdina. The ground floor was Norman: Roger, Count of Sicily, William the Conqueror's brother, came south and took Malta from the Arabs in 1090. Our small dining room consisted of a vault in Norman style as in a cloister or aisle of a cathedral. It had a deep cupboard, which I thought must be very old indeed, and a window opening on to the narrow street. The house was built around a courtyard. A stone staircase with beautiful wrought-iron banisters led up to the various floors to the roof garden. Our drawing room ran from the street to the courtyard. From the balcony one could lean out and touch the lamp on the priest's house opposite. The electric wiring of this house must have been very dangerous – during thunderstorms the whole house used to sparkle with flashes of lightening. The house gave us the utmost pleasure for nearly two years. It was charming and made a home for Jeremy in the holidays. One of the post-war blessings was a system by which school children could be flown out for the holidays. Carol, our middle niece, joined us and went to school at the Sacred Heart Convent. The youngest niece, Susan, now seven, also joined us in the summer. Our landlord, Philip Pulichino, lived next door – the rent was ten pounds a month.

When Susan came it was rather difficult to cope with such mixed ages. Their father offered help and I asked him to provide a cook. Jenny came. We already had Rosy, a dear little girl whose family lived in Mdina and kept us in touch with what was going on. Tom also had Buttersheesh, a naval steward, who was a proper caution. When we entertained, the families of both helpers came and crowded into the kitchen and sometimes war ensued. I can remember once the row in the kitchen, as we waited for the next course, being even worse than that of an English cocktail party. They carried home the remains of the dinner, which I had cooked. Rosy's father was a guide at the Cathedral and her mother and I conversed happily each week over our washing. We got on very well – with a tot of gin always offered. She had only two words in English, "All right – all right", which she always said twice to give emphasis.

We became very fond of the tranquillity and peace exuded by the nuns of the Sacred Heart. The Mother General was a particular friend and I think she enjoyed visits from Tom wearing his naval shorts. They sat opposite each other to discuss his niece's progress. Sadly, when he offered to lift the nuns by boat to their summer residence on the coast it was turned down by authority as being "too much pleasure", which was excessively mortifying to all souls – we all lost out.

A transaction I always enjoyed, as being linked to the past, was the arrival of the fishman who would sit on the doorstep and weigh the fish – delicious lampuki – on hand scales he held up with a few stones for measure on one side.

At weekends, boat trips to one or other of the islands were a great luxury. I can remember swimming to a tiny island covered in wild thyme, in which I lay and breathed the hypnotic scent. Of course there were contrasts and, as nothing is perfect, I think the battle of the flies could be stated as the reverse of the coin. "Flit" was a commodity then and a flit gun was an essential in any house. Whoever woke first flitted. It did not kill cockroaches – only a foot did that. At picnics, if you wanted to snooze, you had to cover your head with a newspaper like Benjamin Bunny. Against such disadvantages one had to balance that we had gone back in time – when walking along the cliffs of Dingley on the south coast as the light faded, the classical phenomenon appeared – the wine dark sea, as the Greeks saw it – there it was.

A very serious reverse was the fate of the migratory birds who arrived in spring and autumn, often exhausted. Alas, the Maltese called it "hunting." It broke the heart to see golden orioles, hoopoes and other lovely species in nets being carried home for pets or the pot.

We had one thing that greatly plagued us during our time in Malta – it was the waywardness of our car. She was second-hand and was looked after lovingly by Tom and by Borg Ginger in Sliema. The trouble was getting her to start. We would push her down the hill inside Mdina until we reached the moat at the bottom, without a twitter of co-operation from her. Then Nichole, our grocer, would come out of his shop and say, "Oh Signor, I get my children," (of which he had many) "to push her up again." I don't think we ever resorted to this drastic measure. She would run beautifully in wet weather but there was not enough for her liking. A bus once gave me a tow back to Rabat with the towrope fixed to the front bumper of the bus. This meant that the driver had to reverse along a windy lane, which somehow he managed to do. The Maltese have so much goodwill. We managed to sell the car just before we left. As we walked away from Giner's garage the new owner stopped to offer us a lift. In agony, we assured him that we liked walking and waved him on. To our relief the car kept going. Mary Milburn wrote after she had returned to England, "I wonder who is pushing the little car around these days." A lot of people had been involved.

Twice, during the two years we were there, I had to return to England as my mother's health was failing. It was not possible for her to make the journey to Malta as we had hoped. In each case Tom stayed at the Casa Inguanez. The second time was before the Coronation and Ian was selling the family silver in order to come to London to the ceremony as the senior "Most Noble." His sisters did not agree with this sale and disapproving silence hung over the breakfast table in the Casa.

On my second visit home my mother died. On my return Tom took me to the Island of Gozo where, high on a cliff, I found a fossil of a sea flower from many millions of years ago. Eternity is a long time but this little flower comforted me.

Collected photographs

Peggy in her father's De Dion

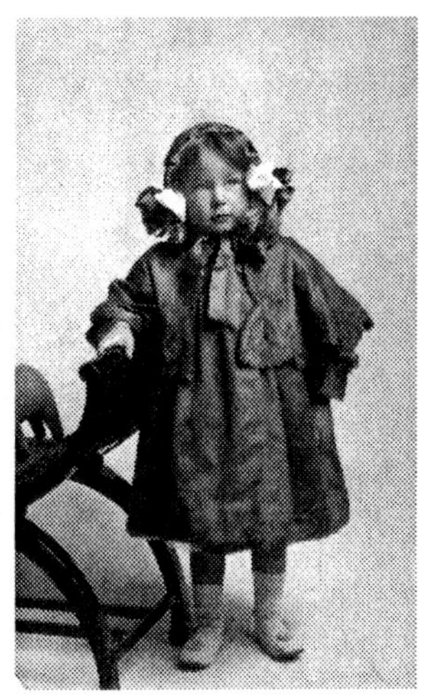

Peggy

Growing

Pat on Jane the donkey with Albert

Pat Shackleton

Greenwich Wedding

The decorator

Peggy and Tom

With Baby Juliet

Juliet and Jeremy

On Dee Sands with John Warren

The Conversion team – 1947

The Sitting Room – Photo Alex Nicoll, Southampton

Leaving the Quai D'Orsay for the office
Photo Mirrorpic, London

Cruising past the Eiffel Tower

On the Seine

Jeremy and Wendy – 1961

Five Sisters
Photo Eileen Ramsay, London

The Gasworks site – 1962

On the ice at Yarmouth – 1963

Bus and Train through Spain

Our return from Malta comprised a variety of transport. We took passage for the first leg in the Royal Fleet Auxiliary Fort Dunvegan. To me, who had travelled in West Indian banana boats, our cabins were the height of luxury. They were designed with very adequate sleeping accommodation but were also used, when necessary, as offices, so they had bookshelves and writing desks as well. Fleet Auxiliaries carry provisions to ships and fleets in waters far from home: the Fort Dunvegan was on her return voyage. After five somnolent days gliding down a tranquil Mediterranean, we reached Gibraltar with some regret as we had decided to disembark and go overland by bus and train.

We just managed to see Gibraltar and to have lunch in Algeciras before we took the train up into the mountains to Ronda, a town which seemed to have had an axe strike it down the middle. It is built on two halves of a split in the mountain, a bridge joining the two halves. Overhead above the dividing ravine vultures circled, hoping, I suppose, that someone would fall in. On board the Fort Dunvegan our last meal had been tea at 5 p.m. and by the time we reached Ronda our gastric juices were beginning to tell us that it was time to eat. It was an intense shock to discover at 6 pm that dinner would be served at 11 pm. We nerved ourselves to adjust to Spain and luckily found that a troupe of Flamenco dancers were practising in the hotel so that the hours of starvation passed while we watched.

It was December and it was getting very cold on the plateau of central Spain when we reached Granada. There was a marvellous system of keeping warm at meals in the hotel where we stayed. Under the table was a brazier which burnt olive stones and the table itself was covered with a thick rug like an old-fashioned horse rug which you tucked around your knees and felt very snug. The top half of the body was kept warm by the excellent food.

We spent a whole day in the Alhambra which left us dizzy with its Moorish beauty and proud to learn that the English dancer, Norma Shearer, had danced on some special occasion, no doubt before Franco, in one of its courts. Beyond the splendours of the Alhambra across a valley was the grimmest looking prison imaginable. "From old days?" we asked from our language book. But no. "Prisoners from the war." they said. The war was their civil war of the thirties when so many generous young men from other countries had come to fight. One wondered if any of them were incarcerated within these ghastly walls.

The next step was the bus part. It took all day to get to Madrid. As we approached each stop it looked as if we should be overcrowded. It always turned out that there were about two passengers and their friends were seeing them off. Everyone on the bus was extremely friendly and we swayed happily along with torrents of conversation. I battled with "Hugo's" Spanish. We arrived in Madrid at the very moment that a two-year drought broke. We were drenched trying to find a restaurant and when we did dash inside it was, unmistakably, a brothel.

Our hotel was also in the same district and appeared to be a trifle dubious. Tom and I lost our heads and behaved like a Victorian uncle and aunt, forbidding Carol to open her door should anyone try to enter. This might have been sound advice if the suitcases had not got mixed so that Tom's was in her room and nothing would induce her to open the door!

We spent all day in the Prado and hardly scratched the surface. My memory of Barcelona is sketchy, as we were anxious to get on to Carcassonne which we very much enjoyed, before taking the train to Paris where we stayed with our friends in Neuilly.

We reached England a few days before Christmas to find that my dearest Aunt Beresford was in University College Hospital having broken her leg. As soon as we had re-established the barge she was freed and hopped about Five Sisters. Sadly, despite her efforts and our pleasure in having her she had a stroke and died later in the spring in a nearby hospital.

High Life in London

The year 1954 was extremely pleasant for both of us. Jeremy by this time was at Bryanston where he was happy with friends from his prep school. Our niece, Carol, parted to continue her erratic education in Switzerland. In London Tom was appointed to a course at the Imperial Defence College as it was then called. It was a civilised course for further education, intended really for higher office, one might say, but with no guarantee that higher office would come one's way.

Tom spent many happy days visiting institutions of every kind, factories, colleges, the Houses of Parliament and listening to lectures by experts on every imaginable subject. During leave time they went away on tours abroad; they debated among themselves and with experts all the knotty problems of the world. His fellow students were drawn from the fighting services but also from other sort of services – consular, Foreign Office, Home Office and from the Commonwealth, also including Americans and other Europeans. In fact they were a happy band of brothers who seemed to enjoy their time immensely. It was an ideal break for reflection in anyone's career. Every Wednesday wives were invited to tea followed by a film and drinks afterwards. It was so well mannered and relaxed giving one ideas above one's station in life as one hurried through wind and rain by bus to an imposing building in Belgrave Square.

In Chiswick, Five Sisters blossomed into social life especially at the Oxford and Cambridge Boat Race which finished just below Chiswick Bridge. Still under rations it was easy to feed parties with soused herrings and stuffed eggs – we had eaten our dear chickens long ago but could now buy eggs galore.

On a particular day the College was visiting some establishment southwest of London. Tom arranged for some of the course to call in on their way back to see the Barge. In the morning before he left he asked me to be sure there was a bottle of gin on hand, “without fail.” he added and returned to the subject as he left. It was, therefore, imprinted indelibly on my mind.

There was a grocer nearby, only five minutes’ walk away from the Yacht Basin. They had a licence. I called during the morning and ordered a few things besides the gin. The manager was insistent that they would send the goods down to the boat within an hour and I unwisely agreed, having another call to make. “Without fail.” I stipulated rather hesitantly, as I left.

During the early afternoon, I realised that the delivery had not arrived. I was worried that the gin had not come. Soon, however, I heard a step on deck and went to the main hatch to receive the things. To my surprise it turned out to be the Vicar. Jeremy was being confirmed that term and there was correspondence in this connection from the Padré at school who, good man, liked to follow up his work, which was fair enough but rather alarming. Before I could restrain myself, I said, "Oh, I thought it was the gin." I tried to smooth over this remark, offering him a cup of tea. To put me at ease he began, very kindly, to top and tail some gooseberries I had been working on. Time wore on and someone else came on deck. I rushed to the hatch again. The boy had brought the groceries but there was no gin. "No gin." I cried. My anxiety became acute as I sent the boy packing to go and fetch it. I tried to concentrate on religious matters. Then the worst happened – I heard, before their expected time, several male voices approaching the gangplank, followed by a heavy tread on deck. "A terrible thing has happened," I cried in anguish, "my husband has come home." I dashed on deck to intercept the arrival and caught sight of the poor man looking startled and bewildered as I glanced over my shoulder. On deck I met Tom. "I haven't got the gin," I said, "but I have got the Vicar." "Bloody Hell!" was his remark, just above where the Vicar was sitting below. I fled up the path on my bicycle to the shop.

They had already shut and were drinking tea inside. I banged on the door. They made infuriating signs that they were closed. I made more urgent signs indicating drinking, making my hand cup shaped. At last they opened the door. "What is it, Mrs. Larken?" asked a young assistant. "The gin." I gasped, "you promised it this morning – remember – it's half past five now." He gave me a long, pitying look. "I will give it to the boy – better than you taking it on your bike." He just did not add "in your condition." The bad boy had already started and I snatched the bottle from his basket. When I got back, the Vicar had left and the only thing I wanted was a stiff gin. The company were quite settled and content with some white wine Tom had produced, while my reputation on all fronts was in ruins.

When August came, we took Five Sisters down under the bridges and, after a refit at Grays in Essex, set off for the East Coast once more. It was not good weather, as is so often the case in August. It is my belief that this is due to the hurricane season in the Caribbean; the ones that don't hit America travel along the Gulf Stream and blow themselves out on our shores. Anyway, we once more split our foresail while crossing the Buxey Sandbank. As a result of this we met a man who was to prove a true friend to us and to Five Sisters from that day on: Captain Fred Cooper, a famous barge skipper since his seventeenth year, son of a barge skipper, with his two brothers.

Fred was skippering a barge, the Ventnor, owned by Judge Blagdon, noted for his original remarks in court. The Judge kindly let us borrow a sailmaker's palm – we had one, of course, but it enabled two people to work on the repair of our sail. Before we had finished, the Ventnor left the mooring and Fred came right up to Five Sisters before 'going about', shouting, "Wakey, wakey." into our portholes. We managed to dash up on deck to wave and to ask for an address to which to return the palm. "It's all in 'Who's Who." shouted the Judge and away they sailed.

When we got back to the river again we were a little disconcerted to find a letter asking us to return the palm. We returned it a little huffily, Tom remarking that we did not carry a 'Who's Who' at sea (nor did we possess one). The Judge's reply was somewhat confusing. "Have you heard." he wrote, "of the ram who died of a broken heart when he heard Frank Sinatra play 'There'll never be another you'?" We supposed that judges must always have the last word.

The year ended as happily as it had begun. Early in 1955 Tom was appointed to command a flotilla of destroyers – he was made Captain D8. His own ship was to be HMS Cossack, named after the one that was sunk a few days before Ark Royal and which Admiral Vian had commanded in Norway. The Eighth Flotilla operated in the Far East and Tom was to take HMS Cheviot from England to join the others. I think there were five others, their names all beginning with 'C'. They were based on Singapore.

I rejoiced for Tom but was highly nervous about going on board as the Captain's wife. However, my first visit put me firmly in my place. Invited to join Tom for a weekend, I was met at the top of the gang plank by a nice looking young sub-lieutenant with the news that Tom had been called away on urgent business for an hour or so. But Tom, ever resourceful, had suggested that I might be escorted to the galley in order to explain to the Chinese cook how to make 'Fudge Pud' – a wartime but favourite family pudding. Tom liked Chinese cooking himself, but he had soon to give lunch to the Mayor of Reigate, the town of Reigate having adopted the ship, and he thought 'Fudge Pud' would be just the thing. I thought it questionable.

There was no means of communication between the cook and myself other than by signs with spoons and bowls and much smiling. Our systems were obviously so different, as east is from west. Eventually I was present when the dish was served to the Mayor and his wife. I gathered from the smiles of the steward who handed the dish that it must be 'Fudge Pud', orientalised, but that was only a guess.

HMS Cheviot sailed away and I was left in Cubitts Yacht Basin. Five Sisters and I were well placed with other friendly boats around us and shipwrights at hand. Our nieces and nephew adopted the habit, learnt in Paris, of turning up at weekends to help maintain the ship, bringing friends with them.

Jeremy took to rowing at school and I spent many a freezing wet or cold afternoon that spring on various tow-paths, including our own, adding my voice to those shouting for Bryanston to win. Dear Mrs. Farmer, who helped clean in Five Sisters, had a son at Chiswick Grammar also rowing. We loyally stood together cheering for our own.

Then, in the summer of 1955, came the suggestion that I should visit Jamaica once more. My Great Aunt Gertrude, my Grandmother's sister, had become 100 when we were in Malta but now it seemed a good moment to make such an expedition into the past.

Return to Jamaica

Tom had sailed away to the Far East in the Cheviot, Jeremy was camping on the continent with school friends and I went to Jamaica. Aunt Gertrude was the only one living of the old people from the household with whom I had stayed in 1929. They had all lived well into their nineties. Gracie Thursfield, sister to Busha, and herself now elderly, met me in Kingston after a fairly uneventful crossing of the Atlantic in a Norwegian Banana Boat. Elders and Fyffes, like so many other things, seemed to have disappeared by that time. We drove by the old route up to the mountains, Clarence, the chauffeur in immaculate white uniform.

As I entered the drawing room from the veranda I realised that nothing here had changed – it was exactly as I remembered it with the exception of a photograph of Tom in naval uniform and one of Jeremy as a small boy. People had disappeared, though not Aunt Gertrude who sat in a low chair looking wonderfully alert for her 102 years. Due to her great age and her perennial wisdom I felt very emotional as I knelt at her feet to embrace her. She had written such affectionate letters down the intervening years, packing parcels of dried bananas for us during the war.

Outside, the estate was a sad travesty of its former self. Buildings were in a state of decay and disrepair: the old pimento factory was a ruin, red coffee beans no longer dried on the barbecue. In the old days, coffee had grown enjoying the shade of banana trees beneath which pigs had rootled, now these had all gone. The whole economy had changed: the islanders now searched the soil for Bauxite, which was extracted for the manufacture of aluminium. After the deaths of Uncle Townshend and Busha, managers had come and gone, leaving the old ladies with an ever diminishing and less productive property. Now Gracie was trying to run it herself – an uphill job shared with that of looking most lovingly after my aunt.

The people themselves had changed: they had grown up but were not yet "come of age." It was no longer the custom in the country to chaff with the servants and to expect a cheeky answer. They were still attentive and kind with their inimitable sense of humour peeping out, but everyone was looking forward to Utopia which would blossom with Independence in two years' time.

The day passed very slowly listening to my Aunt's reminiscences of nearly a hundred years ago, how she had fallen off a horse when she was only four. I knew that she had been near death as a baby with cholera. I had a family tree from a cousin spread before me and I managed to astonish by naming her own aunts and uncles, the tail end of a family of twelve, with whom she, like my grandmother the daughter of the eldest son, had been at school in England. Sometimes she fell asleep and I would fill the time writing feverishly all that she had been saying. This, together with what I remembered from earlier days, provided me with material for the novel I was to write later.

One thing was difficult. I became very hungry: Aunt Gertrude had a tiny appetite, Gracie was too busy to bother with food, and the old planter's breakfast had shrunk away. I would slyly buy myself packets of raisins and chocolate when we went shopping. The chauffeur, Clarence, used to drive me down to Black River to swim at Gracie's instruction which was refreshing and helped my secret larder.

It was on my way home that I really encountered the New Jamaica. I began my lonely return with a certain amount of apprehension. My Aunt had told me that if it appeared that the County of Vere, thirty miles below, seemed to be in the garden beneath my window, then for sure, there was going to be a hurricane. It was the month of August, the most likely month for hurricanes so I was none too pleased to find on the morning of departure that this phenomenon lay before me: Vere was in the garden'

With infinite misgivings I set off in the train from Williamstown. I was to spend the day in Spanish Town, the ancient capital. Later in the day I would take the train to Port Antonio whence I would embark for England. The weather was hot and the day long, but I enjoyed wandering about the old town and wondering in which lovely red brick Georgian colonial house my forebears had lived. Grass sprouted between the cobblestones. The façade of old Kings House, scene of so many bygone festivities where my grandmother had danced as a girl, was all that remained, but was still beautiful. The house had been burnt many years ago. The other buildings, which made up a magnificent square, were the Rodney Memorial and the House of Assembly. My Uncle had taken me there in 1929 and I had sat where my great grandfather had sat as a member and wandered on to the famous open gallery where so much had been discussed by the members of the day. The middle of the square where a garden had flourished was entirely filled with vegetation of man height.

There were a few black and coloured people about but no white. In the Post Office where I queued for stamps I felt self-conscious, hoping that the smell of my skin was not offensive to my fellow customers. I have heard that this is a problem between races. People looked curiously at me. I gave myself a meal at a little restaurant and caught a late afternoon train.

The train ambled through the mountains that divide the south from the north of the island. The north coast has always been the most beautiful and Port Antonio a picturesque town. Sophisticated American bungalows throughout the island now replaced the old planters' dwellings built on stilts for coolness, with a distinctly rustic appearance. The old houses may have boasted marble steps leading to the entrance, brought as ballast in ships, but inside, table legs stood in bowls of water to defeat ants. Sitting in some old houses in the cool of the evening, I remember, one was sometimes startled to hear the snap of a rat-trap being sprung. Nowadays, however, there could be other invaders – one did not, I was told, sleep happily in one's bed for fear of armed robbers who thought nothing of using a gun in these more prosperous districts.

Everywhere there was a child-like enthusiasm for Independence and an entire disregard for facts. In some ways everything seemed so hopeful and one hoped. Bustomente, the bad boy of the twenties, was now Sir Alexander Bustomente, with flowing white hair, retired ex-Governor and elder statesman. The chief and real worry was unemployment, but a further anxiety was the exodus of the most skilled workers to England. And this I met on the boat.

I sat on deck in the cool night air and watched the stevedores checking aboard the cargo of bananas we were to carry. They stood on high platforms and each man who ran past up the gangplank with a huge bunch on his head was accounted for. Sometime after midnight we sailed.

The ship was Swedish and was very comfortable. She carried six passengers – five were black so that I was a little taken aback to find that I was the only white. The first pasenger I met was emerging from a door over which was written “Bad Room.” This turned out to be a “Bath Room.”

The Swedish Captain was a clever seaman and managed to avoid the hurricane which was a true one called “Clara.” When we finally finished rolling in her wake I got to know my fellow passengers. They were charming, friendly and appeared to be very happy to be on board. There was a record playing machine, which was always on – it gobbled up six-pences but there seemed to be a permanent supply. “Happy, happy Africa” was in vogue and imprinted itself on my mind. The company was voluble and fun when not at meals.

Meals were a nightmare. They were very formal. I sat next to the Captain and the First Officer sat at the opposite end of the table. The Captain was an all-round silent man. None of the other passengers was inclined to conversation in such circumstances. In desperation I used to look at a clock that faced me and wonder if it was time for me to try a further remark, hoping it might get taken up. I once ventured a story I thought was funny and emphasised this to the Captain – "Well, it was funny." His reply killed it instantaneously: "I naw." and he then told me a very sick joke in retaliation.

One evening when we were drawing near to England "Swedish Rhapsody." popular at the moment, came out of the machine. The Swedish bar steward rushed in, seized me round the waist and propelled me round the smoking room. The ship was rolling and he was drunk, but I felt at all costs I must hold him up for the honour of Europe.

That same evening, as were approaching the Channel and England, we all got very serious and I asked them what they hoped to find in England. To my astonishment their reply was "the White Boss." My heart sank when I thought what reality was going to produce for them.

Next morning we saw the coasts of both England and France before we turned round the Foreland into the London River and Tilbury. Here I had the greatest difficulty in preventing them from setting out in taxis for places like Birmingham and explained that trains were better. I managed to be threatening enough to taxi drivers, hoping to persuade them not to take their black passengers to such places thus using all of their small reserves of money. I think I succeeded.

Back home in Chiswick I was gardening one Sunday when they all swooped down on me. I had invited them to come but left it to them to do so when they liked. They sat all afternoon in the Five Sisters, playing my gramophone and told me all their news. Alas, it was as I feared: all were cold, sleeping in overcrowded places with friends, looking for accommodation which was too expensive and so on, but they still laughed. Mr. Price, the headman on a sugar estate, was putting plastic handles on plastic handbags. Eventually we all lost touch. One desperately sad misunderstanding, which I found hard, was with a nurse who wrote often from Leeds. She came to London to see us, just when we had taken the barge to sea and so we missed each other. She never understood my explanation and disappeared forever.

The Far East

I arrived home in England for the summer holidays. I had not been in the barge for more than an hour or two before a heavy tread on deck above preceded my son's descent down the main hatch with the heaviest, bulkiest rucksack I have ever attempted to lift. He had been walking with two friends in Germany. We passed the rest of the holidays, as far as I can remember, maintaining the barge.

The following year, 1956, my mother-in-law gave me a present of a trip to Singapore. It was a wonderful present. I flew in a Constellation aircraft in July. The journey was uneventful if tedious: for forty-eight hours children flying out to join their parents abroad climbed over me and round me, passing the time as best they could, eating sweets, going to the loo and playing various games together.

We landed six times but never long enough to see anything other than another airport. Time honoured names – Cairo, Karachi, and Rangoon had no significance whatsoever – just more of less hygienic loos and always food in cellophane packets. Bangkok looked so enchanting from the air but the uncertainty of "take off" made it imperative to remain in the stuffy, dehumanised building, which resembled the previous one – Dum Dum in Calcutta.

During the last lap the thought of release and the urgency to clean up made it seem very short. I peered out at the Malay jungle and caught sight of the China Sea as we flew down the peninsula to land at long last in Singapore. On the roof among the spectators was Tom. He looked pear-shaped from the tarmac but to him it appeared that my knees went on to my feet, my legs having swollen with two nights' sitting.

There are few moments when the astonishment at human life is overwhelming. Even the earth produced different shapes; the vegetables and roots in the market stalls were of different design from ours. The trees, flowers and of course birds and butterflies were all a different species. But what was more astonishing was that things that came out of the Eastern mind were utterly different from what the Western eye would expect. In Europe, for instance, one is at first surprised to see how many ways there are of making a wheelbarrow but it is obviously a wheelbarrow, whether designed by a Frenchman or a Yugoslav. Not so in the East.

The climate with its great heat – Singapore is much nearer the Equator than Jamaica – and the deluge of rain every afternoon was exciting. In the evening across the Jahore Strait was an imitation of Armageddon with electric storms of spectacular lightning. We were staying in a house beside the Strait and used to play tennis in a distracted sort of way as these storms lit the sky. I do remember what in these thirsty climate a gin and tonic could mean!

Both ships the Cossack and the Cheviot, were in dry dock at the same time, both were old ships from the war. Tom took leave and was anxious to go up country in Malay to the Cameron Highlands where a hotel indulged in log fires at night. I was reluctant to leave the tropics, having got here, but glad to arrive. The Dakota we travelled in fell erratically in heat pockets over the jungle, an afternoon habit due to the build-up of heat in the morning. Luckily this did not seem to worry the pilot, though I found it terrifying.

Once arrived, the Cameron Highlands had everything to recommend them, especially for Tom's prickly heat. In those days our warships were not yet air-conditioned. There was gentle rolling wooded country with a wonderful climate, ideal for walking. There was one fly in the ointment: Malay at that time was suffering from communist or rebellious uprisings – pockets of so-called soldiers who had been armed to fight against the Japanese in the jungle now turned against the British who managed finally to overcome them. While playing tennis one evening we were accompanied not far away by dull thuds in the jungle. These were shells fired from naval ships at sea hoping to clean up a hideout.

This hostility gave us a rather hair-raising experience at another time. We had hired a small Fiat car and driven to Malacca. On coming home we were approaching a bridge over a river in torrential rain. The road leading up to the bridge had become a track of mud. The wheels of the car whirled round and completely lost steerage way so that we began to move side-ways towards the river some twenty feet below. Despite my cries to stop Tom forced on, rightly as it turned out. The wheels suddenly got a grip and we made the bridge in safety. It was revealed to me later that we were really in double jeopardy which I fortunately did not know. It was after curfew time and we ought to have been within a military compound by then. Had we been benighted in the jungle, we would most likely have been captured, incurring much displeasure from authorities who might have felt compelled to rescue us.

After the Cameron Highlands we went to Kuala Lumpur where another astonishment to the eye was the railway station, this time a foible designed by a British Victorian Architect. In Kuala Lumpur I saw for the first and last time the British Raj, so soon to disappear from the earth. I saw it in its most honourable state, preparing to hand over independence to the Malay State which it did with the utmost grace and dignity. The other side of the coin, demanding equal respect was the excellence achieved by the Chinese and Malays in serving the British – they were so clean and efficient – the difficulty would be how on earth to be worthy of such service.

I think our hosts were so. We were staying with an old childhood friend of mine whose husband was ADC to the Army's General in command. Tom was astonished that I had such august service connections. A thing that I found of great interest while staying with them was monkeys up the trees in the garden. Gurkhas guarded the house and garden.

We returned to Singapore by night train, an experience of superb tropical luxury. The window in our carriage next to one's bed was lowered and the sounds and smell of the night can never be forgotten.

The town that we loved best was Malacca. So many nations had left their "chop" on it – a suitable way of describing it. A "chop" is a piece of ivory carried in a Chinaman's pocket. The end has been carved with the man's name in Chinese characters. Dipped in a sort of ink, it can be used on a letter or paper indicating the person's agreement or ownership. Tom's steward on board had one made for each of us.

Little tinkling bells could be heard from the many small temples, a large Portuguese Cathedral rose above the pantile roofs that had a distinct Mediterranean flavour. Cheek by jowl with eastern houses are pretty Dutch homely houses in pink brick. One of my Brownie Camera photographs shows a Chinese street with signs in hanging silk from crowded shops and a Malayan policeman directing the rickshaw traffic. Rising above the street is a Dutch frontage and above that towers the Portuguese Cathedral. In the foreground is an English dustcart with the Malaccan coat of arms on its side and next to it a red G.P.O van.

Two personalities played a large part in our lives. The first was Ah Ku, Tom's Chinese steward and the second was Midnight, Tom's Siamese cat. With Ah Ku we exchanged Christmas cards and visits whenever he came to England until he died. The great joke each morning for me was that, Tom, already up, would call as I opened an eye "Ah Ku Missie wakes bring tea." Ah Ku would arrive at once, as if the kettle had been waiting for this cry. Tea would be poured and the bath prepared. When I got there I would find that toothpaste had been squeezed on to my toothbrush No wonder people enjoyed this sort of life!

Midnight became ill and caused great anxiety. One morning I awoke to find there was no cry for tea and I feared the worst. Not at all. The two men, Tom and Ah Ku were kneeling on the floor, their heads pressed close to Midnight's saucer, both watching with intense pleasure as Midnight began to lap milk. East West, but the twain can meet.

The flight home from Singapore, like all flights from East to West, seemed to go on forever – the clocks were always taking a two-hour backward step. Fortunately there were no children this time. Eventually we saw the sun rise over the desert and we landed at Cairo for breakfast. Then England and Chiswick once more.

The day after my arrival home found me in Potter Higham in Norfolk on the Broads, where I spent two weeks chaperoning, or more correctly, cooking for four people all about 16 years old – two boys and two girls. It was the summer holidays. I had left Jeremy to arrange the party and it went very happily. The contrast in weather, environment, hemisphere and style of living was quite a shock to my system and made a dash of gin in the evening glass of cider quite essential. The cruise was a great success. The still waters of the Broads and the ambling pace seemed tranquil when compared to the thrashing of a Thames Sailing Barge at sea.

The next excitement that burst upon the world was the crisis of Suez. This greatly complicated Tom's return in December. He was due to fly home with the whole ship's company but they were unable to fly across Egypt and so landed at Mombasa. Here ill fortune overtook Tom and the First Lieutenant. They were ordered to fly to Aden to take part in a court-martial. This was a dismal blow to all concerned – no doubt most of all to the accused being tried. The court-martial came to an end on 23rd December and had there not been a fog in England, which had delayed the weekly plane's take off, they would have to have spent Christmas in Aden. As it was, they rushed to the airport without much hope, to find the aircraft revving up for take-off. They managed to persuade the pilot to start again and to take them on board. They worked all night on the report and the Naval Writer must have typed the last words as they landed at Heathrow. England was indulging in one of its Arctic spells so they presented a sorry sight in tropical shirts and shorts when Jeremy and I met them at 3 am on the 24th December. Quite an epic return. We spent Christmas with the Milburns in Suffolk.

An even grander London Town

As the next page in our history turned, we were fed by the shipping world. Tom had a curious title which sounded very grand – Director of Trade – not of Cabinet status as might be thought, but of the Trade Division in the Admiralty. This was a department responsible for liaison between the Navy, the shipping companies who built the warships and the Merchant Navy. The effect on our lives was odd. I hardly ever had to feed Tom. He lunched on so many days in some City guildhall, Trinity House or some place like Simpsons with shipping magnates that the sight of food on his return was not attractive. The year was 1957.

Some crumbs from the rich men's tables fell my way. When, for instance, a ship was to be launched, special carriages were laid on or planes hired to take people to the shipbuilding yards where we were entertained to no mean tune. Usually the launching took place on the following day, when we climbed to the platform set up for the occasion beside the ship to be launched, wearing the kind of hats usually seen at weddings. Below in the shipyard the shipwrights would cheer as the great hull slipped away into the water leaving, rather garishly, the Mayfair party (as I learnt we were called) crowded on their now isolated platform, high and dry above the yard. Later, after the lunch that followed, the lady launcher's breast would sparkle with diamonds presented, after much congratulatory speech making, by the builders.

Diamonds! One unforgettable and astonishing evening showed us the City of London in full regalia, a magnificent sight. Thc new Lloyd's building was to be opened by the Queen Mother. The sparkling tiaras and 'colliers', chains of office and buckles, the strange uniforms of the various companies made a dazzling spectacle.

In order to show us at our best, we and another couple were driven from the Admiralty in a smart car with a marine driver and another beside him to open the door for us on arrival. We were then ushered along a red carpet and formally announced to the astonishment of some neighbours in Chiswick, who knew us as those crazy barge people who scraped and tarred their old barge down on the waterfront.

During the speech making we sat on little gilt chairs. There were about twelve rows in front of us. It was odd to observe an extraordinary change of shape that overcame ladies in backless dresses in front of us as they sat down. The bones of their corsets forced the flesh beneath the shoulder blades up into square cushions one and all, a point I am sure no one had thought of in the dress design world and one which must always recur. Never sit down in a backless evening dress is the only way out of the dilemma – that is, unless you are under twenty-five.

The year wore away without much trouble. As time went on, Tom was exercised in his mind as how to return the lavish hospitality he received at lunchtime. No one would want to trail out to Chiswick for lunch and at weekends everyone was in the country. The problem was solved by our taking the barge down to the City and berthing her in St. Catherine's dock. St. Catherine's, beside the Tower, is a very old dock and today is a flourishing and most successful yacht basin. In those days it was a ghostly ruin after the wartime bombing. The London River's Harbour Master was an old friend, Gilbert Parmiter, the man who had passed the hat round in Paris to retrieve my mother from the hairdresser, and he once more came to our rescue arranging a berth for us. During the whole of our visit there we enjoyed a marvellous spell of hot summer weather.

We entered the dock on a Saturday afternoon. We had a slight mishap as we got inside. A young man, an experienced member of our crew was down in the engine room wrestling with the G.B. but unfortunately he misunderstood the directions for astern and pushed the lever to ahead at a critical moment. We were stopped by a sturdy balk of Tudor oak with immense iron fastenings forming lock gates. Rust poured out from the hinges, but all held. The odd thing about this episode was that Tom's sister came to stay and seeing the gate remarked, "Oh, I dreamt that you ran into that gate last night."

Once inside, the expanse of water was immense. There was one other boat in the whole vast dock and so nothing to impede any breeze that might blow, for which we were truly thankful. The buildings on one side had been completely destroyed and yellow toadflax flourished in great profusion with forests of pink willow herb. Between the old paving of the West India Sugar Wharf grass sprouted and wild flowers bloomed most charmingly over all the ruins. The effect was delightful. The cats adored ratting in this paradise but the toadflax was infested with fleas and we had a struggle to rid Five Sisters of this menace, as fleas were resistant to DDT. Keatings was the messy answer.

The buildings that stood were all beautiful, designed by Telford, I believe. The ruined warehouses had stored the richest cargoes for Victorian merchants, such as ivory, ostrich feathers and carpets. Since 1957 the whole place has been re-designed into an attractive yacht centre.

With my sister-in-law I spent much time shopping for the lunch parties either in Leadenhall Market or, more economically, in Jamaica Road and Tooley Street across Tower Bridge. Beneath Tower Hill are huge wine vaults and on one of the hottest days we were escorted down into this cool paradise to choose wine. Our evenings were a complete contrast to the gastronomical efforts of mid-day. We would wander about the deserted streets of the City getting cool. Stepney and Whitechapel hummed with life. Nothing ever seemed to close and you could shop for groceries all night. Pubs at the dock gates were still open at 8.0 a.m. for the night shift dockers. All the pubs left their doors open and pianos thumped away inside. East Enders think that life is for enjoying judging by the good humour and laughter one met at every turn and there was a village atmosphere in all the streets. The curious thing was that newspapers at that time were full of the vice carried on in these parts, particularly the notorious Cable Street. If vice makes people so merry and friendly, it ought to be encouraged.

The Tower, on the other hand, threw a sinister shadow. Those black ravens that strut about its lawns seem to be direct descendants of those who witnessed the tragic executions of the past.

Altogether, the experiment was most successful. In a sort of Pepysian way it was fun for a captain to entertain on his own ship the masters of the shipbuilding world, even those august people, the Brothers of the Trinity.

La Jeunesse Dorée

The children of the original crew of Five Sisters had grown up and, in doing so, had become very strong with inexhaustible energy. During the next five or six summers Five Sisters became more and more active. Each summer young people would arrive to stay for a few days or longer, their eyes shining with eager expectation. Tom and I might have eased off a little but we had not the heart to disappoint those high hopes. These young people – nieces and nephews, children of friends – had all become students, apprentices, Naval cadets and were, as yet, unlike our own generation, uncommitted for a large part of the summer or for weekends. They earned the name of Jeunesse Dorée partly by their youth and good looks but, chiefly, by the immense lengths to which Tom found he went to get the barge to a suitable place for these changing crews. The proceedings took on a pattern. After spending time consulting railway timetables and tide tables, the dinghy would row ashore at some remote spot where a telephone box had to be found. This might dovetail in with a pub or, in daytime, possibly with a launderette but it always worked because at the appropriate time the new people arrived and the outgoing crew left.

Time spent in Five Sisters was described by Tom as an unrest cure. Nevertheless it had, even taking the rough as well as the smooth, an inimitable atmosphere of tranquillity.

From the log I built up a perfect day in Five Sisters which I will repeat here: it was a rose coloured day. There were others when we struggled with the sea in gales, which split our sails, lost topmasts and caused seasickness. These days, however, proved as satisfactory to the young as the one I am going to tell you about.

The log begins: "Very calm morning." Two young men bent to the windlass turning the iron winch handles, one at each end of the windlass, steadily weighing the anchor, the cable coming in through the big iron fairlead and winding itself methodically round the drum ...... the cable lying on deck is stowed in two neat skeins before the coach roof ......

During this time various sails have been made ready and some actually set. The foresail was undoubtedly got ready for spreading by lowering it to the deck and unwrapping the sheet that bound the long sausage when stowed. In a semi-chrysalis form it was then hoisted again, to be set with one tug on the downhaul. The cry of "Anchor up and down" from the people at the windlass was answered by "Set foresail" from the Master (Tom) at the wheel and the foresail would come clattering down the forestay into its triangular position and tacked down. At the cry of "Anchor away" the wheel, which had already been pushing the great rudder to take us in the appropriate direction, was now seriously engaged in propelling Five Sisters sedately, on this calm morning, through the water in the desired direction, someone meanwhile having lowered the appropriate lee board. We were away.

Now the time had come to set the mainsail. Its heavy block was carried aft while someone on the main brails winch below the mast would let out the main brails (the mainsail in a barge is raised and lowered like a theatre curtain). The block was hooked on to a traveller on the main horse; vangs and sheets adjusted after the sail had been tacked down at the foot of the mast. Everything now had to be checked and in the light winds of the morning the staysail most probably was set.

Breakfast at sea and all meals were eaten in relays. Breakfast might be at any time from 5.0 a.m. until 11.0 a.m. because sailing always came first and eating when convenient. On this particular day the demands of the sea were not arduous and people dropped down the hatch to an interior suffused with sunlight. The sound of water rippling past her sides, together with the smell of freshly brewed coffee steaming on the Rayburn and of bacon and eggs frying gave a delightful sense of well-being after the effort of getting under way. The sound of lazy conversation from the watch on deck, pleased at being left in peace to navigate, came drifting down as they bent over charts or adjusted the sails or leeboards. Gradually, with the sixth sense that familiarity bred, each member of the crew became aware of what was happening even when below, with a few exceptions who never knew what was happening, but they held an honourable place of their own.

Breakfast over, work began. Below, housework had been reduced to a minimum, all signs of adornment had been banished and stowed away, carpets rolled up and the sitting room (saloon at sea) left bare but for armchairs, books and piano. At night, camp beds turned it into the men's dormitory. I used to think it looked rather more handsome when thus reduced.

On deck where everyone wanted to be, there was an endless supply of requirements. If the sailing was less demanding – as on this hot, windless morning recaptured from the log – adjustments to sails could easily be accomplished by the watch in charge of navigation, leaving others free to catch up on countless jobs always waiting to be done; new whippings on rope ends, splicings or even a turks head could be found for an enthusiast, decks could be washed down – very cooling to the feet and popular to a one man one girl team. In these golden days of young labour, there were even volunteers to clean brass – brightwork to sailors.

Later in the morning, becalmed near the Columbine Buoy in the Thames Estuary, we had swum in complete isolation despite its being August Bank Holiday, had eaten our lunch and possibly stolen some time with a book. Then, all of a sudden, a breeze – hauling the wind, which meant much activity as a new course was set with full advantage taken of the new condition. Excitement over navigation assailed everyone as buoys were searched for and landmarks ('objects conspic') identified from the chart. As evening wore on and the huge navigation lights were literally lugged up on deck, after being lit below, and placed on each side of the ship, the temperature dropped and pullovers were brought out, their rough surfaces feeling alien to sunbaked salty skins.

Finally, intense activity would start as we began to enter harbour, picking up navigation buoys to port and starboard. We would begin to reduce speed when necessary by getting rid of sail as we picked our way between craft already at anchor and finally, someone sounding with lead and line, Tom would choose our anchorage.

At the cry of "Down topsail" and "Down foresail", we moved speedily to various ropes, halyards and downhauls, throwing ourselves on the downhauls to ensure the sails running down correctly. No sailorman ever runs and this was forbidden to us. At "Let go anchor" the cable was flung twice over the barrel of the windlass and out it ran through the fairlead, then twice again over the barrel and so on until Five Sisters was considered to be swinging correctly to the tide with sufficient cable laid out. Navigation lights were exchanged for that old horror, the riding light, which was hoisted on the forestay while all was tidied on deck and we were snug for the night.

Everyone tumbled exhausted down the hatch for first a 'nip', then supper from the ever friendly Rayburn, bed and a dreamless sleep, Five Sisters riding at anchor, gently swinging to the tide.

The high note forever came in 1958. Tom had left the Admiralty Trade Division and had many weeks before him without employment. The future was unknown to him. We went first, after a refit at Goldsmith's Yard at Grays in Essex where our sails had been stowed from the previous summer, to Whitstable which we had left ten years before. During that time great changes had come over the Barge World. Barges had become a rarity. When we had sailed away in 1948 there were still 210 trading barges under sail alone. Alas, the sailcloth had become as expensive as a diesel engine, deckhouses sprang like mushrooms and sails were abandoned. So it was that holidaymakers crowded to the harbour at Whitstable to see the genuine sailing barge, albeit a barge-yacht. As we threaded our way through the throng staring at Five Sisters I heard a voice say, "Well, you brought back a better barge than you took away then." There stood stalwart Albert, our first skipper and teacher who took us up the Thames and beside him was Joe. This was praise indeed from the monosyllabic Albert, master of his trade. The reunion was a very happy one.

From Whitstable we proceeded to Ramsgate, then 'Calais and beyond the Seas', as our clearance papers when leaving for France had put it. We managed, that memorable summer, to cover 760 miles and indulged ourselves most happily in the canals of Holland. Here, as the Master put it in the log, the luxuries of life – meat and vegetables – were dear. The necessities like gin and bols were cheap.

Our continually changing crews were always at the right port at the right time and one member, a most charming girl, was, unbeknown to us then, to become our very dear daughter-in-law, Wendy Hallett.

Life was on the change, because in the middle of that cruise a communication arrived for Tom telling him that he was to become an admiral. Instead of returning to our beloved Chiswick, we turned right at Dover and sailed down the Channel to Gosport. Here it was that someone mentioned to the Commander-in-Chief at Portsmouth that "Captain Larken has arrived with Five Sisters." to which the great man replied: "How very singular. I am sure they are very nice women, but why tell me?"

Before leaving Chiswick we had informed the Post Office of our intention to sail and requested them, very properly, to disconnect our telephone. Nothing happened so Tom did the job himself and coiled the line up on a tree. In mid-channel I was reading some letters picked up in Dover and one was from the Post Office informing us that if we did not pay their bill they would be forced to disconnect our telephone within seven days.

It took us a little time to settle to the new life in Gosport. The Solent is not barge water and we felt oddly exiled from the London River and also our lives were now circumscribed. There was one terrible gift, which to us was a cause of dismay; we had a house and staff that went with the job. We were thunderstruck.

Double Life

The house with its staff and our home, the barge, was an 'embarras de richesses' – we only needed one. The difficulty was that if we refused that offer of the house then those who followed and might need it would find that it had gone from the job to which it was attached. We resolved the trouble by cutting our lives in two. We spent from Monday to Friday in the house and on Friday evening we piled into the car with the cats and set off for Five Sisters, home and cosiness – also hard work. Five Sisters fared well too as our niece, Muff, who knew the barge from Paris days and had sailed with us, had decided to finish the book she was writing with our cousin, Eddie Shackleton, the explorer's son. She stayed in the barge, looking after it and feeding the cats in Camper and Nicholson's yard. The next year was more difficult, as Muff married and we moved the barge to H.M.S. Hornet.

Up at the house we virtually kept an hotel. Tom was Flag Officer to the Interview Board for cadets entering the Navy. Part of the job seemed to be to entice the headmasters and directors of education to send their best boys into the Navy. As well as visiting headmasters there were always a headmaster and a county director of education sitting in on the Board, so a great many came our way and we enticed like mad, I putting flowers in their bedrooms and selecting the books I thought would amuse them. This became a great game. They used to arrive in the evening and while they were having a drink in the drawing room I used to slip upstairs and make my choice for their bedside reading. Next morning at breakfast I used to hear if I had struck lucky and often I had – PG Wodehouse for Sherborne, Lord Haldane's Ghost Book proved a success for another headmaster, and so on. Sailors are said to have a wife in every port but I found, when trying to entertain these eminent men, that I had a foot in almost every camp – I shamelessly brought in my Catholic relations to Catholics, my Quaker heredity to Protestants, I was Irish with the Celts but English when it seemed to be required. They themselves, whether from public schools or grammar schools, were all people of great interest and were mostly very amusing, making the part I had to do very simple.

The difficulty at the beginning was that we had a staff, which sounds wonderful and for which people would almost give their eyes, but I soon learnt that there are staffs and staffs. We had, in those early days, the 'and' sort if those are the awkward ones. The Chief Steward was a sadist. I had not appreciated that anyone could have such subtle ways of manoeuvring things to go their way as opposed to mine, which I felt I must struggle to establish.

We had several stumbling blocks: one was food – the sadist had the lowest possible standards of what to offer guests – and the other the headmasters who, without rings on their sleeves to establish their seniority, I found were not getting much in the way of VIP treatment from the Naval Stewards. In the end, by saying we were an hotel for headmasters, that we must be five star and that I was only the manageress, the sadist cheered up. Luckily he left and the eventual replacement was of quite a different calibre, gentle, kind and perceptive. Everything ran beautifully and happily from then on.

The contrast between the house and the boat made me a very quick-change artist. I would spend a morning painting the barge or stopping leaks with a tarry mixture called Hercules Glue and sawdust, then suddenly find that time had run out and would dash back to change and get my hands fit to help myself to the dishes handed to me at lunch. With the help of our old friend, Skipper Fred Cooper, and a charming man called The Boatswain, Five Sisters was beautifully maintained during these years. Every weekend during the summer we set out with different people as crew, one of the happiest was when we took the stewards and their wives, sweethearts and families. From then on Cookie was on my side. He himself turned out to be a very good helmsman.

The entry into the Services was apt to be a political issue in the 1960's and MPs often came down to see Tom. After we had been there about a year there was a General Election and a remark from the Labour benches sparked off a controversy that ended in an invitation being issued for a representative to come and sit in on the Board. It had been stated in the House of Commons that the Interview Board favoured Public School boys for entry into the Navy, whereas the Board was actually bending over backwards to encourage the Grammar School headmasters to consider a naval career for their boys. However, in these early days when new grammar schools flourished everywhere, the possible recruits were more anxious to gain entry into a University. In fact, in those days Dartmouth tried to turn itself into a University, but that method was abandoned and was unpopular with the young cadets themselves.

Dr. Horace King, who later became the Speaker of the House of Commons, was selected to come down to sit in with the Interview Board. He was a delightful guest in the house and the evening that he spent dining with the Board was an uproarious one. The cigar smoke that clung to the dining room next morning was nobody's business. I hold most dear my copy of Hansard on the debate that followed. Rising in the House of Commons, using a well-known quotation, Dr. King began, "To spend thirty six hours with Rear Admiral Larken is a liberal education in itself." and he went on to exonerate the Board and to falsify the previous misconception. He also invited Tom and me to dinner in the House of Commons, which was an equal eye-opener on the workings of democracy and also to the good humour between the parties outside the Chamber.

In May 1961 we celebrated our silver wedding which coincided with Five Sister's seventieth birthday. An enormous ice pudding was produced, modelled in the shape of a Thames Sailing Barge, rice paper dyed brown for sails and rigging ingeniously contrived from a little model that I had noticed was missing from the Barge. It was a happily celebrated event with family, crews, friends and staff and was divided between the house and Five Sisters, who really stole the thunder.

During the remainder of the summer, our third, we repeated the practice of weekends at sea. There were an immense number of candidates for crew and we managed as best we could. It was during this summer that we returned to France and the Seine where Five Sisters met with an accident for which the French admitted responsibility. They offered us full compensation after a floating crane had dragged her anchor and rammed us during the night. We sailed back to England in a damaged ship with incessant pumping and a rising gale, a most hair-raising experience. Despite the repairs it was a death blow to the old ship. Although she sailed again, her middle-aged energy was gone and she declined into old age, but with all her usual grace.

Very early, before first light, on an extremely cold morning in December 1961, Five Sisters slipped from her mooring in Haslar Creek and leaving Portsmouth Harbour and the Navy behind she set course for Yarmouth, Isle of Wight. The Master was alone on deck. As he bent to the wheel and the old barge responded in her deliberate way his voice was clear in the crisp morning air singing, "I'll go a'waltzing Matilda with you." For over forty years he had served the Navy, man and boy. For Five Sisters and ourselves, the double life was over.

Single Life

Five Sisters, like us, could only advance into old age. She was already showing signs of decrepitude since her accident on the Seine. It was prudent to search for a backwater for her which would combine ease for ourselves. A good mooring beside a riverbank cottage would be ideal. Five Sisters would serve as an annexe for summer and for visitors particularly for grandchildren, should we have any. It proved difficult to find.

Then a friend who was an architect told us that planning permission could be obtained if a property possessed some sort of convertible building, even a ruined one, barn, boathouse or shed, which one could then convert into one's ideal home. We began to search for a ruin with rather too much emphasis – it had of course to be beside water – and before long we found one; the old disused gas works at Yarmouth, Isle of Wight. A ruin it possessed 'par excellence'. Scrap merchants had extracted all the metal they could get out of it, but two enormous boilers were too much for them and they lolled at impossible angles across the half-demolished brickwork. Doors hung on half remaining hinges and there was a rather pathetic little Victorian chimney rising from the rubble.

Turning our backs on this monstrosity, there were some recommendations. There was an old wharf with deep water at high tide on a creek leading from the River Yar. There was an old manager's cottage still structurally sound. There was an orchard. Best of all, there were acres of woodland and marshland that were undeniably beautiful, that is, if one disregarded one point where there was a rubbish tip. This, however, served a purpose in reclaiming some of the marshland for hard standing. The place carried planning permission for a boatyard, which might come in handy somehow, especially as another recommendation was the price.

We wandered in the woods picking primroses and bluebells and round a bend in the river found a breathtaking view into deep country without a house in sight. It was May and we fell.

Before actually producing our money we had to be certain that the bridge carrying the road from Yarmouth to the west part of the island would always be an opening bridge, as the present one was. At the time Tom was too busy with the Interview Board to go himself so he asked me to go over to the planning office of the County Council to make sure. I returned with the information that in the event of a replacement of the present bridge an opening bridge would certainly be envisaged. I had seen a Mr. Davis and he pointed out that the navigation rights were of the utmost importance. All this would be extremely important in future years. Even before we arrived with the barge to live there, people approached us, asking if they could bring their boats to work on them, either on land or in the creek's mud berths. There was plenty of space and the enquiries began to build up.

Tom himself, when retired, discussed the bridge question with the Chief Planning Officer and I was with him. He was received with courtesy and his opinion was sought as to what angle a new bridge should be in relation to the bank and tide for navigational purposes. It was clear that the one hundred year old, creaking, Victorian bridge was considered obsolete. The boatyard project began to look inevitable with the interest and pressure from outside. Our first objective must be to clear the land.

Our first winter was that of 1962/63 when the sea actually froze so that we could walk on it. The pipeline along the dyke froze solid so that we had no water for ten weeks. We melted snow on the ever-loving Rayburn and saved as many birds as we could. The two things took all day.

It was during this arctic spell that Tom fell on the frozen ruin and badly concussed himself. About the same time we suffered a fire on board, generated by the generator, the Little Bitch. Together we fought it and put it out. It was a gloomy time as all England knows and we seemed isolated. When the thaw came, we set ourselves to clearing the site and also the rubbish tip. It was a long task and an arduous one. A bulldozer did a great deal but by no means all. There was an unexpected source of labour: boys from the local Approved School were allowed out on jobs, if you satisfied the authorities of your suitability. We passed as OK and it proved a two-way benefit. The boys liked getting out and earning some money and we profited from their help. As they were young, we had to work alongside them to keep their interest up and for the most part they worked well. The boys were from all sorts of places and were happy at their school, which was run by an Irish brotherhood. They were taught crafts, rowing and sailing and played much cricket and football. They also boxed which we were invited to watch. I learnt a great deal about deprivation in large towns and broken homes. It was, for us, a happy relationship and when summer came we took them to sea.

One day we were all gleaning. This meant that after the bulldozer had scraped up its bucketful of potted meat jars, which seemed to abound with everything else imaginable, and deposited them on the foreshore, which itself was lined with wire netting and brushwood, we gleaned from the rear for oddments left behind. The boys were allowed five minutes each with a long boathook to break bottles in a creek. We imagined that in some thousand years hence archaeologists will put together the shards of potted meat jars from the war of 1939/45.

One particular day, we had a friend from London who joined the team. He was anxious to set fire to the brambles, which had been bulldozed with the jars. He was so persistent that we reluctantly agreed. Then, from the direction of Yarmouth, came the unmistakable sound of an approaching fire engine. It crossed the bridge and turned up the lane. I had just brought tea out when it drew to a halt. Tom explained that we were burning brambles on purpose. The firemen sat down and readily accepted cups of tea too. Soon a motor bicycle came screeching up the lane and a young man drew up with a flurry of brakes, "It's not here, you bloody fools, it's Hallett's Shute."

We worked very hard indeed – in fact working with the boys was almost time-off. I used to add a baked potato to their sandwiches for lunch and became very fond of them in an auntish way and they in turn taught me London slang – it has special construction of reversing letters, which I have now forgotten. Peter Richardson lived in the cottage, which we restored, until his wife Barbara came with her two small sons. They then found a house in Yarmouth and we let the cottage, which was a great help financially. We gradually managed to clear the site, made a good workshop and a Gents out of the old gasworks and began to feel established. Barbara controlled the Office excellently. I drifted from outside labour, trying to make the yard attractive with trees etc. to helping in the office and chandlery. We bonded together and had all sorts of adventures.

The making of the slipway was memorable. We woke at 3 am taking advantage of the low tide. and the fact that Jeremy was with us so that Peter, Tom, Jeremy and myself were the work force. Laboriously we laid the cement and shaped it between planks of wood. We had acquired a sturdy winch and Peter had made a cradle to fit any boat to be hauled out and it served very well. By morning we had a slipway.

The end product of our striving, when the new sewn grass took over, was a place described officially as one of 'Outstanding Natural Beauty'; it also contained a small boatyard. The pressure from people to lay up their boats, for which we had unlimited space, as well as mud berths and room for storage huts, was overwhelming. In fact the boating fraternity had us in their grip.

At the same time a young man, Peter Richardson, turned up from the mainland and offered himself as a junior partner in such an enterprise as ours, so in September 1963 we opened officially. Peter, a redoubtable young man, built a slipway, cut down trees from the woods to build sheds, using bricks from the old ruins for the first building. We bought two cedar huts for office and chandlery and we were away. We employed one other shipwright. Agonisingly, we waited for further customers who gradually trickled in.

In the spring of 1964, rumour leaked out in the press that the County Council had changed their minds. The old bridge was to be replaced by a bridge with a fixed span. The Planning Officer had won a competition and the prize had been a trip to the States. Having seen Brooklyn, flyovers and 'clover leaf' junctions, he became fascinated and returned home with the burning desire to build something of the sort himself, particularly a bridge. The question was where? The marshes of Yarmouth seemed ideal with the old juddering Victorian bridge ripe for replacement. The lead-in roads over the marshes presented a serious item of expense so that economy could be practised by having a fixed central span. The idea became more and more attractive to members of the County Council and more and more unpopular with the boating fraternity.

A war on paper was fought in the local press, with ferocity, for a year and a half until one day it was announced that there was to be a Public Inquiry to take place in October 1965. We were all shattered. Tom was never to attend the Inquiry. He died in July.

My Lords Spiritual and Temporal

TO MY LORDS SPIRITUAL AND TEMPORAL IN PARLIAMENT ASSEMBLED

"May it please your Lordships...."

When in typing school long ago I had had to study forms of address, the above amused me greatly. Little did I imagine that one day those words would be put into my appeal to the House of Lords. My appeal began with the words, "May it please your Lordships", and ended with the words, "and I will ever pray." My appeal was technically "a prayer."

It all came about thus. Some things are too painful to record. Suffice it to say that from July until October of that year I passed the time as best I could, sheltered by Jeremy and my daughter-in-law, Wendy. Jeremy was attached to the submarine HMS Valiant building at Barrow-in-Furness and they lived nearby at Ulverstone. In their wonderfully kindly company and that of our tiny granddaughter, I managed to live from day to day. In fact we all began to mend our wounds.

The next seven years might be described as chaotic, in one sense. In another, the sturdy hard work and equable temperament and good humour of our partner, Peter Richardson, and the skill and patience of his wife, Barbara, pulled the whole show through the maddening intricacies and unpredictable difficulties that beset small businesses. We had to make decisions and for me, unaccustomed to the commercial world, it was like having to dive off a springboard on a cliff into a turbulent sea below.

The first dive into the troubled waters was the Public Enquiry into the River Yar Bridge held in October of that year, 1965, in Yarmouth, Isle of Wight. This brought us all down south. The Clerk to the County Council who sat just in front of us was scathing on the subject of the importance of our boatyard. We were, he emphasised, "under-capitalised." I was outraged. With the utmost dislike at that moment, I stared at the back of his neck. The battle was on. There followed three more days of argument between the factions, with the boating fraternity solidly against the idea of a fixed bridge, while the bus companies and the County Council were in favour of it.

Despite the uncertainty over the bridge, Jeremy and I agreed with Peter and Barbara that we would run the boatyard until the spring when the future would, we thought, become clear. Instead, we were left high and dry by the Ministry of Transport, with no decision for two years. It was not possible to stop expansion of the boatyard, so we plodded on adding pontoons, further storage huts and improving, where possible, to cope with the increasing number of customers. It grew into a very happy community. Peter and one shipwright, Fred, coped with repair work and people worked on their own boats. There was plenty of room for boats to be laid up and an added little hut, Tom and I had bought, for a chandlery shop.

At Easter 1967 I went to stay with friends in Suffolk. I was about to set out when the postman handed me the morning's delivery. I was already in the car and put the letters on the back seat and drove away. When I arrived at my friends' house, I remember, I helped stoke a bonfire in the garden and then went in to wash and change. In my room I opened my mail. I left one long official looking envelope to the end, broke the seal and there lay the long given-up communication from the Ministry of Transport, from the Minister herself, who was Barbara Castle.

We had lost the opening bridge. The Minister had the grace to mention that she regretted the delay from Mrs. Larken's point of view. However, at the bottom I was advised that I could appeal to the House of Lords if I wished to do so, but that this must be within 24 days. Three days for Easter was too much. Monday morning found me scurrying back to the Isle of Wight.

We opened the campaign by appealing to a very good friend in Yarmouth, Charles Phipps. The first step, he thought, was to contact our MP, Mark Woodnut. From him I learnt that it was possible to appeal to the House of Lords even without a solicitor, whose services would have been beyond our resources. It would be necessary to get instruction from a Clerk to the House of Commons. I waited nervously for the first lesson. Peter felt that he was better working down on the boatyard where he was essential. Meanwhile our friend roused the Harbour Commissioners who were comatose over the whole thing. My friend said, "What will future generations of sailors think, that you left it to a woman to appeal.." This, I am proud to say, upset them and so they joined us. Finally the Royal Yachting Association came into the picture.

With this change, it became unnecessary for me to take those alarming instructions. I was no longer on my own. Instead, I set off with a cousin of Wendy's called George Wightman, a very all-about young man who helped us enormously, to the office of Dyson Bell and Co., Parliamentary Agents in College Street, Westminster. Parliamentary Agents are solicitors who manage things like petitions, as ours was, and they conducted our case.

We were most cordially received. There were about six men in the room including the charming agent himself, Mr. Liddell. Two were representing the Royal Yachting Association. The R.Y.A. was unable to contest the decision unless they had what was called a "locus standi." This we were able to provide, being riparian owners, that is owning riverside property and with a financial stake. (Incidentally we also owned half the riverbed, a rare thing.) Everyone seemed to be thoroughly satisfied with the proceedings, especially as we had a letter from Tom to the Ministry saying, "When I bought the old Gas Works Site I was assured by the County Council that there would always be an opening bridge of the Yar and if it had not been for this I would not have purchased the property."

Cups of tea arrived in pretty china and were handed round amidst general affability, which I found most attractive and reassuring. It was a lovely day; open windows let in warm spring air. Mr. Liddell then asked casually how the expenses of the project were to be met – "between you all?", he added. Impulsively, I opened my mouth to make some offer but George's hand fell heavily on my knee. I waited while he got out some paper and wrote something down which he handed to me. Now George had the smallest handwriting in the world. I stared at the paper unseeing and then fumbled in my handbag for my spectacles and put them on. I bent my head to read. The note said, "Don't speak." I took off my specs as nonchalantly as possible and put them back in my bag. Six pairs of eyes were focused upon me. Inside I felt thoroughly baffled, sat like a complacent cat and waited. At last the Commodore of the R.Y.A. said, "Of course we shall be responsible for Mrs. Larken's expenses." or words to that effect. I felt extremely embarrassed as George got out his writing pad once more and we repeated the operation as before. I read "Go now." Explaining that we had to get back to Yarmouth immediately, without any delay, which was all I could think of on the spur of the moment, we shook hands all round and left.

From that day until the middle of July, hardly a day passed without some communication arriving from Mr. Liddell's office. Halfway through this time Mr. Liddell himself rang up to say that the time had now come when they would like to see the assurance which Tom's letter said he had had from the County Council that the new bridge would be an opening one. I was floored. I had never seen an assurance in writing. On the other hand, I had been with Tom when the County Council had asked for his opinion and discussed the whole project with him. In vain I searched everywhere to find an assurance in writing, but nowhere could I lay my hands on such a document. Finally, I had to accept that in my woolly-minded way I had somehow manoeuvred these busy men into helping me on insufficient evidence. "Well," said Mr. Liddell, "we shall just have to hold to your evidence."

It is not surprising that when the day in July came, I entered the House of Lords with a certain lack of confidence. With me came Jeremy, George and our partner, Peter, as well as several neighbours from the Isle of Wight who were interested.

The whole set-up in the House of Lords was most impressive. The corridors were immensely wide and carpeted in deep red. Double doors, reaching to the high ceiling, gave access to the Committee Room. Within, where the proceedings took place, we were ushered into a large rectangular room on the first floor. After being told by an official in frock-coated uniform to be "Upstanding in Court", we settled down to take stock of our surroundings and company. Across the top of the room was a large table at which sat three lords and three members of the House of Commons. The public, which included ourselves, sat at the opposite end of the room and in front of us were the Queen's Counsel, two for each of us, the Ministry and ourselves. Down each side were tables at which their clerks sat. At the top end, in a corner near the Committee, sat two young men with a Bible and a Crucifix for the swearing-in of witnesses. In the centre between the two opposing tables were two girls, each with some sort of special machine, who recorded the proceedings. They wore the most vacant expressions on their faces as they typed away.

I could not help thinking to myself that our original investment in the land of £6,000 was like a pebble dropped into a pond with the rings always spreading out, giving further and further satisfaction. In the island, the reclaimed land gave immense pleasure for picnickers watching the dinghy sailing, the Cottage was let to holidaymakers, the moorings in the river were available for people's boats afloat and on shore, boats laid up in winter were worked on by their owners. Now, in this room alone, a lot of money was being earned. One could go a long way in giving pleasure and satisfaction even if "under-capitalised."

The first people to be called were the Royal Yachting Association, followed by the Harbour Commissioners. One could almost hear their knees knocking together as they took their place. These witnesses took up all the first day. The next opened with Jeremy on tides, he being a navigator, followed by the County Council. Last of all, I found myself in the witness box in the early afternoon on the second day.

It all seemed to last forever. Mr. Jupp, the Ministry of Transport's Q.C., bombarded me: "Didn't we want everything to be done for us?" This was absurd. We did everything ourselves, working long hours. Finally, of course, came the crucial bit; "Where was the written assurance from the County Council?" I explained that I had been with Tom when members of the

County Council discussed with him the type of bridge to be built. I also explained that I had gone over to the Island for Tom and had seen a Mr. Davis. "You mean, this was before the purchase?"

I felt as if I was rowing in a dinghy that was sinking, the water was rising all the time up to the gunwhale. I must hold on. I had lost hope of anything I said being taken seriously by Mr. Jupp, so his reply surprised me as much as Mr. Davis' name surprised him. "This", he said, "is rather a surprise, because we had not prepared for Mr. Davis."

However, we were soon back on the assurance again. I managed one saving spurt when asked if I did not consider it all an assumption. "But it is an assurance if you are talking to normal people." Before I could explain, I was interrupted but I managed to edge in: "In normal life, a word is an assurance, but perhaps not with County Councils." Here the stenographer girls failed to record that there was laughter. Our own Q.C., Mr. Marnham, then rose and gathered our case up from the wreckage by saying "On what did you base your assumption?" To which I replied "On the word of the County Council." "My Lords – my case." ended Mr. Marnham and I was allowed to withdraw.

The Chairman, Lord Strang, replied, "Mr. Marnham, the Committee are of the opinion that the Minister has a case to answer."

Despite this encouraging remark, next morning found all our side assembled to discuss what steps to take if the Larken case failed – in other words, compensation. Everyone seemed rather gloomy. When we reassembled for the third day, to my surprise, Mr. Davis was called. He had been brought up from the Island overnight. He confirmed the meeting I had had with him and very soon we were dismissed for the Committee to have further deliberations. One of the Lords, looked rather sympathetically towards me, I imagined.

In the enormous corridor where we all waited, the Clerk to the County Council was handling a great pile of files. "Are those all against me?" I asked him. "Yes, all." he said in a rather good-humoured way. We both laughed. Then we were summoned back into Court again. "Upstanding" once more. Then we sat to hear the result of the deliberations. After a somewhat breathless silence, Lord Strang spoke.

The statement was extremely short but, as I later understood, very sweet. "The Committee is of the opinion that the instrument be not approved. A special report will be made to both Houses in the near future."

"What the hell do they mean?" Everyone rose to their feet. I realised that it was all over. People crowded round saying "You've won. You've won." I began to believe them. Mr. Marnham shook hands and then accepted an invitation to lunch with Mr. Jupp. Mr. Liddell was delighted. He had another successful petition going on in another room. Despite my feeling of poor showing and agony to keep afloat, he remarked to Jeremy "I thought your mother's transparent honesty would pull us through." A remark I greatly treasured, as it restored my self-respect

The Aftermath

All outsized moments in life require celebration yet somehow anti-climax is sure to follow. Peter, Jeremy and I left the House of Lords and found nowhere around Westminster where we could even get a drink. All bars were full of hot sweating civil servants queuing at the counters. Wendy had gone with her baby, Juliet, into the Park – no one was interested in the outcome of what seemed to us to have been a desperate ordeal. Jeremy had come up from Chatham under great personal and professional inconvenience and wanted to get back as soon as possible. Peter was anxious to return to the Boatyard. As I still had the right of entry I decided to go back to the House of Lords which I did and listened to a debate on Abortion. Everyone except Lord Longford seemed to be asleep. The most surprising thing was that the Bishops wore their surplices, rumpled and in disarray, they looked like bundles of washing on the seats. However they would suddenly rise up like other members and speak with great energy and spirit.

You might think that we were at the end of our trouble for all time. It was not to be. The night of my return my neighbour rang up to congratulate us in the most flattering terms but with a sting in his tail. He mentioned before he rang off that I was sitting on a gold mine – and one which he hoped to share. He thought that the deeds of our property were incorrectly drawn up some time ago and that our boatyard was situated on part of his land.

He had hinted at this startling bit of information before but it seemed so improbable that no one had taken it seriously. We had bought our land from the National Gas Board but no one could trace the deeds showing exactly what the old Gas Company had handed over to the National Board. We were forced now to embark on investigation, solicitors and research. The litigation dogged us for the next five years.

The Richardsons and I managed to run the boatyard until 1972. The first winter was a difficult one and I used to drive along the South coast visiting yards in case they could give us extra work they could not manage. They were friendly and offered tea, chat and cigarettes in smokey little offices but no work. Peter and Fred, whom we employed, went out decorating. Then things improved: the customers grew in number, we put pontoons on the river for dinghy sailing and the reclaimed land offered a delightful picnic area. The house let easily and Barbara's mother supervised the hand-over for holidaymakers. As well as the happier situation in the yard I had my very good friends, Avice and Charles Phipps, who lived above the Boatyard with whom I could stay. All sorts of unexpected things happened as the days went by. Once when the Richardsons were on holiday, which indeed they needed, a man turned up claiming to be an old friend of Peter's whom Peter himself, disowned. He wanted to use our slip to get his boat out but Peter instructed me to refuse. The man announced that nevertheless he would do the job himself on the next Sunday.

Sunday came and the only thing I could think of doing was to erect a deck chair on the slipway and to spend the day there sewing – my strategy worked!

One night when I was sleeping in the cottage I feared I had not locked the sheds adequately and went out at 2 am to find that some people were robbing boats on the pontoon.

The place was very spooky to me especially at nights. I used to avoid the footpath through the woods to get up to the Phipps house. When I got there a most glorious dry Martini awaited me. During this time I had frequent sessions with people wanting to buy the boatyard on their terms and rumours clustered around us. I was instructed to beware. With my dear friends' hospitality I knew all was in safekeeping with them. Once when the famous Flower Festival took place in the Isle of Wight I was alone at the yard with their Border terrier, Ruggles, who used to come and sit outside the office. A bunch of Flower People came along the Bank. I felt a little anxious but they were charming and responded with great sympathetic ardour when I said I worked for a very strict demanding boss. After this I had no fear of showing them round.

The years wore away. I used to sit in our Solicitor's Office in Southampton and watch the roundabout of traffic outside wondering if another year would see me sitting there. Then a buyer turned up who was willing to buy the property including the litigation. We sold. Unfortunately the gold mine never materialised but the impasse to the business was resolved. On completion our accountant said that ours was a most happy inspiring partnership but one that would never make much money.

In a way during these years and those that followed I was often free to see a lot of my grandchildren which was I hoped a two-way benefit. There were several other families with children who used to stay in a house I had bought in the village of Buriton near Petersfield; these included friends and nieces as well as families from South Africa where Tom's sister had founded a dynasty after the first war. I became quite good at ironing. I wrote my first book. I inherited some excellent slides from Fred Cooper, the Barge Skipper. and used to give talks on the development of Thames Barges emphasising my amateur status; these were mostly to Yacht Clubs whose members fortunately knew little of my subject. After one talk a lady in the audience told me that the five sisters, after whom our barge was named, were her aunts. All this activity was a great consolation to me helping to establishing my new life. I was very occupied. I was continually on the road in a little green and cream Ford Anglia.

My old age is blessed with my family – my nearest and dearest kith and kin, friends, nieces and nephews. I have four grandchildren and five great-grandchildren, all of whom I love dearly and who are extremely kind and tolerant to me. There are also old hands (once young hands) from barging days; also older friends we have picked up on our way; these alas get fewer as time passes. I live in part of the old 'Poor House 1791' in Buriton a most attractive Saxon downland village with my two cats.

Printed in the United Kingdom
by Lightning Source UK Ltd.
101635UKS00001B/385-423